THEORIES OF WORLD GOVERNANCE

THEORIES OF WORLD GOVERNANCE

A Study in the History of Ideas

CORNELIUS F. MURPHY, JR.

The Catholic University of America Press

Washington, D.C.

Library of Congress Cataloging-in-Publication Data
Murphy, Cornelius F.
    Theories of world governance : a study in the
history of ideas / Cornelius F. Murphy, Jr.
        p.   cm.
    Includes bibliographical references
        1. International relations—Philosophy.   2. In-
ternational cooperation.   3. International organization.   I. Title.
JZ1308.M87   1999
327.1′01—dc21
99-25222
ISBN 0-8132-0955-2 (cloth : alk paper).
ISBN 0-8132-0937-4 (pbk. : alk. paper)

In Memoriam
Myres Smith McDougal
(1907–1998)
Scholar and Friend

[T]heir goal must be to stir the heart of the world. It must not be merely practical, it must be sheer poetry . . . It must be a mirror for the world to gaze in and blush . . . For this His Highness had made the inspiring suggestion: "The Emperor of Peace" . . . What was to be achieved was nothing less than the rediscovery of that human unity which had been lost as a result of the great discrepancies that had developed in human interests. Here, admittedly, the question arose whether the present time and the nations of today were still at all capable of such great ideas in common . . .

—Robert Musil, *The Man without Qualities*

The Empire will neither claim to elevate itself to the heavens or to appropriate the heavens for its earthly purposes . . . It would accept being only a functional mode and knowing that that is all there is . . . That will be its fragility and its grandeur. . . .

—Jean-Marie Guehenno, *The End of the Nation-State*

Today the universal common good poses problems of world-wide dimensions which cannot be adequately tackled or solved except by the efforts of public authorities endowed with a wideness of powers, structure and means of the same proportions: that is, of public authorities which are in a position to operate in an effective manner on a world-wide basis. The moral order itself, therefore, demands that such a form of public authority be established.

—Pope John XXIII, *Pacem in Terris*

CONTENTS

Any person who seriously studies international relations is eventually led to raise a fundamental question about this unusual form of human association. One comes to wonder why the world is composed of independent and equal sovereign states, interacting in the absence of any established higher authority when, within states, effective government is deemed to be indispensable to any reasonable expectations of justice and peace. The conventional answer to this question comes from diplomatic history. The beginnings of the present international system are traceable to the European Peace of Westphalia of 1648, which ended the Thirty Years' War. That settlement gave formal recognition to the mutual independence of the modern nation-states. Subsequent events such as the Congress of Vienna, the Concert of Europe, and the international institutional innovations of the present century, expand the membership and fill out that history. By studying this sequence of events, one comes to understand how through a mixture of law, diplomacy, and multilateral practice a global society composed of nearly two hundred separate and autonomous communities has been held together, in spite of violent interludes, for more than three hundred and fifty years.

This chronicle explains what has occurred, but it does not explain why it has happened. The curious mind wants to know more than can be revealed by the empirical evidence. Throughout its turbulent existence, international society has been shaped by the relative political military and economic strength of its members. But it has also been directed by deeper intellectual forces. Beyond the details of universal action and reaction there lie elementary conceptions about the purposes of international life which can only be understood by the powers of reflective thought.

This is not a matter of idle speculation. Ideas of global order are important because thought and action are integrally related in ways that are often overlooked. Many international lawyers assume that the rule of law will eventually prevail, in spite of the absence of organized sanctions by which the law among nations can be impartially enforced. They would be less sanguine if they were more familiar with state of nature theories which, in any earlier age, nullified similar juristic expectations. Comparable observations can be made about those who believe that the world can be morally integrated while it remains in a pre-political condition; or about those who, being sociologically inclined, assume that the nation-state will finally just "wither away." These various misperceptions can be corrected when the mind takes into account the theoretical justifications for that sovereign insubmissiveness which is the foundation of the whole international system.

In the present work, which builds on my earlier studies,[1] I explore the conceptual approaches to the problem of world order that have arisen in Western history from the close of the Middle Ages until our own time. These cover a wide range of intellectual disciplines. Theology, philosophy, ethics, jurisprudence, political science, and sociology are among the various ways of knowing which have inspired leading minds in their struggles to understand the essential conditions of harmony and reciprocal respect among sovereign nations.

Some had specific ideas of how the world should be organized. At the beginning of the fourteenth century Dante proposed that the Holy Roman Emperor should rule the then-known world. I consider this proposal at the outset of these reflections. Although I address some of the specifics of that imperial project, I prefer to concentrate upon the imaginative and philosophical resources which inspired this seminal plan

---

1. See, e.g., my *The Search for World Order* (Dordrecht: Martinus Nijhoff, 1985); and my "The Conciliatory Responsibilities of the United Nations Security Council," 35 *German Yearbook of International Law* 190–204 (1993).

of universal authority. Dante wanted to draw the contentious kingdoms of his time into a hierarchical order, and he articulated that order
in terms of a speculative union of time and eternity. By grasping these
higher parameters of his conception one can understand the enduring
significance of the *De Monarchia* in the international literature of politics.

The jurist-theologians of the Spanish Renaissance rejected Dante's
imperialism. They were struggling to balance the assertive independence of the new nation-states with the transnational spiritual solidari-
ties traditionally nurtured by the Christian faith. The fruit of their reflections was a universal jurisprudence which has been of lasting
influence upon international relations. But they also made important
contributions to the political dimensions of the problem of world
order. Where Dante saw political authority descending from above,
Spanish thinkers, such as Suarez, saw it coming from below. Ultimate
governing authority arose from the multitude, which formed a kingdom and submitted to the rule of its monarch. As our study develops,
the importance of this distinction should become apparent to the careful reader. It introduces a theme which is central to our study: that the
problem of global governance is intimately linked with the principles
and conceptions that derive from a comprehensive political theory
which mediates between intranational and international order.

Suarez was convinced that there was no temporal jurisdiction beyond state frontiers. Yet he also held that rulers were bound in conscience to obey the *jus gentium*—the unwritten law of nations. With
Grotius, and the beginning of the modern age, international theory
began to be less interested in transcendental sources of authority. The
preference is now for a more mundane and humanistic grounding of
international order.

Grotius sought to lay the cultural foundations for a global jurisprudence which would determine, and limit, the rights of states to use
force. The foundations of this quasi-legal edifice would soon be
shaken by developments in political thought. In the final section of
the initial chapter I demonstrate the influence which the naturalism of
Hobbes and Spinoza had upon international theory and practice. The

anarchism implicit in the idea that states are like individuals trying to coexist without government would have a profound impact upon all subsequent reflections on the nature of our unorganized world.

The impress of European culture upon the understanding of international relations came essentially from two primary sources: one Latin, the other Germanic. The first emphasizes the practical needs for the coordination of any social endeavor. For example, ideas of law and hierarchy, first perfected by the Romans, have made their impression upon all aspects of international jurisprudence. The Teutonic spirit, by contrast, is drawn to the boundless. It tries to grasp the whole in some overall form of comprehensive unity. Germanic conceptions of order are inward and abstract, prone to obscure distinctions between subject and object. This northern culture is also inclined to give absolute sanction to impalpable norms. In the second chapter I examine the important ways in which this movement towards immanence affected the development of modern international theory.

Leibniz was the leading figure in what was to become the German Enlightenment. For him, the mind was an internal power which can penetrate the preestablished harmonies which govern the unfolding of the cosmos. This order had an inclusive global dimension. The order established by God, and the values which governed that order, took the form of a rational natural law whose principles would guide the conduct of sovereigns in their mutual relations. Leibniz's disciple, Christian Wolff, tried to extend the universal jurisdiction of reason. He imagined the world to be a supreme state of which all states were presumed to be members. This *civitas maxima* was subject to the governance of the wise.

Wolff's conception assumed a universal sociability which defenders of state independence vigorously denied. The counterattack was led by a cultured Swiss diplomat, Emeric Vattel. Vattel transformed the rationalism of Leibniz and Wolff into an immutable Law of Nations which, at least in theory, justified the mutual independence and equality of states.

Vattel's system demanded a deference to sovereign discretion which was attractive to both established states and the emerging nations of the Western Hemisphere. However, the extensive liberties which it attributed to powerful states were bound to provoke a moral reaction. In the middle section of the second chapter I consider the attempt of the great philosopher Immanuel Kant to temper the growing injustice and anarchy of the international system. Kant's theory of cosmopolitan right was conceived as a self-imposed normative order for the governance of a society of autonomous states. Kant realized that states would not accept a higher political authority but he believed that, as moral beings, all would accept the authority of an inward law. The principles of this subjective authority would lead nations to a covenant of nonaggression. But Kant's proposal was no match for a new philosophical idealism which, by the force of its own logic, would enhance the unrestricted freedom of the absolute state and accentuate the competitive rivalries of the leading powers.

Christianity impressed upon Western culture the conviction that all forms of human association took their ultimate meaning from encompassing realities that originated beyond the created world. Up to the time of Grotius, a reaching out for a higher good marked the uniqueness of this remarkable civilization suspended between time and eternity. The transcendent orientation was terminated by the German Enlightenment. All knowledge was now being drawn out of the resources of a self-conscious, autonomous reason. The mind would subjectively comprehend all that was previously thought of as coming from some reality Beyond. The immanence begun by Leibniz culminates in the thought of Hegel.

In the final part of the second chapter I address the influence of Hegel's ideas upon the expanding international state of nature. In Hegel's political philosophy the state was an absolute, self-contained substance. Its being is within. Each state projects this inwardness upon the world with a ferocious, but legitimate, independence. The inequalities of power among states required the weak to submit to the strong. Hegelian thought further justifies the domination of ancient communities by a Eurocentric *Weltgeist* which would take the odious form of a racist colonialism.

For Kant, a pacific union was appropriate for states governed by the same self-imposed law; to Hegel, enduring peace would corrupt the virtue of nations. There was no juridical or political authority to which an autonomous state could be compelled to submit its international disputes. Moreover, there was an implicit understanding that force was the ultimate expression of hostility. While visionaries hoped that global injustice could be corrected by moral reform, Hegelian principles and ideals were increasingly taking over the direction of universal human destiny.

After the calamity of the First World War the assumption that humankind could flourish within the isolated boundaries of separate nation-states was increasingly called into question. The monopoly of geo-governance by a minority of Western states was also being challenged. Principles of state equality were revitalized and claims were beginning to be made for the extension of democratic values from national, to international, arenas. In the third chapter I recount the attempts to revive the lawmaking potential of a system which, although timidly experimenting with international organization, adamantly refused to accept any form of higher temporal authority.

Distinguished jurists eloquently defended the existing rules and the collaborative practices, such as multilateral conferences, which increased participation of smaller states in the international legal process. It was also hoped that standards of reason and justice developed within mature legal systems would gradually become universal in their range and application. In this new century, it was expected that as states matured they would begin to prefer the international to the national interest. Progress was becoming associated with evolution.

New ideal conceptions of world order also began to appear. The United States, while refusing membership in the League of Nations, began to assert its own moral leadership. American diplomats and jurists insisted that upholding the sanctity of treaties, and strict compliance with other traditional international obligations, would do more

In his *Eunomia*—depicting the good order of a self-ordering international society—Allott attempts to reconcile Comte's Social Idealism with the Pure Theory of Law. Allott's objective is to affirm, by the articulation of a collective consciousness, the creation of a society of societies which represents, in ideal form, the whole of the human race. Law becomes the means by which this unification of all humanity is to be achieved.

Allott is also influenced by the principles and methods of scientific naturalism, and he acknowledges his indebtedness to Teilhard de Chardin. At the beginning of the final chapter I explore this intellectual affinity in some detail. Like the Jesuit paleontologist, Allott looks forward to a future which is ordered by structures and systems that are different from, but integrated with, the order of the physical universe. The two thinkers share a fascination with the powers operative in the evolution of the universe, for they see these powers as constantly creating ever more complex forms of unification through the self-development of thought.

In a scientific anthropology the epistemology of the positive sciences defines the boundaries of human thought. The distinctiveness of the human being recedes as the individual is seen as part of a larger biological order. The multitude is no longer the ultimate source of political authority; as the masses, they are a passive phenomenon. As such, they are properly subject to a universal regulative order imposed by law on behalf of the collective consciousness of Humanity. I object to this denigration of the human person and I do so in the name of reason as well as human dignity.

In my critique of *Eunomia* I argue that aspirations for universal justice and peace will never be satisfied without a recognition of the uniqueness of the person and of his, or her, powers of thought and deliberation. Such recognition is indispensable to all constructive human action, including that related to the formation of a political community which, potentially, may embraces the whole of the human race. I also defend the application of a practical reasonableness to moral questions of international significance.

Addressing the issue of universal human rights, I suggest that timeless preferences will not lead to global reform. The only hope of progress lies in the development of a new *jus gentium* which is authentically transnational and mediates between inflexible principle and the contingencies of cultural diversity and experience. This approach navigates the streams of entitlement in a way that avoids the allure of idealism on the one hand and the ethical relativism of radical pragmatism on the other.

The acceptance of legitimate differences in the area of human rights leads on to issues of political pluralism. Following the thought of His Holiness John Paul II, I defend the legitimate differences that are represented by the variety of established and nascent state-societies, against the sterile uniformities implicit in a socio-juridical organization of the world. All forms of universal utopianism ignore the good which can be achieved through a just balance of the rights and duties of the nation-state. Socio-scientific anthropology is no exception, for it sees communal pluralism as an obstacle to general unity. For a humanistic anthropology, however, respect for difference is the only basis upon which we can hope to approach the goal of a universal solidarity.

I also emphasize the importance of the immediate problems of order in a decentralized world community. Hopes for the future must not displace responsible concern for the present. I suggest some ways that the existing society of states, with its established structure and practices, can advance beyond the minimalist goal of negative coordination of the actions of its members and develop a greater degree of cohesion. But I am careful to insist that the search for a more substantive unity within the existing system is, in the nature of things, provisional. If states will learn to take their existing international obligations as seriously as they now take their national self-interests, considerable progress will be made toward the creation of a world civilization. But we must not forget that the structure within which this reform might occur is essentially imperfect. A state of nature can never evolve into a political society.

A study in the history of ideas about international relations would be incomplete if it did not contemplate a future which may be substantially different from the present. Those who expect these pages to contained a specific constitutional proposal will be disappointed, but those who understand the primacy of thought over action should be reasonably satisfied with my concluding reflections.[2] The first speculative consideration is determining the appropriate intellectual discipline within which the mind can fruitfully prepare for changes which may, at some indeterminate time, become the responsibility of men and women of action.

Dante thought that world disorder could be overcome by the power of an imaginative philosophy. Others have looked to some kind of universal jurisprudence to regulate relations between states. Still others believe that international anarchy can be cured by a strong infusion of moral theory. Some are now convinced that universal harmony falls within the jurisdiction of either practical or theoretical sociology. It is my contention that if we wish to understand the possibilities of universal peace we must open our minds to categories of thought which are within the province of political philosophy. In the spirit of that discipline, I detail some of the practical improvements which can be made within the existing organization of the world with its ingrained principles of state sovereignty. But I also point out the insoluble difficulties which will be experienced as aspirations for global justice and harmony are increasingly frustrated by the legitimate independence of member states. Rather than opt for a transnational sovereignty of dubious authority to resolve the expected impasse, I recommend a strengthening of the powers of self-governance within states as the only reasonable way to build the conditions necessary for a further advance in the political organization of the world.

Unless the peoples of the world can control despotism, protect freedom, and advance social justice within their own countries they will be unable to create an acceptable worldwide political community. Historically, ruling power has been established as much by conquest as by consent. However, the evolving common conscience of humanity insists that governments be created by the deliberative choice of those

2. Compare Stanley Hoffman, *The State of War: Essays on the Theory and Practice of International Politics* (New York: Frederick Praeger, 1965), chap. 1.

who will be subject to superior authority. In the modern world, political communities are primarily composed of heterogeneous populations and it is they who have the considerable burden of making inclusive societies which can unify all in spite of divergences of ethnic or national identity.

To be responsible, the modern citizen must also have a genuine interest in the human condition beyond borders. I follow the teaching of the Catholic Church, first articulated by John XXIII, that we all have obligations toward the whole human family that do not exclude a legitimate allegiance to one's own state. The ultimate reconciliation of universal and municipal authority will depend upon a proper balance of these two obligations.

The growth of a wider congeniality is the immediate task of a growing international civil society composed of private groups and individuals who are devoted to public purposes of global scale. These activities are of immense importance to the development of a universal common good. Yet they do not represent a final development. A global civil society can temper the harsh realities of an international state of nature but it cannot replace that primitive pre-political condition which is the current status of the world.

As the study is brought to a close I grapple with the differences between an international civil community and a world political society. A world body politic would build upon, and perfect, a civic friendship whose unities are now being formed by the labor and sacrifices of devoted men and women from every corner of the globe. The planetary *polis* would be composed of diverse peoples of varying states and cultures who, desirous of lasting peace, and determined to give a stable form to their living together, will establish a permanent framework within which changing circumstances, and the conflicts they engender, can be resolved in a nonviolent manner by legitimate institutions of government. These universal organs will participate in the supreme authority of a world body politic under a fundamental law which designates their competencies, restricts their powers, and holds them accountable. None of these characteristics are part of an international civil society.

If the idea of a world political society is to have any substantial influence upon the unknown future its unique characteristics will have to be widely understood. Otherwise a sovereign people of the world will not adequately grasp the full nature of their own authority or be empowered to relieve the disparities between their hopes for national well-being and the burdens, financial and otherwise, of international anarchy. The establishment of a world government which protects and enhances life within national societies will not occur as a matter of natural evolution. Because it belongs to the realm of contingent possibilities, it may not happen at all. History is a matter of human acts which can not be precisely anticipated and are never fully determined. For now, it is important that we see that what is at stake is something more than a deepening transnational fellowship.[3]

The idea that human freedom and prosperity may best be secured through the formation of a world political society seems alien to much of modern consciousness, which is drifting more deeply into private concerns and is unwilling to form more than provincial attachments. Such a mentality is easy prey for those who preach an immanent fulfillment of human history. Perhaps the positive possibilities will be best understood by those who see the vital connection between time and eternity. They may realize that ultimate concerns cannot be separated from a commitment to the preservation and flourishing of life on earth. These will also understand that the deep desires for universal happiness and peace which are striving to break through an archaic international system correspond to a natural law of growth within the human person, which law bears the imprint of a Supreme and Providential Wisdom.

Cornelius F. Murphy Jr.
Pittsburgh 1998

3. Confusion between the political and the social began with Aquinas, who held that to be "a social and political animal" was a condition that was natural to man (*de Regimine Principum*). As for the time that must pass before humanity is ready to form a world political society, see the speculations of Mortimer Adler in *The Common Sense of Politics* (New York: Holt, Rinehart & Winston, 1971), chap. 16.

CHAPTER I

FROM WORLD STATE TO STATE OF NATURE

I

From the beginnings of recorded time there have been official relations between political communities. Treaties were concluded by ancient rulers and some form of diplomatic and commercial intercourse occurred among states and empires. However, the present form of the international community traces its origins to developments in Europe at the end of the Middle Ages. Distinct national societies were then beginning to replace the existing city-states as well as the sprawling feudal arrangements. As the antagonisms between these larger associations intensified, there was a perceived need for some higher authority which might impose order upon the growing turmoil.

By the ninth century there were two distinct poles of higher authority within Christendom: the papacy and the office of the Holy Roman Emperor. These spiritual and temporal spheres were thought of as integral parts of a hierarchy, an ordered unity which represented the subordination of all existence to an ultimate Beatific Vision.

The separation of these two powers was not absolute. The Church was not directly concerned with political affairs, although the Pope, as Vicar of Christ, intermittently exercised his supreme authority with respect to civic concerns. But in a maturing Europe there was a felt need for more decisive political governance. The papacy had once been the supreme arbiter of political differences, but the conciliatory power of the office had gone into decline. Other forms of ecclesiastical intervention were widely resented. A mood of anticlericalism was beginning to spread through the European continent. Within this Christian society, the only other likely source of supreme authority was the Holy Roman Emperor.

By the middle of the thirteenth century the office of the emperor had also lost its preeminence. Its authority was more symbolic than real. But a great humanist, Dante Alighieri, sought to revive its past magnificence. Dante ardently hoped that a renewed temporal power could vindicate its political supremacy by severing its legitimacy from any intrinsic dependence on the authority of the Church.

Dante knew from personal experience the adverse effect of anarchy on the flourishing of the human spirit. As a citizen of Florence he had lived through divisive municipal conflicts from which there was no effective appeal. He also knew that the peace of citizens could be shattered by encroachments from beyond municipal boundaries. It was not just a matter of unwelcome papal intrusions; around the city-states larger states and kingdoms were coming into existence and their contentiousness was threatening the general peace.[1]

These developments convinced Dante that political diversity was not always an unqualified good. Pluralism was a mark of vitality, but it could also be a source of great discord. As differences multiplied,

---

1. Dante Alighieri, *De Monarchia* (On World Government), trans. Herbert W. Schneider (Indianapolis: Bobbs Merrill, 1957). See "Dante and World Government," chap. 5 of *The Social and Political Ideas of Some Great Medieval Thinkers,* ed. F. J. C. Hearnshaw (1923); Hans Kelsen, *La Theoria Dello Stato in Dante* (Bologna: Massimiliano Boni Editore, 1974). See also Etienne Gilson, *Dante and Philosophy,* trans. David Moore (New York: Harper & Row, 1963), chap. 3; A. P. D'Entreves, *Dante as a Political Thinker* (Oxford: The Clarendon Press, 1952). In a letter of April 30, 1921, Pope Benedict XV honored Dante as a "teacher of Christian truth." *Praeclara Summorum* in vol. 6 of Claudia Carlen, ed., *The Papal Encyclicals* (Ann Arbor: The Pierian Press, 1981), at 213.

On the Holy Roman Empire see Frederick Heer, *The Holy Roman Empire,* trans. Janet Sondheimer (New York: Frederick Praeger, 1968); James Bryce, *The Holy Roman Empire* (London: Macmillan, 1904). For the possibilities of world government in ancient thought see S. M. Stern, *Aristotle on the World State* (Columbia, S.C.: University of South Carolina Press, 1968).

The earlier forms of international relations are discussed in Michael A. Rosvotseff, "International Relations in the Ancient World," in *The History and Nature of International Relations,* ed. Edmund A. Walsh, S. J. (New York: Macmillan, 1922), chap. 2. See generally Arnold Toynbee, *Civilization on Trial* (New York: Meridian, 1958), chaps. 4–5; Arthur Nussbaum, *A Concise History of the Law of Nations* (New York: Macmillan, 1962); and Antonio Cassese, *International Law in a Divided World* (Oxford: The Clarendon Press, 1968), chap. 2.

conflicts between communities increased. Through such confrontations between independent peoples a *libido dominandi* was making its appearance as the "she-wolf of the world at large."[2]

In his *De Monarchia,* written early in the fourteenth century, Dante argued with great passion and intelligence that the emperor, as heir to the Roman tradition, was the only one capable of enforcing a regime of universal peace and justice throughout the known world. The need for order arose out of the specific needs of human nature as well as the requirements of a civilized Christian existence. In developing his theory of a universal state Dante drew upon observations favorable to empire which he had made in his earlier poetry, essays, and epistles. He also made use of classical pagan sources and the best of prior Christian thought. The political philosophy of Aristotle and the theology of Thomas Aquinas were particularly influential. Dante creatively reimagined the principal themes of these venerable authorities and made them relevant to the problems of his own age.

The theology of Aquinas had drawn upon earlier juridical reflections in order to place the phenomenon of law within the framework of a universal order whose origins were divine. All creation was subject to the eternal law and all human regulation that purported to have inherent authority was ultimately derived from, and justified by, transcendental sources of absolute sovereignty. Rational creatures participated in this supreme order in a way which corresponded with their unique human dignity. Unlike the rest of the created world, mankind was not compelled to reach its fulfillment through any inherent necessity. Instead, through its understanding of the natural law, mankind participated directly in the order of Divine Providence. Natural reason, through which we discern what is intrinsically good and learn to avoid what is essentially evil, is the imprint upon us of a divine light which guides the quest for the proper use of freedom.[3]

To Aquinas, the understanding of the natural law fell under the domain of practical reason. In its disposition toward action, reason

---

2. D'Entreves, *Dante as a Political Thinker,* at 24.

3. St. Thomas Aquinas, *Summa Theologiae,* Ia IIae q.90 a.1.

guided the will in its desire to affirm the good. Dante recognized the practical aspect of reason as it was understood in the tradition of the natural law. But he also drew a deeper meaning from the linkage between the mind of man and the mind of God. Employing his vast imaginative powers, Dante tried to penetrate more deeply into the relationship between the love that moves the universe and the human desire for unity and peace.

Dante's understanding of order was more speculative than practical. He believed that the world is moved by thought. He did not share the modern instrumentalist view that thought exists for action. Dante's intellectualism led him to articulate a philosophical politics whose principles were derived from an ennobled conception of human nature. The substantial reality of the human creature mirrored a divine creativity. Man was the art of the Eternal.

Dante's conception of human nature is creative and developmental, manifesting a profound ontological disposition towards fulfillment. The divine purpose was not just to bring individuals into existence. They were also endowed with intelligible principles that directed their flourishing. Such a plenitude of being calls upon all the powers of reason, for reason is the paramount expression of what it means to be human.

For Dante, culture was of greater importance than politics. As the temporal venue of human fulfillment, culture is constantly threatened by the forces of barbarism. The elementary opposition between these positive and negative possibilities creates the need for order. Dante was convinced that the full flourishing of reason could only be achieved in circumstances of tranquillity; the undisturbed life is the fundamental condition of every flourishing civilization. An ordered existence is the core principle of the common good, and it must be secured upon foundations that are shared by all. There can be no genuine human happiness without universal peace.[4]

4. Dante Alighieri, *De Monarchia,* bk. 1, sec. 4. Compare Josef Pieper, *Leisure: The Basis of Culture,* with an introduction by T. S. Eliot, trans. Alexander Dru (New York: New American Library, 1963).

When strife and disorder abound, the highest aspirations of human nature become subject to destruction. The consequences of violence are incalculable. The culture which records mankind's intellectual and artistic accomplishments is lost or seriously damaged whenever humanity becomes enmeshed in strife and compromises its natural ascent to the divine. This squandering of human capital is the price which is paid for conflict within existing communities. For Dante, an inexorable descent into disorder is the condition of the whole of human society so long as it is not subject to the restraints of general government.

In the Dantean philosophy of the political, the preservation and advance of civilization is the supreme objective of international authority as well as the responsibility of the leadership of every particular kingdom. The earlier classical and Christian writers who had inspired Dante did not seriously consider the possibility of a universal political society. But in the imaginative mind of the poet, the substance of their thought was susceptible to expansion. Both Aristotle and Aquinas had attributed a positive, natural cause to the origins of human communities. They did not think of civic life simply as a remedy for evil or sinfulness; rather, it springs from the roots of human nature. Man is a political animal because humanity is inherently disposed toward society.

The natural inclination toward the political was usually thought of as being fulfilled in conventional forms of human association, with the State as the highest form of political organization. Dante saw that the Aristotelian idea had more inclusive potential. Dante's genius lay in his ability to transpose traditional ideas of the *polis* into a universal model that could accommodate the communal needs of the whole human race. In smaller communities, the need for order was obvious. What was not sufficiently understood, according to Dante, was the degree to which the growing interdependence of otherwise separate peoples required the articulation of a comparable, appropriate order of universal scale.[5]

---

5. On the basic inclination to political life, see Aristotle, *The Politics,* bk. 1, trans. B. Jowett, ed. Stephen Everson (Cambridge: Cambridge University Press, 1988); Aquinas, *Summa,* Ia IIae q.91 a. 2. The idea of natural inclination is controversial, even within

To understand Dante's theory of world government one must remember the theocentric ambience of the culture in which he lived. The problem of universal political governance was seen in the context of a vast cosmological order whose structure had been ordained by God. Within this framework the state is not the highest form of organization. More importantly, human society does not, of itself, approach self-sufficiency, even when the immense number of particular kingdoms is taken into account. The indispensability of further governance arises when the requirements of human peace and well-being are considered with reference to the divine order that permeates the whole created universe.[6]

For the complete realization of the *humana civilitas,* there must be a single, universal power of government. Dante's central argument was that the Holy Roman Emperor, by office and tradition, is best suited to fulfill this supreme temporal responsibility. Through his reign righteousness will prevail. Elevated above the petty interests of lesser men, the emperor is freed from that greed which too often perverts the local administration of justice. Supreme above all other rulers, the emperor would be able to accomplish more than was possible within lower forms of political association.

In Dante's scheme, all other governments are essentially imperfect. For Dante the imperfection of the unorganized world is most obvious in the case of quarrels between the smaller societies. Conflicts between lesser sovereigns are interminable. Intractable differences exist between those who consider themselves equals and there is no higher authority which can pass judgment upon the merits of their disputes. Since neither is subordinate to the other, their controversies can only be resolved by "a wider power which can rule both within its jurisdiction."[7]

---

the Thomistic tradition. Compare Jacques Maritain, *Man and the State* (Chicago: University of Chicago Press, 1951), with John Finnis, *Natural Law and Natural Rights* (Oxford: The Clarendon Press, 1980), chap. 13. See generally Servais Pinckaers, *The Sources of Christian Ethics,* trans. Sr. Mary Thomas Noble (Washington, D.C.: The Catholic University of America Press, 1995), chap. 17.

6. *De Monarchia,* bk. 1, secs. 6–7.

7. Ibid., bk. 1, sec. 10.

Dante also believed that all peoples would have a deeper allegiance to the governor of the world than to their more immediate rulers. Loyalty to the power closest at hand is provisional because domestic government tends to be tyrannical. The rule of the Emperor would inspire because his perspective would be the common good, and his superior power would correct those local injustices which were a perennial threat to personal liberty.[8]

As a political humanist Dante hoped to transpose to the temporal world an imaginative expression of the divine cosmological order. The *De Monarchia* was a deductive conception which demanded the essential subordination of lower forms of political association to the dominant idea of universal sovereignty. From imperial heights, humanity would be drawn into a conceptual edifice of supreme unity symbolized by the single will of the Emperor. The Emperor would be able to achieve the highest good of which humanity is capable by directing the uniform movement of many wills toward the supreme objective of universal peace.

Dante's *De Monarchia* did more than passionately expand the corpus of traditional wisdom to embrace the emerging need for universal order. Dante also drew upon newer intellectual currents that were beginning to influence the culture of Europe. These novel strains of thought would give a more transcendental thrust to his idea of a world state.

Dante's theory grew out of the Aristotelian-Thomistic synthesis. One may also detect the influence of Plato upon his thought. But the *De Monarchia* is, in important respects, an application of the metaphysics of Averroës and his followers to the realm of the political. Averroës, the great Arabic philosopher, thought of the world as an eternal reality which was endlessly moved by a self-thinking thought or mind. Men had no intellect of their own, and did not think; they were *thought into from above,* by a separate intellectual substance. Averroës postulated an eternal being in order to account for the complete realization of the intellect which is potentially accessible to the whole human race.

8. Ibid., bk. 1, sec. 12.

Complete knowledge cannot be realized all at once, or over a limited period of time. It can only be realized in a universal community which is thought of as having an existence of its own.

The *De Monarchia* is an intellectual approach to the problem of world order. Dante gave Averroës' concept of total comprehension a more concrete human form. He envisioned an abstract community, governed by an absolute ruler, which could actualize all of the knowledge and culture available to man.[9] Dante constructed in his mind an idea of the Holy Roman Emperor as the incarnation of a comprehensive moral ideal which promoted the goal of human cultural fulfillment. The political was absorbed in the philosophical. In seeking to overcome universal disorder through an imaginative conception Dante was a creature of his time. But, as we shall see, his abstract and speculative approach to global governance would be repeated, in different forms, throughout the history of international relations.

II

Dante's vision failed. The failure was, in hindsight, predictable. To strengthen his thesis that the Holy Roman Emperor should rule the world, Dante had appealed to collective memories of the glory of Rome, the sanction of divine providence, and the ideal of a supreme temporal power acting independently of the authority of the Church. But his imagination was no match for reality. However elevated in thought and tradition, the Roman *imperium* was gradually being superseded by the independent state. The emperors had to compete, on a practical level, with princes whose material resources were often superior to their own. And, in spite of Dante's theory, the emperors did not have an authentic base of common allegiance.

Human freedom flourishes when it is ruled by reason. Dante thought that the human race, being reasonable, would be drawn to esteem, above all, a world ruler who guaranteed their peace and their liberties. But as national sentiments grew, citizens became increasingly

9. On the influence of Averroës see Etienne Gilson, *Dante and Philosophy,* chap. 3, and his *Reason and Revelation in the Middle Ages* (New York: Scribners, 1938). See generally Philip H. Wicksteed, *Dante and Aquinas* (New York: Haskell House, 1971).

attached to more immediate authority. Imperial status declined in respect and power as political authority within national boundaries became more centralized. These changes stimulated new reflections on the nature, and range, of sovereignty.

The writings of the Spanish scholastics during that country's Golden Age were of decisive importance. These jurist-theologians struggled to reconcile the realities of national independence with traditional ideals of Christian and human solidarity. Like Dante, they wished to distinguish political from religious authority. As for Christendom, they affirmed the ecclesiastical sovereignty of the Church, but they held that the Pope did not have direct jurisdiction over political affairs. They rejected the idea that the Church possessed a universal temporal authority as nothing more than an invention of canonists to please and flatter the Pope.[10]

The Spaniards also refuted Dante's idea of world government. They did so through a process of reasoning which combined ethical, political, and legal arguments.

During the period before Charles I of Spain became the Emperor Charles V, the Dominican Francisco De Vitoria asserted that universal political sovereignty was incompatible with natural law. By nature all are free from any subjection other than that of the immediate family. If global political authority were to exist it would not, as Dante thought, be given directly by God. Such power would have to be conferred at some point in time by a political community which freely appointed a specific ruler. A Lord of the World would have to be designated by an appropriate body politic. This would require a gathering of a greater part of the world. Such an extraordinary political event had never taken place, nor was it practically conceivable that it would ever occur.[11]

10. *The Principles of Political and International Law in the Works of Francisco De Vitoria,* ed. Antonio Truyol Serra (Madrid: Ediciones Cultural Hispanica, 1946), chap. 2.

11. Ibid. Compare the position of Domingo Soto in Bernice Hamilton, *Political Thought in Sixteenth Century Spain* (Oxford: The Clarendon Press, 1963), chap. 4. The similar position of Suarez is discussed in his *De Legibus ac Deo Legislatore,* bk. 3, chap. 2, in *Selections from Three Works of Francisco Suarez S. J.,* vol. 2 (Washington, D.C.: Carnegie Endowment, 1944).

The idea of world government was also addressed, and decisively refuted, by the greatest of the Spanish thinkers, the Jesuit Francisco Suarez. He reaffirmed the position of the earlier scholastics, and in doing so he gave special attention to the concept of jurisdiction:

> [The] power in question does not reside in the whole community of mankind, since the whole community of mankind does not constitute one single commonwealth or kingdom. Nor does that power reside in one individual since such an individual would have to receive it from the hands of men and this is inconceivable in as much as men have never agreed to confer it. Furthermore, not even by title of war whether justly or unjustly has there has there at any time been a prince who made himself a temporal sovereign over the whole world. Therefore, the ordinary course of human nature points to the conclusion that a human legislative power of universal character and worldwide extent does not exist and has never existed nor is it morally possible that it should have done so.[12]

The reasoning used by the Spanish scholastics to refute claims of universal monarchy was also applied to questions concerning the origins of national sovereignty. The original sovereignty of the people was an essential principle of their political thought. And they applied it bravely in resisting the theory of the divine right of kings.

A monarch, once legitimately established, ruled with absolute authority. The power was greater than the popular authority that conferred it. But political dominion is not conferred by God upon any particular individual. By the force of natural law it belongs to a community as a whole. This is by divine plan. For God, in creating men, gave them the power necessary for their preservation and self-government.

For Suarez, supreme political authority did not reside, as it did with later contractarian theory, in separate individuals. Nor was it possessed by a people considered simply as a formless mass of individuals. This ultimate power only arose when men gathered in community and were collectively sustained by a bond of fellowship which united them in a shared political purpose which they were committed to pursue.[13]

12. Suarez, *De Legibus,* bk. 3, chap. 4., para. 7.
13. Ibid., bk. 3, chap. 2, para. 4.

The major issue facing the Spanish thinkers was essentially the same as that posed by Dante three hundred years earlier: the need for order beyond state boundaries. With the rise of exploration and commerce, and increasing contact with a non-Christian world, it was necessary to find a new harmony among the disparate states of this expanding international society. A political solution was foreclosed by the rejection of universal jurisdiction and assertion of the sovereign independence by the major powers of the time. In addition, the juridical orientation of the Spanish scholastics led them to reduce problems of order to problems of law. The great jurist-theologians had the uncommon ability to draw the various forms of divine and human law into a single system. They were also able to subject the whole to an ethical interpretation which was vindicated by divine sanction. The Spanish mind was a mind that "contemplate[d] the universe as subject to the reign of jurisprudence."[14]

The main step in their reasoning was to affirm the existence of a transnational community. The Spanish scholastics referred to the world society in language which sometimes implied the existence of a political community, but it is unlikely that they had an organized society in mind. They thought more in terms of an amorphous *humana civilitas* or general community of the human race. This was not just a metaphor. This universal society was substantial and real enough to have some juridical authority with moral sanctions. The existence of a whole human community imposed upon every head of state the obligation to consider that his responsibilities, both as a ruler and as a human being, were not restricted to the interests of his subjects:

> Therefore, although a given sovereign state, commonwealth, or kingdom may constitute a perfect community in itself, consisting of it own members, nevertheless, each one of these states is also, in a certain sense, and viewed in relation to the human race, a member of that universal society; for these states when standing alone are never so self sufficient that they do not require some mutual assistance, association,

14. John Neville Figgis, *Studies of Political Thought from Gerson to Grotius 1414–1625* (New York: Harper, 1907), 188–89, 215.

and intercourse, at times for their own greater welfare and advantage, but at other times because of some moral necessity or need. . .[15]

The need for universal law arose out of an awareness of general human interdependence. The normative order of the world would not be imposed by a universal political authority. It would, nevertheless, be an order of reason, and it would be guided by a philosophy of law whose range and moral force was felt to be an appropriate measure of international coexistence.

Within the scholastic tradition the concept of law was comprehended under three broad jural divisions which were meant to integrate the human understanding of legal obligation with the divine order of the universe. This comprehensive sweep led to the trichotomous division of jural phenomenona into the natural law, the *jus gentium,* and the positive civil law of particular states. The first, which dealt with the essentials of human nature, was the expression of divine wisdom. Its immutable principles regulated the articulation of the other two forms of law, which were of human origin.[16]

The Spanish scholastics could pass between these gradations of law (and the canon law as well) with relative ease and with due regard for the hierarchical priorities. As their jurisprudence was ultimately theocentric, they maintained an ideal of universal law which subjected the jural sphere to the demands of reason and objective justice. The breadth of their conception also prevented the sphere of the legal from being reduced to an expression of arbitrary will.

In the reworking of the phenomenon of law into a system of international law the idea of custom was of central importance. Aquinas had recognized the existence of a law of nations distinct from but related to the natural law. He had also recognized that custom can have the force of law.[17] For a jurist of the stature of Suarez, it was relatively easy to combine these two sources into a new unity.

15. Suarez, *De Legibus,* bk. 2, chap. 19, para. 9.
16. Aquinas, *Summa,* Ia IIae q.95 a.4; Ia IIae q.94 a. 3. See also Jacques Maritain, *Man and the State* (Washington, D.C.: The Catholic University of America Press, 1998), chap. 4, pt. 3.
17. *Summa,* Ia IIae q.97 a.3.

Suarez reasoned, by analogy, that as custom can make law within a state, it can also make law for the entire community of nations. For Suarez, this universal law was drawn from two sources: the practices of states, and the laws and practices within states, which, by their substantial similarities, are of universal validity. The habitual and general character of these practices give them a jural character of sufficient weight to bind the consciences of sovereigns and regulate their behavior in the field of interstate relations.

The teaching of the scholastics was that all are bound to observe this unwritten law, or *jus gentium*. The duties which these principles imposed were not, to their minds, onerous. The scholastics were optimistic in believing that such norms, being recognized by most civilized nations, have an inherent reasonableness which should elicit the consent of any just and honorable ruler.[18]

The *De Legibus ac Deo Legislatore* of Suarez was published in 1612. In 1625 a devout Dutch scholar and lawyer, Huig de Groot, or Grotius, published a work which has come to be respected as the foundation of modern international law. *De Jure Belli ac Pacis* reflected the author's revulsion towards the prevalence of warfare among the rulers of his time who purported to adhere to the Christian faith. Grotius was a realist. Rejecting the extreme views of the pacifists, he hoped to persuade his readers that it was possible to distinguish righteous from unrighteous wars. He also laid down the jural principles which should govern the conduct of hostilities.

Grotius's *magnum opus* reflected the culture of the seventeenth century. By that time, the Reformation and the Counter-Reformation had affected the political as well as the religious aspects of European life. Grotius's native Netherlands had thrown off the yoke of Phillip II and established itself as a small, independent state desirous of attaining legal equality in the family of nations. Like other states, it was redefining the idea of Christendom.

18. James Leslie Brierly, *The Basis of Obligation in International Law and Other Papers* (Oxford: The Clarendon Press, 1958), chap. 28.

Dante had tried to give the Holy Roman Emperor a divine mandate to universal temporal rule which was separate from the authority of the Church. The Protestant Reformers hoped to raise up "godly princes" whose supreme territorial authority would be equally independent of ecclesiastical control. The power of the princes within their separate domains was to be as absolute as that attributed to the Emperor in the *De Monarchia*.

There were further, more ominous, developments. For scholastics such as Suarez, ecclesiastical authority came from above, while civil authority came from below. The jurisdiction of the Church was based upon divine mandate, while that of rulers was derived from the sovereignty of the people. But in the new Europe the right to command was being legitimized without reference to popular consent.

To secular theorists such as Bodin, civil strife within states and kingdoms required greater centralized control. This assertion of complete authority was reinforced by religious thought. Luther counseled complete political submission. Every well-ordered community, especially one spiritually inspired, required a single center of supreme and indivisible authority to which all godly subjects should submit. Sovereignty was now understood as the absolute power of Christian rulers over all who resided within their jurisdiction.[19]

These changes influenced the life and work of Grotius. The *De Jure Belli ac Pacis* was written while Grotius was in exile in France, having escaped imprisonment because of his involvement in the Arminian predestination controversy in the Netherlands. In spite of the injustice which he had suffered, Grotius believed that the power of the ruler must be severed from the consent of the citizens. He rejected the opinion that sovereignty always resided in the people. In the interest of security and good government, the public could completely transfer their political authority to their rulers. And the independent states

19. Jean Bodin, *Six Books of Commonwealth,* trans. M. J. Tooley (Oxford: B. Blackwell, 1955), bk. 1, chaps. 8–10. And see F. H. Hinsley, *Sovereignty,* 2nd ed. (Cambridge: Cambridge University Press, 1986), chap. 5. On Luther, see Figgis, *Studies of Political Thought,* lec. 3. See generally John Calvin, *On God and Political Duty,* ed. John T. McNeill (New York: Liberal Arts Press, 1956).

were free from any pretensions of universal empire, either political or ecclesiastical.[20]

For Grotius, as for Dante, the destructiveness of war was the paramount issue. Grotius's moral and religious fervor was focused on determining how to bring the external exercise of sovereign power under some appropriate regulation. Bodin had taught that the sovereign could not in any way be subject to the command of another. His power was of necessity absolute, both in relation to those within, and those beyond, his kingdom. But since the sovereign princes were established by God to govern the rest of mankind they were subject to His sovereign commands. The rules to which the princes owed obedience were expressed in divine and natural law. Because of its close relation to the natural law, the princes should also observe the law of nations. Likewise Grotius, while affirming the independence of separate states, wanted to convince his readers that such sovereignty was not incompatible with an allegiance to a higher spiritual authority. He, too, would commend submission to the divine will. He further recognized a law of nature whose foundations were to be discovered by reason and ratified by the testimony of a shared civilization.[21]

Grotius's treatment of the natural law builds upon the classical tradition as well as the writings of his Catholic predecessors. He repeats what was affirmed by Cicero: that the law of nature was the law of right reason, commanding duties and prohibiting wrongdoing. This

20. Hugo Grotius, *De Jure Belli ac Pacis,* trans. Francis W. Kelsey (Indianapolis: Bobbs-Merrill, 1962), bk. 1, chap. 3, sec. 8. *Per contra,* Suarez argued in *De Legibus* that although the sovereign power may be transferred, and even pass by way of succession, the community is always regarded as its ultimate possessor. *De Legibus,* bk. 3, chap. 4, 8. The position of Johannes Althusius is the same. Johannes Althusius, *Politica* (Indianapolis: Liberty Fund, 1995), chap. 9, secs. 12–27. For Grotius's deviation from Althusius' view of sovereignty, see Figgis, *Studies of Political Thought,* lec. 7.

21. Charles S. Edwards, *Hugo Grotius: The Miracle of Holland* (Chicago: Nelson Hall, 1981), 51–69. Compare Bodin on the general obligation of princes to divine law in *Six Books of Commonwealth,* bk. 5, chap. 6. For general studies of Grotius see *Hugo Grotius and International Relations,* ed. Hedley Bull, Benedict Kingsbury, and Adam Roberts (Oxford: The Clarendon Press, 1990); W. S. M. Knight, *The Life and Work of Hugo Grotius* (London: Sweet & Maxwell, 1925); and Figgis, *Political Thought from Gerson to Grotius* (New York: Harper & Row, 1960) chap. 7.

higher law was eternal and unchangeable. Being discovered by reason, it was also a law of all mankind. It would be valid even if one might concede that God did not exist. Grotius, as we shall see, was criticized for raising such a possibility; but there is no doubt that he was a deeply religious man. Like Suarez, he affirmed that natural law was sustained by the divine will. But Grotius was not a theologian. He was a Protestant humanist and a man of action who desired to create a legal order within the developing international society. His approach was understandably different from that of the Spanish Scholastics, whose interest in international law was governed by its bearing upon questions of eternal salvation.[22]

For Grotius, the law of nature was confirmed by history and experience. From the treasures of time there had emerged a body of laws, the law of nations, which had been legitimized by the consent of states. States were independent, but not so self-sufficient as to have no need for justice. And Grotius was convinced that justice must become law.

Grotius's reflections were driven by the moral necessity of distinguishing between just and unjust wars. Because justice prohibits the wrongful taking of what rightfully belongs to another, war could be lawfully commenced for the redress of injuries. Where there was just cause, recourse to arms was a matter of right. And as an enforcement of law, war had a pacific, as well as a moral, purpose.[23]

Grotius speaks boldly of the powers of reason. However, like Augustine before him, he was acutely aware of how much reason needs the aid of faith. His treatise is filled with appeals to biblical injunctions, and he draws upon the divine will as a source of moderation to restrain the impulses of violence and the cruelties of warfare. Thus he asserts that in vindicating rights we may, in some circumstances, be required by the precepts of charity to refrain from insisting upon what we are entitled to under the law of nature.

By combining natural, human, and divine laws Grotius sought to create a new international unity. Although he recognized that the

---

22. *De Jure Belli ac Pacis,* Prolegomena, II. The theological significance of jurisprudence is discussed by Suarez in his preface to *De Legibus.*

23. *De Jure Belli ac Pacis,* bk. 1, chaps. 2–4; bk. 2, chap. 1.

world is fragmented into separate and independent states, he believed that through the use of reason the human community could become essentially one. As a humanist, Grotius stressed the cultural foundations of the emerging international jurisprudence; as a devout Christian, he appealed to the divine order as a vindication of the universal need for justice and peace. But the whole Grotian edifice was built upon assumptions about human nature and sociability which would be increasingly challenged by new developments in political theory. These innovations would substantially influence the direction of international thought and practice and move it away from the path of Grotian idealism to a more effective but destructive realism.

III

The new international society, composed of separate states independent of any higher authority, was confirmed by the Westphalian Treaties of 1648. The supreme authority of the Protestant and Catholic princes within their respective territories was recognized. In spite of Dante's hopes, the jurisdiction of the Holy Roman Emperor was limited to the German lands of Central Europe, and the office was stripped of all important transnational authority. The independent states legitimated by the Treaties were still creatures of personal authority and the external policies of each were determined by a ruling prince. If the interactions between these sovereigns were to be subject to some authoritative regulation, the appeal could not be made to the political supremacy of the emperor or to the spiritual jurisdiction of the Roman pontiff.

Although expressed in a juridical form by thinkers such as Grotius, the standards which formed the basis of international law were essentially moral in nature. Appeal was primarily made to the principles of the natural law, the rational nature of man, or the Christian piety of the rulers. But these external restraints were beginning to disappear as normative forces within seventeenth-century European culture.

For Grotius, good faith was a central principle of international order, the foundation of every treaty, and of indispensable value to the preservation of peace. Good faith was a common duty which all rulers should feel bound to observe as a matter of conscience. But these ideals were already in competition with more realistic evaluations of the nature and purposes of personal rule. Machiavelli's ideas on the amoralism of governance were beginning to influence international conduct.

In *The Prince,* which was published a century before Grotius's treatise, Machiavelli acknowledged that the keeping of agreements was laudable, but was not always practicable. It is dangerous for a ruler to always act in good faith. A prince must make preservation of his power and the security of the state his highest duties. And he must also be realistic. The world is full of vulgar and evil men and many rulers cannot be expected to always keep their word. In such a dangerous milieu one must keep up appearances. A prudent ruler must always *seem* to be honorable. But he must not keep faith if it is against his interests or if the reasons which led him to assume an obligation no longer exist. In the actions of princes—from which there are no appeals—the end justifies the means.[24]

By revealing the darker springs of human action Machiavelli provoked an ethical debate over the nature and limits of sovereign power which continues to influence our understanding of the role of morality in foreign affairs. However, there were other factors at work in European philosophy and culture which would pose an even greater challenge to those who hoped to bring justice and stability to the emerging society of independent states. As a consequence of the Renaissance and the Reformation, a new subjectivism was abroad which was beginning to affect the general understanding of human nature.

In the seventeenth century there was a growing conviction that there were no higher, or final, ends to which the will of the individual could rationally adhere. As the world became less and less intelligible, human connectedness diminished. An isolated self was forced to create his own world out of his inner resources. The scientific revolution further encouraged the belief that the internal structures and powers of the individual mind were all that was left of a human nature which

---

24. Niccolo Machiavelli, *The Prince* (1513)(New York: New American Library, 1952), chap. 18.

previously had given itself an exalted position within the cosmological order of the universe.[25]

These profound epistemic changes began to be reflected in political theories. While these theories were primarily concerned with the relation between the individual and the state, they would also influence the understanding of international relations. Hobbes was a critical figure in these developments. He postulated an original state of nature inhabited by separate individuals who had no shared desire to live together. In this unorganized environment the relations between the self and others were characterized by mutual isolation and chronic enmity. Each was independent and driven by his own desires and aversions. The separate individual used his reasoning powers to achieve his self-preservation and to direct the expansion of his existence in the direction dictated by his emotional life.[26]

The state of nature is also a state of equality. The obvious differences of power among individuals were to Hobbes more apparent than real. The weak, by cunning or confederation, can always bring down the strong. Most importantly, the state of nature is a state of war. Hobbes did not mean that there was constant armed conflict in a state of nature. His point is that whenever individuals try to coexist without government a propensity toward combat is unavoidable. Here Hobbes's thought surpasses the practical advice of Machiavelli. In Hobbes's logic, discord is not caused by the presence of evil adversaries, nor is it based upon innate malice or aggressiveness. Rather, for Hobbes, it is a universal truth that natural insecurities, coupled with incompatible desires for prestige and advancement, inevitably lead to conflict in any society that is not formally organized.

Hobbes's essential insight is that unorganized society is inherently unstable. Every individual is subject to the potential of violent death

25. Charles Taylor, *Sources of the Self* (Cambridge, Mass.: Harvard University Press, 1980); Roberto Mangabeira Unger, *Knowledge and Politics* (New York: The Free Press, 1975). See also my *Descent into Subjectivity* (Wakefield, N.H.: Longwood Academic, 1990), chap. 3.

26. Thomas Hobbes, *Leviathan* (1651), ed. Michael Oakeshott (New York: Macmillan, 1962), pt. 2, chaps. 17–18.

because order cannot be created out of this chaos of passion. According to Hobbes, a peaceful life is only possible through a covenanted undertaking by which all submit to a supreme and absolute political authority.

In Hobbes's political theory the relationship between states which recognize no higher temporal authority is the same as that between individuals who attempt to coexist without government. Independent states, like independent individuals, are enemies by nature. For Hobbes, the natural state of nations was not as chaotic as that between individuals. Preparations for war provided employment for citizens and strong nations could, in that prenuclear age, arm themselves sufficiently to avoid complete destruction. Nevertheless, the underlying enmity persisted. Because of their mutual equality and independence commonwealths are

> . . . in continual jealousies, and in the state and posture of gladiators; having their weapons pointing, and their eyes fixed on one another; that is, their forts, garrisons, and guns upon the frontiers of their kingdoms; and continual spies upon their neighbors; which is a posture of war. . . [27]

The philosophy of Hobbes was a direct challenge to the international idealism of Grotius, and it had a corrosive effect upon the principles of Grotian international jurisprudence. The *De Jure Belli ac Pacis* was directed toward a determination of entitlements. Grotius wanted to ascertain when, and under what conditions, a ruler had a *right* to engage in warfare. The right was an individual moral power, which a ruler could justifiably exercise because of its congruence with the moral order of the law of nature. For Grotius, such rights became, on the international plane, legal causes of action. Hobbes was also concerned with the individual and his rights. For Hobbes, the central idea

27. Hobbes, *Leviathan,* pt. 1, chap. 13. Compare his *De Cive* (1658), pt. 2, chap. 13, sec. 7. And see David Gauthier, *The Logic of Leviathan: The Moral and Political Theory of Thomas Hobbes* (Oxford: The Clarendon Press, 1969). For a summary of Hobbes's influence upon international theory see the appendix to Gauthier; see also Edward Dickerson, *The Equality of States in International Law* (Cambridge, Mass.: Harvard University Press, 1920), chap. 3.

was that of natural right. Hobbesian rights were not, as with Grotius, determined by their relation to an objective moral order; for Hobbes a right was a subjective claim which, of itself, becomes the source of law for anyone—individual or ruler—living in a state of nature. As will become evident, Hobbes's understanding of the self-justifying nature of rights would have a pernicious influence upon the development of international law.[28]

Grotius had built his theory of international law upon a premise of sociability. A desire for social life was a unique human quality. It led to the need to live with others, in some organized way, according to the measure of honor, respect, and intelligence. Having a capacity for goodness, man can understand the essential moral principles that flow from his social nature.

In the subjectivism of the new naturalists good and evil were losing their moral connotations and becoming nothing more than effusions of desire and aversion. Man was now understood as being fundamentally asocial and selfish; his claims against others were governed more by passion than by reason. The principal objective of Hobbes's political philosophy was to justify monarchical supremacy, but his pessimistic outlook was widely shared. The growth of this disposition would be reflected in the writings of others who would further undermine the moral idealism of the Grotian tradition.

The darker implications can be seen in Spinoza's theory of human nature and international morality. Spinoza explored some of the deeper implications of the universal urge toward self-preservation and independence. These tendencies are metaphysical, characteristic of all beings. Power is the essence of any particular thing, and the greater the power the greater is the reality. For Spinoza, power is an even greater force in human relations than it was for Hobbes.

In the philosophy of Spinoza natural right is a form of power. Individuals living in a state of nature have to vest supreme power in one man, or group, in order to secure peace. But the sovereign serves the

28. See generally Leo Strauss, *The Political Philosophy of Hobbes,* trans. Elsa M. Sinclair (Oxford: The Clarendon Press, 1936).

individual's interest just so long as the superior force of the ruler exists in fact and not merely in theory. Force is to be applied by those who govern in a way that will hold the community together. According to Spinoza there is no covenant, or natural law, which guarantees the permanence of the political community.[29]

Spinoza applied his conception of human nature to the relationship between the individual and the state, and then transferred these ideas, *more geometrico,* to the relations between states. The formation of territorial states did not eliminate the state of nature; it simply transferred it to a higher plane. States are in a state of nature in relation to each other. Each has an innate urge for self-preservation and independence. Every political society has as much natural right as it has the power to exist and find its place in the universe. This *potentia* is formed by bringing all desires within the state into unity, combining reason with all the impulses of existence. Yet such natural power is nothing else but the power of God, which is absolutely free.[30]

Like Grotius, Spinoza had a deep desire for peace among nations. Spinoza urged rulers to be content with what they had, not to be covetous, and to ". . . strive, therefore, most eagerly by every means to avoid war and preserve peace."[31] But the international state of nature structured the relations between rulers in a way that made peace an impractical ideal.

In a state of nature wrongdoing is virtually impossible. If anyone does wrong, it is to himself and not to another. Since men are chiefly guided by appetite and emotion, the good is measured by their desires. Moreover, the people's welfare is the highest law that the ruler must

29. *A Political Treatise* in *The Chief Works of Benedict De Spinoza,* trans. R. H. M. Elwes (New York: Dover Publications, 1901), vol. 1; A. G. A. Baltz, *Writings on Political Philosophy by Benedict De Spinoza* (New York: Appleton-Crofts, 1937); Robert M. McShea, *The Political Philosophy of Spinoza* (New York: Columbia University Press, 1968); Stuart Hampshire, *Spinoza* (Harmondsworth: Penguin Books, 1952); F. J. C. Hearnshaw, ed., *The Social and Political Ideas of Some Great Thinkers of the Sixteenth and Seventeenth Centuries* (New York: Barnes & Noble, 1967).

30. H. Lauterpacht, "Spinoza and International Law," 8 British Yearbook of International Law 89 (1927).

31. Benedict Spinoza, *Political Treatise,* chap. 7, secs. 7, 28.

observe. It is to that end all other laws, both human and divine, must be adjusted.

Higher norms must also be subject to the desire for independence. Although a state can protect itself from attack more effectively than can an isolated individual, the state is not truly independent so long as its actions are motivated by fear of its adversaries. Subjectively, fear is a form of dependence. The need for help from others also compromises the desire for complete autonomy. Under such pressures, the distinctions between just and unjust wars lose their restraining force. All that is necessary to wage war by right is the will to do so. Treaties may relieve conflict and, when multilateral, they can reduce fear and lessen the power to make war. But like all international agreements, such security arrangements should be sustained only so long as there is fear of loss or hope of gain. For when one supreme authority promises another but then finds that the promise is contrary to the welfare of its subjects "it is surely bound to break its word."[32]

In the *ethos* of the seventeenth century the advance of science renewed the aspirations for an intellectual autonomy that had been introduced into European culture at the time of the Renaissance. The dominance of theology was being challenged by the new rationalism. Rationalism insisted upon separating science from ecclesiastical control and also demanded independence for philosophy and the other humanistic disciplines. Since the Middle Ages the relationship between human reason and revealed dogma had been in a state of tension. As Europe became more secularized, theology lost its preeminence and began to play a more instrumental role in cultural life. It was increasingly used to give a spiritual sanction to natural ethics and to endow the logic of the new theories of government with a supreme, and decisive, authority.[33]

32. Ibid. See also chap. 3, sec. 17.

33. Peter Gay, *The Enlightenment: The Rise of Modern Paganism* (New York: Alfred Knopf, 1967); E. Cassier, *The Philosophy of the Enlightenment,* trans. Fritz C. A. Koelln and James P. Pettegrave (Princeton: Princeton University Press, 1951); see generally Gilson, *Reason and Revelation in the Middle Ages* (New York: Scribners, 1938.

All these tendencies were reflected in the work of the distinguished Lutheran jurist Baron Samuel Pufendorf. Pufendorf sought to mediate between the individualism of Hobbes and the idealism of Grotius. For Pufendorf, individuals in a state of nature were not isolated, nor were they essentially enemies. Hobbes's theory did not sufficiently account for either the natural sociability of humankind, nor of the nobility of a human nature distinguished from the rest of creation by the faculty of reason.

Pufendorf believed that in their primeval state—as set forth in Scripture—humans were not bellicose. Particular hostilities were understood as deviations from a norm of preexisting harmony. In such a world the fundamental rights and obligations of natural law were operative, and man had some power to use reason to discipline his passions. Most importantly, he was inclined towards the peace recommended by his reason.[34]

Pufendorf is an important transitional figure because he was, in one sense, the last of the scholastics. His jurisprudence was theocentric as well as humanistic. For him, the order of the human world was not, as with Grotius, intelligible to reason without reference to its divine source. Law was a dictate of conscience. To give a full sense of accountability it had to be the command of a superior who had the power to coerce obedience. God was both the Legislator and Executive of the natural law. He was also the Supreme Vindicator of its justice. Although he often "walks with a slow step," God will not allow those who violate the law of nature to go unpunished.[35]

Men have an appetite for society, but Pufendorf thought that they are not naturally drawn to it. The classical idea of an inclination to political life as an inherent part of human nature was incompatible with the new individualism. Men become political animals *after* they become citizens. The Baron also did not believe that submission to sovereign political authority was a contractarian undertaking. He rea-

---

34. Samuel Pufendorf, *De Jure Naturae et Gentium* (1672) (Carnegie trans., 1934); *Elementorum Jurisprudentiae* (1660) (Carnegie trans., 1931); *The Political Writings of Samuel Pufendorf*, ed. Craig L. Carr, trans. Michael J. Seidler (New York: Oxford University Press, 1994).

35. *Elementorum*, bk. 1, def. 12.

soned that the fathers of families establish states to surround themselves with protection from the evils threatened by other men.

For Pufendorf human evil was not as pervasive as it was for either Machiavelli or Hobbes. Yet disputes reflect human failings. Conflicts arise because some have an insatiable desire for material things or because they are ambitious or vindictive. Thus the wise understand that "unless there were courts of justice, one man would devour another."[36]

Men who are able to reflect upon the human condition see the value of political association. In using their reason to reach such a conclusion they are following a fundamental law which bears the imprint of the Creator. In this larger perspective self-love and sociability are not incompatible. Pufendorf realized that self-love inclines the individual toward self-preservation, and he needs others to sustain those desires. Egoism and need, when coupled with the awareness of evil in oneself and others, make men sociable.

What arises by nature is supplemented by convention. When men are organized together into states they gain security from mutual injuries and enjoy their material advantages. These potentials become facts through the growth of the customs and positive laws which give substance to sociality. Pufendorf was a historian as well as a jurist, and this immersion in time protected his thought from the *a priori* reasoning of a more abstract individualism. But he was also sensitive to the value of personal freedom. He saw that an anthropology of social evolution, supported by express or implied consent, preserves individual freedom while, at the same time, it draws attention to the textured realities of human association.[37]

Pufendorf felt that individuals who suffer injustice at the hands of the sovereign can legitimately defend themselves from such abuses. He also believed that the people can impose restrictions upon sovereign power at the time it is instituted in order to secure some general safeguards for their liberties. But in Pufendorf's theory of government the people can never rebel. For it would be wrong for them to take back

36. Pufendorf, *De Jure,* bk. 7, chap. 1, sec 7.
37. See the introduction to Carr, ed., *The Political Writings of Samuel Pufendorf.*

the authority which by their consent they have given to the sovereign. Their submission is to a supreme ruler who, while he may be subject to some legal limits in relation to his subjects, is not otherwise accountable to any other earthly power.

The general premises of his reasoning led Pufendorf to the conviction that international relations were beyond the realm of any human law. Recall that for the Spanish jurist-theologians such as Suarez the *jus gentium,* as a form of unwritten law, could oblige in conscience. All law based upon reason could create moral obligations. The reasonable principles of customary law, when affirmed by most nations, are related to, even if not declaratory of, natural law. The *jus gentium* is constituted and imposed by practical human reason. Because of imperative human needs both within and beyond the state, the community of nations has established general laws for itself. To Suarez, therefore, the *jus gentium* was a form of obligatory positive law.

Pufendorf, anticipating the positivist jurisprudence of the nineteenth century, held that there can be no positive law of nations because any law, properly so-called, can only bind if it proceeds from a superior sovereign. Positive laws imposed upon citizens within the state satisfy the definition; but sovereign princes, not being subject to any higher political authority, are not, in their international relations, subject to any human law. For this Protestant jurist the *jus gentium* could not have any independent binding power. Its precepts could have meaning only in terms of their relation to natural law because the only law by which the sovereigns of states were bound was the higher law imposed by the Divine Sovereignty.

Pufendorf did not accept Grotius's theory of a natural law that culturally unified the whole of international society. As a Lutheran, Pufendorf was determined to correct what he saw as the excessive humanism of his Dutch predecessor. For Pufendorf, the natural law was transcendental in its origins. Being a divine command, it applied immediately to the conscience of each separate sovereign.[38]

38. Pufendorf, *Elementorum,* bk. 1, def. 13, sec. 24. See generally Alfred P. Rubin, *Ethics and Authority in International Law* (Cambridge: Cambridge University Press, 1997),

Dante's vision of universal imperial authority also had no place in Pufendorf's understanding of internationalism. The Holy Roman Emperor was an impotent absurdity, and other ideas of collective security were not worthy of serious consideration. To Pufendorf, all such ideas tended to compromise the dignity of earthly princes. Their sovereign authority was enhanced by the absence of any higher political power with jurisdiction over them. One who is supreme within his own territory can have no earthly superior. Having no master, he should govern himself by reason. Sovereign rulers, like individuals, should be disposed toward that peace which is commended by reason. But coexistence in a state of nature leads to inevitable instabilities which the natural law is powerless to prevent.

Pufendorf was not a follower of Spinoza, but he was realistic enough to grasp the ethical dilemmas which a conscientious ruler must face in his foreign relations. As far as possible, the justifications for the use of force should be free from doubt. Suspicions or fears may motivate the construction of defenses, but unless there is moral certainty that another state intends to cause harm, there is no right to engage in warfare. However, in the absence of more positive regulations, these general ethical restraints were subject to substantial qualifications. For example, in Pufendorf's international jurisprudence the "excessively swelling power" of a neighbor would have a legitimate influence upon a ruler's deliberations over the possible initiation of hostilities.

Similar difficulties surrounded the general duty to keep the peace. Pufendorf was acutely aware that international obligations are reciprocal. If one prince violates the relevant precepts, the injured party is forbidden to use unlimited force in reply. Nonetheless it is not unjust for a sovereign to repay a lesser harm with a greater evil because the principles of proportionate justice apply strictly only to tribunals with superior established authority.[39]

---

chap. 2, and Leonard Krieger, *The Politics of Discretion: Pufendorf and the Acceptance of Natural Law* (Chicago: University of Chicago Press, 1965), chap. 3, sec. 2.

39. Pufendorf, *De Jure*, bk. 8, chap. 6, secs. 4–7. The authority to inflict disproportionate punishment is qualified by the duty imposed on sovereigns to try to approximate the conditions of a civil society in their international relations.

Uncertainties also surround the stability of international agreements. Treaties of peace have no independent value because they duplicate obligations already imposed by natural law. Pufendorf believed that a ruler who is conscious of his dignity and his duties toward his Creator should not make profane agreements which purport to extend his responsibilities beyond what the law of his nature requires.

The rule that everyone should fulfill his promises is a sacred precept of natural law. Observance of that higher principle should promote the stability of treaties. In spite of those affirmations, there are loopholes in Pufendorf's theory. No one can be bound by what he is prohibited from observing by some law, and the primary duty of sovereigns is to the subjects who have submitted to them for their defense. Thus it is foolhardy for one ruler to trust in a treaty whose preservation is not in another's interest.[40]

The state of natural law reflections in the seventeenth century comes to a close with Locke. Locke, in contradistinction to Hobbes, defended the principles of representative government against the pretensions of absolute monarchy. Locke had read and admired the works of Pufendorf. He agreed with the German jurist that sovereigns were in a state of nature and that their mutual conduct was regulated by natural law. Locke also agreed with Pufendorf that a state of nature was not, as Hobbes had claimed, a state of perpetual conflict. The state of nature was a state of liberty but it was not a state of license. The state of nature had reason for its law.[41]

The impartial enforcement of the natural law goes to the heart of early modern international theory. The critical issue is whether a moral law governing the actions of independent states can be objectively applied in the absence of government. The difficulties begin to emerge in the Grotian theory. Grotius held that those who had sovereign power could punish not only injuries to themselves and their subjects, but also all gross violations of the law of nations and of nature. He acknowledged that individuals may have had such a right "in the early

40. Compare Pufendorf, *De Jure,* bk. 8, chap. 6, sec. 14, with bk. 3, chap. 4.

41. John Locke, *Second Treatise on Government* (1690), chap. II, in *Two Treatises of Government,* ed. Pete Laslett (London: Cambridge University Press, 1967).

stages of the world" but he believed the universal punitive power was now exclusively within the judicial authority of sovereign states. The reasoning is of permanent interest. According to Grotius, the right no longer belongs to individuals because, being interested in their own cause, they can not render impartial justice. Furthermore, the right of enforcement had to be that of sovereigns; otherwise states could never wage a just war.[42]

Pufendorf had a realistic understanding of the difficulties. He acknowledged that the law of nature could not, of its own force, ensure peace. Individuals in a state of nature are independent of each other and each exercises his own judgment about the lawfulness of his own behavior and that of others. Unfortunately, individual judgments on such matters vary. Few have sufficient control over their passions to understand what is of permanent value to themselves or to those with whom they must coexist. Reason alone, as it exists in separate individuals, cannot resolve the serious disagreements which arise among them. Harmony must be found in some other way. For individuals, that way is the establishment of civil government.[43]

Locke agreed with Pufendorf that in a state of nature the law of nature is the regulative authority. Having been established by God, it exists independent of any human will. In a state of nature it must be enforced by individuals who are independent of each other, and who posses an equal and indefeasible right to self-preservation. The same power applies to sovereigns because they are in a state of nature in relation to each other.

Locke expands upon the insights of Pufendorf concerning the difficulties which attend the enforcement of the law of nature in any state of nature. When individuals try to live together without government, each must judge breaches of the moral law by others and apply a punishment that they determine the offense deserves. But in a conflictual situation each is biased by his own interests. He will, therefore, interpret the law to his own advantage. This is an essential inconvenience of any state of affairs which can be called a state of nature. There is no settled law

42. Hugo Grotius, *De Jure Belli ac Pacis,* bk. 2, chaps. 20, 40.
43. Pufendorf, *De Jure,* bk. 7, chap. 1, sec. 10.

accepted by all that can serve as the standard of right and wrong. Nor are there neutral judges to interpret and apply the law to controversies. Finally, there are no authorized agencies of enforcement.[44]

Unfortunately, the insights of Pufendorf and Locke into the impossibility of impartially enforcing the natural law in a state of nature were not aspects of an international political theory. Pufendorf's philosophy of law was directed primarily toward showing the advantages of a civil state for those who leave a state of nature. Locke's political theory was also directed toward domestic concerns, as he sought to justify representative government as a means of securing life, liberty, and property within a civil society.

Both Pufendorf and Locke extended their "state of nature" reasoning to encompass the international plane. The analogies between separate individuals and independent sovereigns coexisting without government were too obvious. But neither made a connection between the *deficiencies* of the natural state of relations between individuals and the comparable defects of the international state of nature. Nonetheless, their theories contain some permanent principles of political analysis which can be applied to the enduring problems of international order.

Locke's ideas on the relations between states are an integral part of his broader reflections upon the basic distinction between pre-political and political societies. Being fundamental, these distinctions are universal. Their relevance to the present study on world governance will become apparent as our reflections progress.

For the present, it is sufficient to observe that Locke's understanding of any situation where there is no government, while more elevated than that of Hobbes and the naturalists, was actually more damaging to Grotian ideals. In order to combat the Machiavellian "reasons of state," which held that nothing was unjust that was expedient, Grotius upheld natural law as an objective reality which reflected the moral and social nature of man. He believed that honorable rulers would justly and fairly execute its mandates. Given the idealism which per-

44. Locke, *Second Treatise,* chap. 2, secs. 6–13; chap. 7, sec. 87; chap. 9, secs. 123–26. See also chap. 19, sec. 242. The relation between sovereigns is described as a state of nature in chap. 16, sec. 183.

meated his theory, Grotius could not have been expected to understand the structural weakness of these assumptions.

The explanatory power of Locke's thought enables us to understand that no human association whose order depends upon the judgment of independent and equal individuals can impartially realize justice. That is because bias, as well as inefficiency, is inherent in any form of unorganized existence. Viewed in the light of political philosophy, the Grotian principle that without law all is uncertain is turned against itself. In the natural state that obtains between sovereigns, the unprejudiced enforcement of the fundamental law, which was an indispensable part of the whole Grotian system, cannot be.

As we shall see in the chapters which follow, Locke's understanding of the consequences of a state of nature had an influence upon international theory, but its full significance was resisted by those who hoped to create a positive international law for the emerging society of states. Others who remained convinced of the power of moral reason to bring order out of the chaos would also ignore the force of Locke's ideas. The significance of Locke's distinction between political and pre-political forms of social life would not become relevant until the concept of the sovereign nation-state was refined and its powers to wage war against other nation-states were more fully developed. At that point, the possible unification of the world would again begin to attract serious intellectual attention.[45]

45. On the development of the right to engage in war, see G. A. D. Draper, "Grotius's Place in the Development of Legal Ideas about War," in Bull et. al, eds., *Hugo Grotius and International Relations,* at 177–207.

In his magisterial treatise, first published in 1906, Lassa Oppenheim stated that "War is not inconsistent with, but a condition regulated by, International Law. The latter cannot and does not object to the States which are in conflict waging war upon each other instead of peaceably settling their differences. . . ." *International Law: A Treatise* (London: Longmans, Green & Co., 1906), vol. 2, chap. 1, sec. 53. Later editions took into account the changes made by the Paris Pact of 1928. See, e.g., 6th ed., vol. 2, pt. 2, chap. 3, sec. 52g. The issue of the legitimate uses of force will be discussed further in Chapter 4 of the present work.

For a study of the developing awareness of the consequences of the international state of nature, see Diego Panizza, "Conceptions of International Order in Eighteenth-Century Political Thought: A Typology in Context" 17 *Quinnipiac Law Review* 61–98 (1997).

———————
ᑾᑿ

TRANSCENDENCE AND IMMANENCE

I

Since the time of Dante, the possibilities of international order had been explored primarily within theological categories of thought. This was the case both before and after the Reformation. With some exceptions, concern over relationships between rulers was dominated by ideas of natural law, conceptions of divine order, and a sense of religious responsibility. But there was a growing awareness within Europe that these remote forms of transcendent authority were inadequate to the concrete problems posed by an expanding international community. A more realistic appreciation of international disorder was encouraged by the state of nature theories, which revealed the futility of reliance upon higher sanction. And jurists began to develop more direct measures for regulating international relations than those suggested by a tradition which had placed its hopes in the effectiveness of divine commands.

By the close of the sixteenth century, international lawyers were advising theologians to refrain from speaking of matters outside of their competence. A secular legalism was developing which would distinguish its competencies from the higher dispositions of the natural law tradition. Diplomats and judges who were responsible for resolving international disputes began to grapple with problematic areas of state practice such as jurisdiction, the immunities of ambassadors, and, with the increasing frequency of warfare, the rights and duties of both combatants and neutrals. They brought to their work a sense of impartiality appropriate to the administration of justice, and applied their skills of analysis and judgment to a broad range of practical issues. Lawyers elevated the legal status of treaties, and sought to reinvent the notion of customary law.[1]

To Francisco Suarez, customary law, or the *jus gentium,* embodied the broadest rules of behavior that could be extracted from the habitual practices within, as well as between, states. As a theologian, Suarez was concerned with the degree to which such rules have a juridical character which might bind in conscience. The customary *jus gentium* was a form of positive law that was closely related to, or at least in harmony with, the superior precepts of the natural law. This connection between human and divine regulation gave these laws a higher vindication as well as a binding force. In the changing climate of secular thinking, however, the weight given to habitual practices was beginning to be qualified by the structure of the new international system.

Beginning with Grotius, scholarly attention was concentrated on the legal qualities implicit in the regular relations between states. This practical jural focus reduced the relevance of general jural principles developing within states to the formation of international order between states. Consent became of critical importance to the quest for order among sovereign princes. To the jurists, evidence of a state's willingness to be bound by a rule determined the existence and extent of an obligation. Treaties manifest the explicit agreement of rulers to enter stable reciprocal relationships, and habitual practices among a large number of states revealed a tacit consent to be bound by rules. In a world of independent states, voluntary obligation was becoming the standard of European international law and diplomacy. An increase in systematic treatises devoted to the empirical *jus inter gentes* reflected a faith in these possibilities of order and a corresponding distancing from the theological orientation of the natural law tradition.

The writings of the German jurist Samuel Rachel exemplified this transition to proximate sources of order. Like Pufendorf, Rachel was brought up in the Lutheran tradition. But Rachel would not allow the

1. Nussbaum, *A Concise History of the Law of Nations,* chap. 3.

imperatives of theology to eclipse the distinct reality of the temporal international realm. He resisted the absorption of custom and state practice into the orbit of Divine natural law advocated by his distinguished predecessor. To Rachel and the other positivists, progress in the understanding and control of international problems was possible only if legal thought distanced itself from the demands of the natural law. This bold assertion was vindicated by reference to state practice. In their mutual relations, states expressed their claims for redress of injuries in terms of the law of nations rather than by an appeal to a higher law.

This approach, while compelled by realistic considerations, would further weaken the regulatory force of the Grotian system. The redress of injuries had been a central theme of the *De Jure Belli ac Pacis*. Grotius was convinced that the distinction between just and unjust international causes was of critical importance to the realization of peace and order within the emerging society of states. Jurists of a more practical bent felt compelled to make a further distinction. They recognized that the morality of war could be evaluated according to the criteria of the natural law. But they also believed that the formalities for the commencement of war and regulation of the conduct of war came under the jurisdiction of the positive law of nations. This approach was understandable. At the practical level, there was no way of determining whether a sovereign who decided to wage war was acting properly. The operative legal standard was whether war was waged by one who had the requisite authority and who also had observed the customary formalities.[2]

There was also a political movement away from the theological regulation of the international world. The Peace of Utrecht (1713), which ended the War of the Spanish Succession, expressed the hope that the order of Christendom could be restored by a just balance of power among the signatory states. Rulers were to seek justice in their mutual relations and conform their policies to the principles of equilibrium. All signatories were ostensibly willing to resist any state which aspired

2. Draper, "Grotius's Place in the Development of Ideas about War," in Bull et al, *Hugo Grotius and International Relations*.

to a preeminent position. The independent states which then made up the European community hoped to preserve stability through such a balance and thus avoid recourse to any higher form of authority. But in spite of these practical political and legal changes, new speculative developments were beginning to appear in European culture. They would have a significant influence upon the theoretical understanding of international relations.

The German Enlightenment renewed interest in the hierarchical structures that had shaped the organic relations between Church and Empire during the course of the Middle Ages. Medieval thought based its ideas of organization on the assumption that Christendom was a single unified society. This human totality was compared with the structure of the human body. Both were composed of different parts; and, in both, the parts were inseverably connected in an integral and harmonious relationship. The unity of the human body was expressed in health; the unity of Christendom in the tranquility of order.

In theory, the general order of Christian Europe was secured by the interconnectedness of Church and Empire and by the subordinate status of the various states and kingdoms within the overall design. The larger whole received its vindication from God, who had freely created the order of the universe. Within this framework, the political and ecclesiastical spheres had their distinctive competences. Nevertheless, they were united in a common faith and they shared a way of life which began on earth and would be completed in eternity.[3]

The speculative destiny of Christendom embraced all of mankind. To the leading minds of the Middle Ages, humanity was a single, universal community that was created, and governed, by God. All that existed bore the imprint of the Creator; each individual, and every community, had an intrinsic value. Whatever was singular was a whole, with a final purpose of its own. At the same time, each was as a part of a larger cosmos and had a destiny that was guided by the final cause of the universe. Within this comprehensive reality reason,

---

3. Figgis, *Political Thought from Gerson to Grotius;* Otto Gierke, *Political Theories of the Middle Age,* trans. Frederick William Maitland (Cambridge: Cambridge University Press, 1900), chap. 4.

guided by faith, had a decisive ruling power. Reason ordered the parts in relation to each other, and in subordination to the higher forms of both temporal and spiritual association.

Dante had grasped the significance of this hierarchical model of existence. As we have seen, he believed that a just relation between plurality and unity could only be sustained if the composite whole was ruled by one supreme imperial government. Gottfried Leibniz, an eminent philosopher, jurist, and political theorist of the German Enlightenment, shared Dante's belief in the importance of universal unity and harmony. But Christendom was no longer either politically or spiritually a single commonwealth.

Leibniz represented what was distinctive about the Germanic spirit: a longing to embrace the whole of reality and a confidence in the power of thought to comprehend that totality. Like the medievalists, he saw that in order to know any of the manifold aspects of existence, one must view its component parts in relationship to each other. One must also account for the larger whole which is presupposed by the existence of the parts.

Leibniz's philosophy was one of immanence. His universe was composed of a pluralism of *monads.* These are individual self-contained and self-sufficient substances. Monads derive their being from what is within themselves. Each is an individual living center of energy, and it is out of the abundance and diversity of monads that the unity of the world is constituted.

Within this pluralism, substance is thought of as activity. In the overall chain of being it is in man that the positive qualities of created substance can be most fully realized. These free agents are self-determining. Each individual is a living force, poised to realize its potentials whenever the occasion arises. Human personality is also expansive. The possibilities of its development should not be inhibited by any external force.[4]

4. Nicholas Rescher, *The Philosophy of Leibniz* (Englewood Cliffs, N.J.: Prentice-Hall, 1967); Herbert Wildon Carr, *Leibniz* (London: E. Benn, Ltd., 1929); Huntington Cairns, *Legal Philosophy from Plato to Hegel* (Baltimore: Johns Hopkins University Press, 1949), chap. 9; "Leibniz," in .J. MacDonell and E. Manson, eds. *Great Jurists of the World,* vol.

Leibniz was a mathematician and philosopher who became interested in political and international questions. He considered Pufendorf to be a second-rate jurist. And while he respected and participated in some of the positivist approaches to international relations, his interests were theoretical. Leibniz's intellectual preference was for Grotius. Leibniz was drawn to the Grotian vision of order because it appealed to systematic principles which could govern the concrete relations between rulers and upheld norms of justice which were valid in themselves, whether or not they were actually affirmed in state practice.

Leibniz was particularly interested in the quarrel between Grotius and Pufendorf over whether the existence of natural law was independent of Divine origin. The idea of an autonomous natural law, as suggested by Grotius, was compatible with the intellectual aspirations of modern humanism. The ambition of the humanists was to contemplate the order of all things as they exist in God. The mind would draw into itself the rational plan which the Supreme Being has established for the happiness of mankind. In this new age, what dwelled in the mind of God would be reflected in the minds of philosophers.

Reason reveals a law which appeals to moral freedom because it is a law of perfectibility. The law made known by reason was not, as with Pufendorf, a normative order imposed by a divine superior upon a servile, or rebellious, subject. Pufendorf's conception of natural law was abhorrent to Leibniz because it revealed the inhuman consequences of an excessive reliance upon theology. Thus the attraction of Leibniz to Grotius, who had seen the need to understand that natural law, as a normative order, was completely within the horizons of human understanding.[5]

2, Continental Legal History Series 283 (South Hackensack, N.J.: Rothman Reprints, 1968); C. J. Friedrich, "Philosophical Reflections of Leibniz on Law, Politics, and the State," in *Leibniz: A Collection of Critical Essays,* edited by Harry. G. Frankfurt (Garden City, N.Y.: Anchor Books, 1972); Patrick Riley, *The Political Writings of Leibniz* (Cambridge: Cambridge University Press, 1972).

5. On the general cultural conditions, see Ernst Cassier, *The Philosophy of the Enlightenment;* Carl C. Becker, *The Heavenly City of the Eighteenth-Century Philosophers* (New York: Yale University Press, 1932); Frank. E. and Fritzie. P. Manuel, *Utopian Thought in the Western World* (Cambridge, Mass.: The Belknap Press of the Harvard University Press, 1979).

The German Enlightenment initiated by Leibniz sought to construct an independent theory of natural law that would break the hold of theological voluntarism upon juristic thought. It would also affirm the autonomy of reason. This required a bold belief in the power of human thought. Truth could not be dependent upon God's arbitrary power. Natural law, as an aspect of moral truth, was founded upon reason, rather than the will of God, although it was included in His understanding.

Leibniz's idea of law bore some resemblance to that of Aquinas, but for Leibniz law was not derived from any will, either divine or human. Rational natural law was immutable and eternal, reigning in the realm of pure reason. There was an important subjective corollary. Conformity to the precepts of the law manifest by reason could not be motivated by fear or a sense of compelling obligation. One adhered to the higher law out of love and an enduring desire for happiness.[6]

Leibniz challenged the political absolutism of Hobbes and the general premises of state of nature reasoning. In refusing to subject international relations to ethical standards, the naturalists had failed to understand the ultimate structure of the universe. When the mind exercises its authority in the highest ranges of the natural order, it enters into a fellowship with the divine. Leibniz saw the mind as being involved in a form of moral governance. Thought participates in a comprehensive and universal order which reveals the harmony established by God for the development and happiness of the whole world.[7]

---

6. In *Opinion on the Principles of Pufendorf* (1706), reprinted in Riley, *The Political Writings of Leibniz*. Suarez sought a middle ground between the voluntarists and the rationalists on the issue of the origins of the natural law. He held that through its participation in the natural law, human reason discovers what is good and what is evil with respect to human nature and that God, as the author and providential guide of that nature, commands that actions should be performed or avoided in accordance with the dictates of reason. See also Suarez, *De Legibus,* bk. 2, chap. 6. The position of Grotius was closer to that of Suarez than to Pufendorf. Edwards, *Hugo Grotius: The Miracle of Holland,* chap. 3. For a further discussion of the problem see John Finnis, *Natural Law and Natural Right,* chap. 2.

7. Cairns, *Legal Philosophy from Plato to Hegel,* chap. 9. See also James Collins, *The Continental Rationalists* (Milwaukee: Bruce Publishing, 1967), chap. 3.

To Leibniz, the study of any social phenomenon had to take moral values into account. This was not for reasons of obedience to transcendental authority, but because morality is an essential part of the natural order of existence. The values which inhere in that order appeal to the best of human aspirations. The good which the heart seeks is a fulfilling good. This comprehensive yearning can not be satisfied by an incomplete theory of justice.

The theories of the naturalists are inadequate because they are restricted to the articulation of individual rights. Such rights are generally understood to imply duties, which obtain in some reciprocal relationship between equals. This was the level of analysis deployed by Hobbes and his followers. As a form of moral reasoning, it was limited to questions of *commutative* or *reciprocal* justice, to wit: if there is an injury there is a right of redress. Within the state, a wrong creates a cause of action at law; between states, it creates a right to make war. But, according to Leibniz, no political order, national or international, can be fully explained in terms of individual rights. The reason is that such a restricted idea of entitlement does not exhaust the idea of justice. Particular rights imply reciprocal duties and the violation of rights calls for appropriate remedies.

This is the elementary level of commutative justice. Beyond that lies the realm of *distributive* justice. Here justice becomes social in nature.

To comprehend the nature of distributive justice, reason refers to the allocation of opportunities and resources within a community. In this field of public law, entitlements are not unconditional. Nor is reciprocity a decisive measure of righteousness. Giving to each his due at this higher and more complex level of justice depends upon discretionary judgments which allocate burdens and benefits among individuals—or nations—in terms of their relative positions in a group.

With distributive justice, differences of social position are more important than relationships of equality. Within the state, demands for distributive justice are imperfect moral claims which may, or may not, become legal rights. On the international plane, such claims are essentially imperfect. They can never be subject to compulsion. States having material advantages may share them with less fortunate states, but the possibilities of such equitable distribution depend upon inner motivations and choices that cannot be expressed as strict obligations.

The theory of justice articulated by Leibniz does not eliminate the international state of nature. In an unorganized society, the desire for self-preservation trumps other considerations. The underlying rivalry among states, and their desires for economic supremacy, was also inconsistent with a genuine understanding of the demands of a universal distributive justice.

Leibniz did not want to encourage the selfishness of states. He simply tried to orient the range of state discretion in a way that would reflect the moral complexities of interstate relationships. Leibniz believed that genuine international progress depended upon the enlargement of understanding and the expansion of benevolence. If rulers had knowledge of all the principles of justice, they would advance international as well as national well-being.

This ideal comprehensive order was in harmony with the deepest aspirations of personal righteousness. For this German Rationalist, justice was the charity of the wise. The just man, or sovereign, will do as much as he can, for as many as he can, in this best of all possible worlds. And he will do so without fear of divine retribution.[8]

Pufendorf had agreed with the naturalists that upon the establishment of government within states, the state of nature that had originally existed among individuals would be transposed into the relations among states. Pufendorf sought to subject this realm to the control of the natural law. The principle of sociability was a fundamental part of this law of nature. Between states there is a modified state of nature rather than any natural form of society.

Christian Wolff, a disciple of Leibniz, tried to improve upon Pu-

---

8. Leibniz, *Meditation on the Common Concept of Justice* (c. 1702) and *Portrait of the Prince* (1679), in Riley, *The Political Writings of Leibniz*. See also the introduction to the cited work.

fendorf's compromise. Wolff wanted to extend the abstract powers of the mind to more fully comprehend the phenomenon of human sociability in its bearing upon international relations. To him, the original human condition was not a state of nature but rather a universal community of mankind. This community of the whole was familial, not individualistic.

Upon the formation of separate states a residue of the original community survived. This is the social ground of all subsequent reflections upon international relations. A natural universal society provides the framework within which sovereign rulers conduct their foreign affairs. Wolff hoped to build, by thought, a universal association which would be able to control the anarchic potential of an unorganized society of states. It was upon this basis that Wolff created his philosophy of international law.[9]

Since sovereigns represent particular societies, they are not in a pure state of nature. Moreover, although separate rulers are independent and equal they are all subject to the natural law. To Wolff, the natural law was not the manifestation of a distant divine will, as understood by Pufendorf. Following Leibniz, Wolff thought of the natural law as something much closer to the human. The natural law is the law of nature—qualified by the representative character of sovereignty.

For Wolff, when the natural law is engaged with international reality it becomes the necessary and immutable law of nations. As such, it is morally binding upon rulers. This special natural law confers natural rights upon nations. But although the necessary law of nations is indispensable it cannot, of itself, adequately govern all of the interactions between separate sovereign states. There is a need for further lawmak-

9. Christian Wolff, *Jus Gentium Methodo Scientifica Pertractatum* (The Law of Nations Treated According to a Scientific Method) (1764), vol. 2 (Carnegie trans., 1934). For a short biography of Wolff, see the introduction to the Carnegie translation by Otfried Nippold. See also Onuf, "Civitas Maxima: Wolff, Vattel, and the Fate of Republicanism," 88 *American Journal of International Law* 280 (1994); Arthur Nussbaum, *A Concise History of the Law of Nations,* chap. 5; Percy Ellwood Corbett, *Law and Society in the Relations of States* (New York: Harcourt Brace & Company, 1951), chap. 2. See also Alfred P. Rubin, *Ethics and Authority in International Law* (Cambridge: Cambridge University Press, 1997), chap. 2.

ing: a positive law established by human reason and wisdom. Nature has established a society between states and compels them to preserve it. Supplementary universal legislation fills that need.

Wolff reasoned that states may be presumed to have agreed to participate in a *Civitas Maxima,* or Supreme State. This body, whose being is conferred by reason, is authorized to enact laws to make up for the unfinished nature of the necessary law of nations. These additional laws are limited by that necessary law and by the immutable rights of nations established thereby that *jus necessarium.* The legal authority of this human law, or *jus voluntarium,* is confined to the purposes for which the Supreme State exists. Wolff believed that such laws would elicit the consent of states because they meet a fundamental requirement of the international society. The primary objective of the society of states is the same as that of any social union: to realize a just balance between the individual interest and the common good. This is the responsibility of the *Civitas Maxima.* If its commands are resisted, the whole community of nations can coerce compliance.

The lawmaking authority of the Supreme State rests with the whole human race. But humanity is now divided into separate states and kingdoms. Being scattered, it cannot assemble to express a general will. However, these lesser communities must be subject to some normative order if the Supreme State is to realize its objectives.

To the geometric mentality of Wolff, this order cannot be found in the received traditions of Western culture. Nature has ordained that right reason should constitute the will of all. There must be a *Rector Civitas Maxima:* an incarnation of the wise ruler advocated by Leibniz. The right to rule belongs to the one who, "following the leadership of nature, defines by the right use of reason what nations ought to consider as law among themselves."[10]

Wolff's use of reason to construct a comprehensive world order, with a fictitious universal state at its summit, dramatically reflects the rational ambitions of the German Enlightenment. It also bears some

10. Wolff, *Jus Gentium,* Prolegomena, para. 21.

resemblance to the vision of Dante. The *Civitas Maxima,* as a form of universal government, has substantially the same authority as the poet wanted to confer upon the Holy Roman Emperor. And the speculations of both Dante and Wolff reflect the influence of the Latin Averröists upon the development of European thought. As we have previously noted, their intellectualism looks upon the world as being perpetually subject to an eternal and substantive reason. Ideal reason imagines some form of community which might realize all of its possibilities.

Such a mentality overstates the authority of philosophical thought. Francisco Suarez was more cautious because he understood the differences between the speculative and practical ways of knowing. For Suarez, the human race may for certain purposes be thought of as a single community, but it is not a *political* society. The peoples of the world had never actually come together to form a more perfect union. There was, therefore, no prospect of universal legislation. For Wolff, this inconvenience is surmounted by the power of abstract thought. For him, if reason demands that there ought to be a world state, it may be thought of as existing.[11]

Wolff exaggerates the power of reason, but his approach to international affairs was not entirely unreasonable. Every society has a need for some ultimate authority, not only to correct for human weakness and evil but also to promote the positive purposes of the entire community. In an unorganized society, this responsibility falls upon the individual or group that has the power and influence necessary to settle the problems of the whole.

In this respect, Wolff's speculations had some subsequent confirmation. For example, in the nineteenth century, the responsibility for general order was assumed by a small group of powerful nations who purported to act on behalf of the whole of European society. This Concert of Europe made territorial judgments, established states, and

11. Suarez's position should be compared with that of Vitoria, who, like Wolff, thought of the world society as a body which possessed its own political authority. See Corbett, *Law and Society in the Relations of States,* chap. 2.

proclaimed principles of public law. While not free from controversy, the Concert was based upon sufficient consensus to bring into concrete form some of the values of governance previously envisioned by Wolff.[12]

Wolff made other contributions to international law which are not sufficiently appreciated. He insisted that the actions of rulers in the international realm must be guided by the law of nature and that their foreign policies were subject to the rule of reason. Like monads, self-determining states were entitled to realize their potential. Yet Wolff wanted them to understand that as they became more powerful their actions should be guided by the higher harmonies that govern the ultimate development of the world.

Wolff believed that rulers of the more advanced nations should try to achieve the highest degree of righteousness, especially in their dealings with weaker nations. These civilizing admonitions presupposed a meaningful social unity among all the nations of the earth. Once that assumption was removed, the principles of sovereign independence would assume an entirely different character. Such a profound change in the conceptualization of international law and society would be accomplished by the work of a cultivated Swiss diplomat, Emmerick de Vattel.

In his *Le Droit des Gens,* published in 1758, Vattel sought to reconcile the philosophical idealism of Leibniz and Wolff with the principles of sovereign state independence which were becoming of primary importance in international law and diplomacy. Vattel was also inspired by the emerging ideals of liberalism, as well as the spirit of scientific understanding which was then shaping the general culture of Europe.

For Vattel, the natural law of nations is the law of nature as applied to political societies. This law, which constitutes the Necessary Law of Nations, reflects the character of those societies. The principles of this

12. C. Holbraad, *The Concert of Europe: A Study of German and British International Theory* (Longmans, 1970); R. B. Mowat, *The Concert of Europe* (London: Macmillan, 1930). For a discussion of the general thrust of human nature toward some form of social authority, see Finnis, *Natural Law and Natural Right,* chap. 9.

law assure the sovereign independence and equality of every nation within the universal society of nations. The other division of the Law of Nations was of human origin. Derived from the will of states, positive law was composed of the conventional law of nations, to which consent was expressed; customary international law, which rested upon tacit consent; and the voluntary law of nations, for which consent was presumed. This general positive law consisted of the rules which promoted the welfare of the whole international community.[13]

There was no *Civitas Maxima* in Vattel's scheme. Vattel agreed that there was a universal society which reflected the natural interdependence of humanity. But there was no *civil* society among states, for a civil society implied the relinquishment of individual rights to a general will and the subordination of all to the authoritative enforcement of law. Such submission was incompatible with the independence of the sovereign state. Individuals have recourse to the remedy of political association in order to curb the violent. But Vattel did not think that there is the same necessity for a civil society among states as there is among individuals. Once united under a government, individuals have most of their needs met by the society to which they give allegiance, and the help of other political communities is not as necessary to them as the care provided by their sovereign.[14]

The law of nations is a law of sovereigns. Sovereignty was understood by Vattel in terms of modern political principles which placed ultimate power in the community. For Vattel the ruler never possesses the full political authority of the society that he governs.

Sovereignty exists when the nation governs itself. The power that is exercised on behalf of the nation makes the well-being of the nation the primary objective of international relations. These principles com-

---

13. Emeric Vattel, *The Law of Nations: Or Principles of the Law of Nature Applied to the Conduct and Affairs of Nations and Sovereigns,* 6th ed. (Chitty, 1844); Francis Stephen Ruddy, *International Law in the Enlightenment: The Background of Emmerich de Vattel's "Le Droit des Gens"* (Dobbs Ferry, N.Y.: Oceana Publications, 1975). Compare Henry Wheaton, *Elements of International Law with a Sketch of the History of the Science,* 2 vols. (London: B. Fellows, 1836).

14. Vattel, *The Law of Nations,* preface.

promised the cosmopolitan and humanistic ideals of Leibniz. This downward adjustment can be seen in Vattel's treatment of international commerce.

Vattel sees freedom of commerce as a common right of nations and he recognizes that trade raises questions of distributive justice. But his empirical logic leads him to admit that powerful nations may advance their own economic prosperity in disregard of the general obligations of humanity. The actions of the powerful may *harm* other nations, but they do them no *injury,* so long as trading policies do not trespass upon a perfect right or render poorer states destitute.[15]

Vattel's treatment of the important themes of international law reflect the refinements of a mind schooled in practical affairs as well as deep philosophical learning. He insists that good faith performance of treaties is a principle of international law and, contrary to Spinoza, he believes that fidelity to these principles is a practical possibility. Yet the primacy of sovereign independence leads him to conclusions which are not far removed from those of the naturalists. Vattel claims that injurious treaties are not unjust, although agreements which would ruin a nation are void. And a sovereign who imposes unequal terms upon a weaker state acts in conformity with natural law if the more powerful state is motivated by its own safety.[16]

Sovereign liberty is the foundation of Vattel's system. There is, therefore, no accounting for performance of internal obligations in the absence of a perfect external right. States cannot take it upon themselves to decide the moral legitimacy of each other's actions. If states were to oppose by force the liberty of other nations whose conduct they found reprehensible, they would destroy the foundations of the natural society within which they all are entitled to exist. A ruler actu-

15. Ibid., bk. 2, chap. 1, sec. 2, para. 9. Compare the importance of international economic hegemony in Lockean conception of foreign policy discussed in Richard H. Cox, *Locke on War and Peace* (Oxford: The Clarendon Press, 1960), chap. 5. Vattel also held that if every nation has a right to whatever is essential to its existence, it is lawful for a state on the verge of starvation to take by force what is needed from a prosperous neighbor who is unwilling to sell from its surplus. *The Law of Nations,* bk. 2, chap. 9, para. 120.

16. Vattel, *The Law of Nations,* bk. 2, chap. 15.

ally in the wrong sins against conscience; as long as there is a possibility that he is in the right, however, he cannot be accused of violating the law of nations.

While his system permits offenses against distributive justice, Vattel does not condone active wrongdoing. He writes with passion against the evils of warfare. He tried to temper the violence, to deepen the distinctions between combatants and noncombatants and strengthen the obligations of neutrals to abstain from an ongoing conflict. He also believed that war is contrary to nature. Yet while he insists upon the importance of the peaceful settlement of disputes, he allows, under the voluntary law of nations, the right of direct recourse to force when the issue is in doubt. If an essential interest is at stake the nation should consult its courage and act without even trying to settle the matter peacefully.[17]

Vattel's rational law of nations enhanced the sovereign independence and equality of states at a time when those values were facilitating the expansion of international society. His works were of great use to the new states of North and South America. But in matters of central importance to justice and peace, Vattel's treatise did not make a positive advance over the theories of Hobbes and the naturalists. The implications of the concept that the world at large was in a state of nature needed to be taken more seriously if there was to be long-term progress. The inwardness of a system that deferred to the will of the state at every critical juncture also had to be taken into account. There was

17. Ibid., bk. 2, chap. 18, para. 332. Vattel says further that ". . . And as in virtue of the natural liberty of nations each one is free to judge in her own conscience how she ought to act and has a right to make her own judgment the sole guide of her conduct with respect to her duties in everything that is not determined by the perfect rights of another . . . it belongs to each nation to judge whether her situation will admit of pacific measures, before she has recourse to arms." Id., para. 335. This is an important, and often overlooked, deviation from the teaching of Wolff. Wolff had held that there is no right to engage in war independent of the duty to seek a peaceful settlement and that armed force could not be used until the adversary refused to conciliate the dispute. *Jus Gentium,* chap. 5.

Vattel balances the liberty to use force with the condemnation of one who wages an unjust war. Such a wrongdoer is an enemy of the human race. *The Law of Nations,* bk. 3, chap. 11.

a need for a new moral evaluation of international relations. This task would be assumed by the most important figure in the German Enlightenment, Immanuel Kant.

II

Throughout the eighteenth century there was a general conviction that European order could be maintained by the wise maintenance of balances of power. Vattel, like Wolff, approved of international equilibrium as a means of maintaining peace, and other major thinkers concurred in this opinion. But there were also serious doubts about the permanence of the desired stability. Reactions of a state to an increase in the power of its neighbors were guided more by self-interest than by a concern for principles of public morality. The insecurity of states, when coupled with the general competition for power and influence, meant that each state's foreign policy included a desire to attain superiority relative to its actual or potential adversaries. The objectives of equilibrium were becoming of lesser importance than the pursuit of supremacy.[18]

The increasing anarchy led to proposals for fundamental reform in the public law of Europe. One of the most important was that of the Abbé de Saint-Pierre. The Abbé renewed interest in plans for universal peace which had previously been put forth by reformers such as Henry IV of France and the Duc de Sully, his minister and confidant. Europe was, in the mind of the Abbé, uncivilized. He was convinced that the prevailing barbarism and constant conflict were primarily caused by the absolute independence that was the prerogative of each sovereign. The exercise of this unlimited power had repeatedly plunged the peoples of Europe into the horrors of war. The Abbé believed that the settlement of differences by right of the strongest was unworthy of a

18. David Hume, "Of the Balance of Power," in *Political Essays*, ed. Knud Haakonssen (Cambridge: Cambridge University Press, 1994), 154–60; Adam Ferguson, *An Essay on the History of Civil Society*, pt. 3, sec. 2 (1767), ed. Fania Oz-Salzberger (Cambridge: Cambridge University Press, 1995). See also the discussion in my *The Search for World Order* (Dordrecht: Martinus Nijhoff, 1985).

people who shared a Christian faith and lived within the tradition of Roman law.

The ideals of the *De Monarchia* were part of the collective memory. The Roman Empire had once united all Europe into a body politic, and the need was to find some contemporary equivalent to this venerable precedent. The Abbé proposed a Constitution for a Federation of Europe. Under its terms the contracting sovereigns would renounce all anterior claims among themselves and form a permanent Diet where all future matters of conflict would be resolved by arbitration or judicial decision. Those who broke the agreement would be placed under the ban of Europe. They would be proscribed as public enemies and their actions could be opposed by force. The plenipotentiaries to the Diet would also have standing powers, under instructions from their courts, to frame measures that they considered to be expedient to the welfare of the whole Commonwealth of Europe.[19]

Rousseau met the Abbé in his old age. Attracted to the plan, Rousseau decided to write a critical edition of the work. As a romantic philosopher, Rousseau was acutely conscious of the moral contradictions which afflicted human nature. He was particularly concerned with the way in which disparities of power could destroy the natural harmony that existed among individuals.

Rousseau thought that these inequalities could be corrected within civil societies by reforms based upon transcendent norms. A higher law, imposed by state authority in the name of a social contract, would lead individuals into a more perfect moral life. The situation between nations was more perilous. Within the state the individual coexists with fellow citizens; with respect to the rest of the world, he is in a

19. Leibniz, "On the Works of the Abbé de St. Pierre" (1715), in Patrick Riley, *The Political Writings of Leibniz;* H. J. Hemleben, *Plans for World Peace through Six Centuries* (Chicago: University of Chicago Press, 1943); Jean-Jacques Rousseau, *A Lasting Peace through the Federation of Europe* and *the State of War,* ed. C. E. Vaughan (London: Constable & Co., 1917). Grotius had advocated Peace Conferences in which controversies among some could be decided by others and in which measures could be taken to compel acceptance of a settlement on equitable terms. *De Jure Belli Ac Pacis,* bk. 2, chaps. 8, 23.

state of nature. The consequences are inhuman. By joining a specific group, one virtually declares oneself an enemy of the whole human race. And, while the "venerable phantom" of the Roman Empire continued to have a unifying influence, the persistent warfare among the European peoples had turned this venerable brotherhood into a cauldron of mutual hatred.

To Rousseau, these dire conditions were the natural result of existing arrangements rather than the expression of inherent human depravity. Any community without laws inevitable falls into destructive quarrels. This was especially true of the powers of Europe, who refused to recognize any earthly superior. Treaties of peace did not completely resolve the underlying conflicts among them, and fresh wars between the parties broke out whenever there was a change of circumstances. The public law of Europe was not supported by common agreement, nor did it embody any general principles. The application of the rules that are supposed to govern international relations varied from time to time and from place to place. The whole was nothing but "a mass of contradictory rules which nothing but the right of the stronger can reduce to order . . ."[20]

Rousseau saw advantages in the Abbé's plan, especially since, once established, its dispute-settlement and security provisions would eliminate the possibility of war between its members. But the plan was flawed because it did not protect citizens from the tyranny of their rulers. Beyond that objection, the plan was too good to be adopted. The whole idea was associated in Rousseau's mind with the processes of reform through force.

Rousseau wished his good citizen to live in a self-sufficient state with infrequent contacts with those beyond its borders. A larger political unity could only be achieved by revolutionary violence and the arbitrary imposition of governance. Few would dare to say that the proposed League of Europe was more to be desired than feared.[21]

A deep pessimism permeates Rousseau's reflections on the prospects

20. Rousseau, *A Lasting Peace,* 47–48.
21. Ibid., 112.

of general peace. His dour assessment of political improvement was accentuated by his feeling that under the prevailing conditions of absolute rule man is not free—either at home or abroad. There is no authentic liberty anywhere.

Within monarchical societies, force masquerades as law; in external affairs, the rule of force is manifest as "reason of state." The limited tranquility man realizes within states is not extended beyond borders. The idea of international right is an illusion because the laws which purport to uphold it lack any sanction. The prevailing situation is worse than when relations between sovereigns were governed by natural law. For then, at least, a law was operative which addressed the heart of the individual. Now, the appeal is entirely to national self-interest.[22]

The most important reflections after Rousseau were those of Immanuel Kant. Kant had at first been attracted by the rationalism of the Enlightenment and the writings of Leibniz and Wolff. After reading Hume, Kant began to develop a critical philosophy which would establish the limits of reason. His intellectual position was that objective reality is known only as it conforms to the essential structures of the mind. The objects of possible experience, or phenomena, are all that can be known. *Noumena,* or things in themselves, are unknowable. Within its experiential limits, reason can only discern a world of natural determinism. Subjectively, however, reason can perceive the requirements of the moral law. Although the ambitions of theoretical reason are radically circumscribed, pure practical reason has the power to determine what duty and justice demand of the exercise of human freedom.

Hume roused Kant from his "dogmatic slumber"; Rousseau awaked him from his moral apathy. Kant learned from the great Romantic philosopher the importance of working to establish the rights of mankind. This ideal called for an understanding of the vocation to be

22. Rousseau, *The State of War.* See also F. H. Hinsley, *Power and the Pursuit of Peace: Theory and Practice in the History of Relations between States* (Cambridge: Cambridge University Press, 1967).

moral. The basic questions which man must ask about his destiny—what can I know, what ought I to do, and for what can I hope— are the fundamental concerns of any self-legislating individual. Once such a person discerns the fundamental significance of duty, he will be able to elevate his life and act so that the maxim of his action could be willed by him into a general law to which he would himself be subject. As the respect due each as an end in himself was honored, the freedom and autonomy of each would be reconciled with the freedom and autonomy of all.[23]

Kant's general theory of right ranged from questions of individual entitlement to the momentous issues of war and peace. The sole original right is freedom. By freedom Kant means independence from the coercive will of another. Such a liberty is fundamental to the progress of humanity. The freedom of the individual is to be advanced insofar as it can coexist with the freedom of all under a universal law. Such security can only be assured when individuals quit the natural nonlawful state where violence is endemic. Kant understood the disorder of the natural state as an *a priori* idea. In this imagined situation, each is entitled to do what seems right for him to do, without consideration of the rights of others. To relieve this condition, the individual must enter a civil state. There he must submit to external lawful coercion so that what is rightfully his is secured by law.

The creation of a civil state is difficult because man is asocial by nature. But the building of civic order is aided by nature. Nature uses the inherent antagonism between men to draw them into a civil society and thereby neutralize the destructive effects of their self-seeking.

Within a lawful state, individual freedom is the political expression of public right as it ought to exist within a republican constitution. Such a constitution has immediate implications for external as well

23. Kant's basic works are *Critique of Pure Reason* (1781) and *Prolegomena to Any Future Metaphysics* (1783). N. Kemp Smith, *A Commentary on Kant's Critique of Reason,* rev. ed. (1962), and F. Copleston, *A History of Philosophy,* vol. 6 (Westminster, Md.: Newman Press, 1950) contain good general summaries and evaluations. See also Susan Meld Shell, *The Rights of Reason: A Study of Kant's Philosophy and Politics* (Toronto: University of Toronto Press, 1980).

as internal peace. A republican constitution affirms principles of self-government as well as enforcing the inalienable rights of man. The consent of citizens is required for all political actions of fundamental importance. These include the commencement of hostilities. Since citizens bear the brunt of war they will be less likely than irresponsible rulers to engage in armed conflict. With that safeguard, the prospects of warfare will be substantially reduced.[24]

For Kant, the state of nature among nations is different from the state of nature between individuals. The primitive international condition encompasses more than the relations between states. Here Kant develops the thought of Rousseau. The international state of nature implicates the connections among citizens of different states as well as among the states themselves. An individual may leave the original state of nature and become a citizen within a civil society, but he remains in a state of nature with respect to citizens of other states and their governments. This deeper conception of natural insecurity makes questions of war and peace of central importance because they involve the fate of individuals as well as the well-being of the impersonal state.

The rights of nations in relation to one another, the *jus publicum civitatum,* arise out a consideration of the state of nature in which these nations exist. As a moralist Kant penetrates more deeply into the significance of the state of nature than do Hobbes or the other naturalists. The relationship between states in such a condition is to Kant one of "lawless savages." This state of affairs is unjust in itself. Even though there may not be any actual hostilities between them, each community is a permanent threat to the other. There is injury in the mere fact of naked coexistence. Because of this inherent wrong, a nation can compel its proximate neighbors to enter into some form of lawful state. However, unlike the situation of individuals similarly situated, nations in a state of nature are not obliged to enter into a legal civil society.

24. Immanuel Kant, *Zum Ewigen Frieden ein Philosophischer Entwurf* (Perpetual Peace: A Philosophical Sketch)(1795), first definitive article. The work is commonly known as *Perpetual Peace.* This study relies upon Kant's text as it appears in *Political Writings,* ed. Hans Reiss, trans. H. B. Nisbet, 2nd enlarged ed. (Cambridge: Cambridge University Press, 1990).

Kant adopts the prevailing opinion that a large universal state is un-desirable because it would be unwieldy and potentially despotic. But he recognizes that the logic of a progression from a state of nature to a civil society is as applicable to the international state of nature as it is to any other situation of unorganized human association. States are like men who live in a natural condition and, like men, they should abandon it. But states are also independent political societies. They have outgrown the condition of subjection to the coercive power of others that would be required to subject them to a legal constitution.

Although he defers to this sovereign insubmissiveness, Kant realizes that there must not be a continuous right to go to war. The dilemma must be settled by pure practical reason which, in moral matters, is the decisive legislative power. Reason absolutely condemns war as a test of rights and demands peace as an immediate obligation. The only rational way to end the lawless state of nature among nations would be to form a *civitas gentium* or international state. But this positive idea of a world republic cannot be realized because it is not the will of nations according to their present concept of international right. Nonetheless, in matters of conflict, lawfulness cannot be decided by the right of the powerful. Kant provides a negative substitute for world government. He demands the establishment of a pacific federation which at least has the potential of putting an end to all wars for good.[25]

Cosmopolitan right is the third level of moral entitlement. It is based upon the experience of commerce between nations. "World citizens" often travel great distances in order to enter into trading relations with others. These encounters must be regulated by moral principles. The right is one of universal hospitality. An alien is entitled not to be treated with hostility upon his arrival. But his right is a limited one: of *resort* and not extensive care and entertainment upon arrival.

Like the Spanish theologians before him, Kant castigates the Euro-pean nations for the violence and exploitation which they brought to distant lands. As the moral sense develops, a wrong done far away

---

25. Kant, *Perpetual Peace,* sec. 2; see also his *Die Metaphysic der Sitten* (The Metaphysics of Morals), secs. 53–54 (1797) in Reiss, ed., *Political Writings.*

reverberates around the world. Kant retains the hope that the proper implementation of universal right will lead to laws which can regulate global intercourse and thus bring the human race closer to a cosmopolitan constitution.[26]

Kant recognizes that the inherent disorder of the international state of nature is exacerbated by the absence of any established judge to whom states can submit their disputes. He also believes that a constitutional arrangement in which states settle their disputes by legal proceedings rather than by war is the only appropriate way of realizing the idea of international public right. But he does not pursue the political implications of the idea. This indifference to the political separates Kant's reflections from those of Saint-Pierre and Rousseau. It also diminishes the force of some of his insights. For example, Kant considers it imperative that standing armies be gradually abolished, yet he does not consider the profound changes in global governance that such abolition would require.

Kant's thinking is also very different from that of John Locke. Locke wanted to promote individual freedom, but, as we have seen, he understood the importance of human association, which was a means to that end. Locke concentrated upon the inherent imperfections of a pre-political society, because an understanding of those imperfections was a prerequisite to any form of societal improvement. Locke's reflections upon the transition from pre-political to political society were not directed towards a correction of the deficiencies of the international state of nature, but analyzed the problem of order in a way that was potentially applicable to any social structure. Kant was not of such a mind. He was essentially a moral philosopher, convinced that the archetypal regulative discipline of moral theory provides the only

26. Kant, *The Metaphysics of Morals* 3, sec. 62; *Perpetual Peace,* sec. 2, third definitive article. In Jeremy Bentham's *Plan for Universal and Perpetual Peace* in *The Works of Jeremy Bentham,* ed. J. Bowering (1843), vol. 2, the object was to reduce foreign colonies. Such dependencies increased the occasions for war with other nations, and Bentham thought that their expense outweighed the advantages gained from possessing them. Bentham also introduced the expression "international law" into the literature as a substitute for the phrase "law of nations."

means by which any community of autonomous beings can govern themselves.

For Kant, the political had no value in itself. It was a subservient discipline. Morality is the theoretical branch of right; politics is the application of the theory. The only conceivable justification for politics is morality, which alone gives humanity its worth. Kant does not consider man to be a *zoon politikon,* a political being. Man's dignity lies in his being a moral being because he is an end in himself. The subject matter of Kant's thought is not the *polis* but rather what *a priori* reason can determine—among states, as well as among individuals—to be the ideal form of rightful human association.[27]

Like Hobbes, Kant wanted to ward off the dangers of politics and subject its chaotic processes to a form of simple order. For both of these philosophers, natural right was the only moral fact. For Hobbes, right was secured by submission to an absolute political sovereign; for Kant, right was to be realized by the identification of the individual will with the moral law. Both thinkers sought to simplify complex questions of human association: Hobbes, by deducing his theory of social peace from the right of self-preservation; Kant, by deriving the imperative of nonviolence from the rights of individual and state autonomy.

The thought of both also had totalitarian implications. Kant's conception, while moral rather than political, shares with Hobbes's the idea that whoever enforces the compact of peace rightfully has a plenitude of power. Such domination is self-justifying; it is not dependent upon any form of conscious delegation of authority.[28]

A sense of opposition runs through Kant's thought. Desire and duty, for example, are antithetical. Impulses of duty conflict with our selfish inclinations. Kant insists that our deepest and most secret motives must

27. "We . . . hypothesize a world which we ourselves govern . . ." Shell, *The Rights of Reason,* at 88. See also Hannah Arendt, *Lectures on Kant's Political Philosophy,* ed. Ronald Beiner (Chicago: University of Chicago Press, 1982).

28. Leo Strauss, *Natural Right and History* (Chicago: University of Chicago Press, 1953), chap. 5. See the discussion of the politically coercive implications of Kantian ethics in my *Descent into Subjectivity,* chap. 1.

be cleansed by a purer reason. Otherwise, our actions can not be authentically moral. Kant applies this methodology with great insight into some of the most destructive international practices. For example, in *Perpetual Peace,* he holds that no peace treaty should contain any secret reservations which can lead to future war, and that any that do are not morally valid. This command is not derived from the natural law or from a *jus gentium* that engages moral reason with experience. The obligation is formed in an ideal world of pure practical reason. The imperatives of this reason impose the norms which will determine the ethical quality of individual actions.[29]

This subjective probing of Kant's ethics often exposes depths of evil which more moderate philosophies might overlook. But this approach, while elevated, leads to an incomplete understanding of moral responsibility. The corrective remedies which are enforced by Kantian ethics upon the wayward will represent limited, although indispensable, values. In Kant's international theory, peace is of decisive importance. It is valuable not only in itself but because, when implemented, it will assure the flourishing of the rights of states. However, his singlemindedness leads Kant to take moral positions with respect to international affairs which oversimplify very difficult practical problems that those possessing actual authority must resolve.

A particular example serves to illustrate the general difficulty. One preliminary article of *Perpetual Peace* prohibits the contracting of national debt in connection with the external affairs of states. The principal reason for the prohibition is that such a credit system can be used by the powerful states to build up their own armies and thus, as debts grow, increase the possibilities of war. While this law need not be immediately implemented, it remains an unqualified imperative which must be realized as soon as circumstances permit.

This example illustrates how far Kant's thought is from that of Leibniz. For Leibniz, as we have seen, problems of international finance

29. Because the content of theory is conceived *a priori,* it should not, according to Kant, pose any danger to the policies of states, which are based upon experience. Kant, *Perpetual Peace,* introduction.

raise issues of distributive justice. Like general matters of international
commerce, questions of finance require an allocation of common
goods among states that are not equal in either power or resources.
The range of debt incurred, the amounts to be paid or forgiven, would
require a fuller exploration of the rights of both the debtor and credi-
tor states to realize their relative entitlements and the proper scope of
their legitimate interests. To adequately deal with these problems as
matters of social justice would also require a more careful assessment
of the different and sometimes antagonistic claims which members of
the international society could reasonably invoke against each other.
All these avenues of inquiry are foreclosed by Kant's reliance upon a
singular and absolute principle—the avoidance of international violence.

Kant's theory is an ethic of simplification. He shares with many
other modern philosophers a conviction that a just order is not something to be developed, in time, through the application of reason to
experience. Rather, the terms of order—international as well as domestic—are decided once and for all through the deductive power of
abstract thought. Pure practical reason creates a union of theory and
practice. There are no existential uncertainties: whatever is universally
valid as a matter of abstract right is equally valid in matters of action.
A fiction of the social contract postulates an agreement among all as
moral agents to implement the categorical imperatives, and this mechanism assures that peace and individual freedom are guaranteed from
the beginning. Righteousness then consists of obedience to the duties
imposed by *a priori* thought.[30]

Kant allows no positive role to a more concretely nuanced practical
reason. Suspicious of human motives, he cannot see that men can be
moved to act, or abstain from action, for reasons more complex than
pure selfishness or the will to dominate. Nor does Kant grasp the po-

30. The avoidance of complexity is noted in Shell, *The Rights of Reason,* and in
Strauss, *Natural Right and History,* chap. 5. But see Terry Nardin and David R. Mapel,
Traditions of International Ethics (Cambridge: Cambridge University Press, 1993), where
the positive effect of the Kantian tradition upon international relations is defended.

tential for good which may arise out of a natural order of existence and a more comprehensive set of core values. And because he has no conception of a common good, he cannot grasp the fundamental needs of international society that go beyond the avoidance of armed conflict.

The tragedy of Kant's *Perpetual Peace* lies, paradoxically, in its exclusive attention to the evils of war. Because of this preoccupation with violence, he fails to address the more difficult questions of how peace can be established; or, more precisely, whether it can be established at all so long as the sovereign independence of states remains the foundation of the international system. Kant's unwillingness to address these issues is caused, in part, by his unqualified commitment to autonomy. Kant follows Rousseau in believing that the purpose of philosophy is not the acquisition of knowledge but rather the enforcement of the rights of man and, by extension, the rights of separate nations.

Kant's failure to pursue deeper questions concerning the future of international life also results also from the lowering of his moral vision. His prescriptions are demanding, but they harmonize with the desires and aversions of those who are subject to the moral law. He accepts the unwillingness of states to be subject to any higher temporal authority, and there is no sustained critique of general disorder in his reflections that might lead, as with the Abbé de Saint-Pierre, to more general proposals of international political reform. In Kant's mind, a pact of nonaggression becomes not only a necessary, but also a sufficient, condition for universal peace.

Kant advises those who hope for human progress to adopt an attitude of detachment. They can then contemplate the evolution of the moral character of mankind as it works through the conflicts which nature has ordained. Through such struggles, humanity strives toward a cosmopolitan existence that will realize the highest capacities of individuals and states. Enlargement of the mental outlook is also recommended as a moral ideal. Only by taking the rights of others into account are we able to overcome our selfishness. This is all to the good, yet Kant is not interested in how we are to *combine* with others in order to act, at a practical level, in a way that will actually promote peace. His world citizen is primarily a world spectator. Kant's ambivalence leaves those who are interested in the development of world order to choose between the alternatives of moral idealism or Machiavellian realism.[31]

In *Perpetual Peace* Kant distinguishes those articles which are independent of circumstances and must be immediately implemented from those which, while equally prohibitive, may justifiably have their enforcement delayed. But he insists that all are eventually binding and he brusquely dismisses the selfish political motives which may obstruct the ultimate goals. The abstract quality of Kant's thought prevents him from seeing that, in the real world, a sense of universal responsibility may be qualified by more immediate obligations.

Kant characterizes Grotius, Pufendorf and Vattel as "sorry comforters," but they all were more conscious than he of the moral dilemmas of a ruler who tries to reconcile his humanitarian instincts with his obligations to his own people. Kant's unwillingness to address those difficulties or the demands which moral ambiguity makes upon reason and judgment impairs the practical value of his theory.[32]

His pessimism further limits the relevance of his ideas. Kant's indifference to any desires for substantial happiness on earth places him at the opposite end of the moral spectrum from Leibniz, for whom the hope for temporal well-being was an integral part of the pursuit of the good. Kant's negative disposition also reinforces his aversion to politics. Never really serious about human affairs, Kant would prefer to bypass politics altogether.

31. Hannah Arendt, *Lectures on Kant's Political Philosophy,* seventh session.

32. These difficulties with the Kantian ethical tradition are noted in a number of critical writings. See, e.g., C. E. Larmore, *Patterns of Moral Complexity* (Cambridge: Cambridge University Press, 1987); E. F. Schumaker, *A Guide for the Perplexed* (New York: Harper & Row, 1987); Nicholas Rescher, *Ethical Idealism* (Berkeley: University of California Press, 1987); E. L. Pincoffs, *Quandaries and Virtues: Against Reductivism in Ethics* (Lawrence, Kan.: University of Kansas Press, 1986); and Bernard Williams, *Ethics and the Limits of Philosophy* (Cambridge, Mass.: Harvard University Press, 1986). The best recognition of complexity as it bears upon the responsibilities of the diplomat is Raymond Aron, *Peace and War: A Theory of International Relations,* ed. Richard Howard and Annette B. Fox (Garden City, N.Y.: Doubleday, 1966), pt. 4.

Yet the political dimension of existence is an essential part of any reasonable understanding of any form of stable human association. Kant placed his faith in the advent of a universal moral community that would spring directly from the noumenal personality of the individual. But this approach is essentially flawed. An exclusive dependence upon morality is a psychological impediment to any genuine human progress, for it is a disposition which is closely allied with despair: "[W]here there is no tomorrow, moralism makes its entrance."[33]

Later pessimists, such as Schopenhauer, looked upon the very idea of a moral law with its categorical imperatives as a form of enslavement. To these thinkers, reason could not establish the moral personality because the inmost being of the individual is nothing more than the voracious subjective will. This insight had social as well as personal significance. As we shall see with Hegel, when subjectivism becomes the *modus operandi* of governance it can cause havoc in the world at large.

Kant could not foresee that his exalted idea of individual autonomy would be gradually replaced by the autonomy of the state. Nor could he anticipate that when the state is considered to be the actualization of an ideal, it will resist subjection to either moral or political authority. Beginning with Hegel, philosophical thought would complete the rejection of transcendence by affirming an immanence of being centered upon the expanding world of collective, as well as individual, consciousness.[34]

III

From the time of Leibniz the German Enlightenment had been inspired by a cosmopolitan spirit. Whether expressed in terms of rationalism or moral philosophy, a universal outlook permeated these magnificent expressions of culture. But this expansiveness occurred during an historical period in which there was little opportunity for leading

33. Czeslaw Milosz, *The Witness of Poetry* (Cambridge, Mass.: Harvard University Press, 1983), 14–15.

34. On Schopenhauer's reaction to Kant's ethic, see Allan Janik and Stephen Toulmin, *Wittgenstein's Vienna* (New York: Simon & Schuster, 1973), chap. 5.

minds to have a national attachment. Before the age of Bismarck there was no great German fatherland to make more particularistic demands upon those who were philosophically inclined. But as the French Revolution gave new meaning to the idea of national glory, divided loyalties began to appear in the field of German thought.

The case of Fichte is illustrative. In his earlier writings he was absorbed in diffuse ideals and he expressed a disdain for statehood. However, by the beginning of the nineteenth century, his work sought to reach a balance between cosmopolitanism and the values associated with a distinctive national community. He also placed the state within a more meaningful whole. Fichte believed that a new and unified German republic would achieve its own greatness; but it would also fully perform its duties to humanity. That broader qualification depended upon vital distinctions between the universal and the particular which would recede before the forces of German nationalism. In the emerging idealistic philosophy, the state was thought of as the incarnation of absolute rationality.[35]

Other changes in the general culture of Europe were beginning to remove all higher restraints upon the ambitions of the state. From its beginnings, European Christendom had been based upon the idea that a meaningful distinction could be made between the spiritual and the temporal realms of existence. These distinctions cut to the core of human life and destiny. Furthermore, from the time of Augustine, there had been a recurring tendency to emphasize the supremacy of the spiritual life over profane activities. From such transcendent perspectives, all political authority, whether particular or universal, was merely part of a human nature which would disappear when time eventually passed into eternity. Sacred history, with its promise of ultimate beatitude, was given priority over the ordinary course of temporal events.

The expectation of an eschatological fulfillment intensified in the

---

35. H. C. Englebrecht, *Johann Gottlieb Fichte: The Study of His Political Writings with Special Reference to His Nationalism* (New York: Columbia University Press, 1933); Cairns, *Legal Philosophy from Plato to Hegel,* chap. 13.

religious reaction to the Renaissance. At the same time, however, the humanistic spirit was becoming more independent. As it did so, it strengthened its resistance to sources of meaning beyond itself. Grotius's ambiguities about the ultimate nature of natural law reflected the beginning of the shift from the transcendental toward an immanence of understanding. This disposition would accelerate with the dawn of the modern age and would take a distinctive form in the German Enlightenment. As a result, the sense of the divine as something existing beyond, but directing, the course of creation, declined.

European culture continued to distance itself from Christian revelation and the spiritual authority of the Church. To thinkers of the first rank it seemed certain that whatever was of supreme importance could be attributed to the inner nature of things. Man would discover his destiny within, rather through any source outside himself. The liberation of man would come through the expansion of the human. For Leibniz, and later for Goethe, the real was itself a rich and harmonious source of being. The world was a work of nature, not of God; nothing of substance beyond it could be conceived.[36]

There was also a growing sense of the inherent value of the individual person. As a logical, ethical, and aesthetic subject, the person was a free spirit capable of realizing immense subjective possibilities. The measure of his fulfillment would be found within himself. For Kant, the individual would become self-determining through a process of moral reform. By subjecting himself to self-imposed laws, he could move from what is valid for his own will to what is valid for all. In this autonomous community each would recognize the right, and all would be doing what reason could expect of any purely rational being. Although no longer a participant in a Divine order, the individual, in his moral vocation, would realize a dignity that had an immortal significance.

36. Romano Guardini, *The End of the Modern World*, trans. Joseph Theman and Herbert Burke (Chicago: Henry Regnery Company, 1968); Joseph Wood Krutch, *The Modern Temper* (New York: Harcourt Brace & World, 1929); Nicholas Berdyaev, *The End of Our Time* (New York: Sheed and Ward, 1933).

Western history was entering a *gnostic* phase. A gnostic believes that he possesses immediate knowledge of reality through the medium of an absolute speculative idea. Through such insight one contemplates the order of things as they exist in God. Ancient Gnosticism was apolitical; it encouraged its disciples to withdraw from the world. Modern gnosticism, by contrast, draws upon the absolute idea in order to transform temporal life. The inward powers of the mind are expanded to a point where the distinction between the divine and the human no longer has meaning. What had in the past been thought of as having its origins in God becomes part of the temporal existence of man. The spiritual mysteries of creation are perceived in a way that matches the penetration of science into the inner structures of the physical world.[37]

The Christian tradition had maintained the distinction between the divine and the human as it drew the spiritual into mankind by way of redemptive grace. With the Reformation, the sanctification of life was removed from the field of contemplation and assigned the tasks of civilization. However, in the growing secularization of culture, all thought of transcendence was beginning to be seen as simply a projection of what was best in man. As the influence of Christianity waned, the domain of human action became more self-assertive and endowed with an inherent significance.

These pervasive changes of outlook impinged upon basic questions of political order. Within the state, their implications were profound. For Kant the moral vocation was a juridical task as well as an ethical responsibility. Since each citizen must act upon a universally applicable principle that respects human beings as ends in themselves, they should be obliged by political authority to honor that commitment. All must submit to a legal regime which will enforce right according to *a priori* standards. The moral good of freedom is to be realized within civil society through a hypothetical social contract which embodies the principles of pure practical reason.

37. Eric Voegelin, *The New Science of Politics* (Chicago: University of Chicago Press, 1952), chap. 4. The gnostic aspect of the moral philosophy of John Rawls is noted in my study *Descent into Subjectivity,* chap. 1.

Kant tried to project this juridical concept into the nonpolitical international arena by way of his moral theory of cosmopolitan right. But the extension did not take hold. With the dawn of German nationalism, the world beyond the state was being substantially reconceived. Interstate relations were coming under the influence of Hegelian thought. Attention was increasingly focused on the nature and significance of the absolute ethical state. This new idealization would have a destabilizing influence upon international law and politics.

There would be a decisive turning away from any meaningful conception of universal authority. A sense of divine order separate from, but enriching, the course of human history remained within European culture as long as human existence was understood as a participation in a more encompassing reality. The essential structures of collective life were thought of as being grounded in an arrangement whose origins were beyond the world of created being.

Before the modern age, its transcendence was not experienced as something hostile to human aspirations. An understanding of a superior normative domain was accompanied by a confidence that conformity to its principles was a source of human flourishing. Order was allied with reason, and reason was nurtured by a higher law which was in harmony with its own nature.

In the premodern West the search for a supreme source of order was fueled by an almost erotic tension. An unsatisfied desire for fulfillment implied the incompleteness of human experience within the whole order of Creation. The yearning for the good and for righteousness was insatiable. Reaching out beyond the given world, these strivings reflected the ambiguous position of the human in the overall order of existence.

The purpose of the Enlightenment was to bring this process to an end. An indefinite search for truth had marked the uniqueness of a culture straddling time and eternity; in this new age, immanence would eclipse transcendence. With the Enlightenment the quest for understanding would be reduced to a purely human conception of absolute knowledge.

The movement towards immanence which began with Leibniz and Wolff would be completed by Hegel. For Hegel, total understanding would be derived from a science of the experience of consciousness. The intellect would no longer mediate between time and eternity. The cosmos would be concentrated in one's mind and knowledge would be drawn out of the resources of one's own self-consciousness. Subjectively one would feel, and understand, all that was previously beyond apprehension. The truth would be unveiled. Reality would be seen for itself within the immanence of self-moving consciousness.[38]

Hegel's understanding of morality was essentially different from that of Kant. Kant directed moral consciousness toward the purity of its own intentions. He thought that the ethical develops independently from social existence. To Hegel, Kant only focused upon that part of moral consciousness which is concerned with strengthening the will's resistance to the passions. But ethics involves performances as well as restrictions, and these wider purposes cannot be understood if the individual disassociates himself from the world around him. Individuals exist but, for Hegel, they are not self-contained. They *coexist* in societies. And while without individuals there can be no societies, it is equally true that without societies there can be no complete understanding of the individual.[39]

A rigorously subjective approach to ethics, as advocated by Kant, neglects the fact that actions are carried out in a public world. One acts against the background of a pervasive and common morality. For Hegel, the history of social experience records something more that

38. Eric Voegelin, *In Search of Order,* vol. 5 (Baton Rouge: Louisiana University Press, 1987), chap. 2. See also Eugene Webb, *Eric Voegelin* (Seattle: University of Washington Press, 1981), chap. 3. Francis Fukuyama, *The End of History and the Last Man* (New York: The Free Press, 1992) is an important contemporary attempt to derive an understanding of the political world from the experience of consciousness. See further *After History? Francis Fukuyama and His Critics,* ed. Timothy Burns (Lanham, Md.: Rowman and Littlefield, 1994).

39. W. W. Walsh, *Hegelian Ethics* (New York: Garland, 1984), chap. 3; Charles Taylor, *Hegel* (Cambridge: Cambridge University Press, 1975); Judith Shklar, *Freedom and Independence: A Study of the Political Ideas of Hegel's Phenomenology* (Cambridge: Cambridge University Press, 1976), chap. 3.

human antagonisms and the evolution of individual freedom. It also evidences a broad pursuit of values. Within the matrix of time, one gains knowledge of how a general good, or spirit, can arise as a consequence of human deeds. To fully understand, one must presuppose a fundamental unity which will make actions intelligible. This unity is not to be found in self-legislation. It can only be found in the state.

Hegel's state is not just a political association. Nor is it simply a juridical order. The state is the spirit of the nation. As such, it is the rational embodiment of power. The state expresses all that is real about the society in which the individual lives. There is no need for the individual to try to escape from the state into an existence which will be determined by himself alone. Such a flight is unnecessary because the state does not suppress personal autonomy. It provides for its expansion by the reasonableness of the demands which it makes upon the individual.

The individual who becomes an obedient citizen leads a universal life. But this is not a cosmopolitan existence. The state is mind objectified and it is only as one as its members that the individual finds his own objectivity. The individual achieves the actuality of his ethical life when his own will becomes identified with the substantial will of the state.[40]

In Hegel's political theory sovereignty is inflated. Each state is absolute. There is no higher *Civitas Maxima,* or other universal form of human association. States are in a state of nature in their mutual relations and each one faces the other as a complete autonomous sovereign. Like Leibnizian self-contained substances, each state's being comes from within itself. There is no substantial interdependence between states. Each is a whole which satisfies its essential needs within its own borders. In its international relations the state projects onto the world stage the actual infinity of everything which is finite within it.[41]

There is no political authority above the state. There is also no

40. Walsh, *Hegelian Ethics.* See also Lionel Trilling, *Sincerity and Authenticity* (Cambridge, Mass.: Harvard University Press, 1972), chap. 2.

41. Hegel, *Philosophy of Right,* translated by T. M. Knox (1952), pt. 3, paras. 321–27.

juridical order to which the state must submit. International law is not based upon a common humanity, nor does it have a decisive binding force. When a state enters into a legal relationship with another state it subjects itself to international law by an act of self-limitation. It can disengage itself from that constraint at any time if it considers that its essential interests require withdrawal. No state can renounce the egotism that belongs to its sovereign nature.[42]

The philosophical idealism generated by Hegel became the policy of the Prussian state. As it did so, it jeopardized the patient labors of international positivists who had hoped to create a general order out of various expressions of a sovereign willingness to be bound. Hegel's international theory revealed the shallowness of Vattel's belief that the relations between sovereign states could be stabilized through a refinement of the law of treaties. Hegel admitted the moral authority of the principle *pacta sunt servanda* but he insisted that it does not pass beyond the normative stage and acquire actual regulative power.

All international rights come into existence through the particular wills of specific states. There is no universal will having constitutional authority over them. Within the field of international practice attempts may legitimately be made to arbitrate disputes over diverse interpretations of treaty obligations. However, such efforts are always subject to the power of the states who confer authority upon the arbitrators. Ultimately, the particular wills of states are decisive.[43]

For Hegel, war is the final sanction of international law. To commence war, a state does not have to suffer an objectively provable injury. In the endless vortex of the international state of nature it is impossible to say when a legitimate cause of war may arise. The state, as mind, can react simply to the idea of injury and can legitimately use

---

42. Id. Compare the discussion of Jellinek's philosophy of law in Nussbaum, *A Concise History of the Law of Nations.*, chap. 7. See also Henrich von Treitsche, *Politics,* edited by Hans Kohn (New York: Harcourt Brace & World, 1963).

43. Hegel, *Philosophy of Right,* para. 333. Vattel had argued that an international agreement that works injury to the obliged party cannot be revoked. He also placed great hope in the stabilizing influence of principles of treaty interpretation. See his *The Law of Nations,* bk. 2, chaps. 15–18.

force to safeguard its honor at the slightest provocation. Justifications for war are not to be found in any higher law beyond the power of the state. As autonomous personalities, states are not subject to any superior moral or political authority. States are themselves ethical substances; they find within their own specific natures the principles which justify their actions. Only the absolute mind, or *Geist,* which manifests itself in the history of the world, sits in higher judgment.[44]

Kant believed that the international state of nature was unjust in itself. The inherent disorder of this natural condition implies the dominance of the stronger and such a heteronomy is offensive to the ideal of equal dignity. It was imperative that this state of nature be overcome by a federation of peoples who, acting under the idea of an *a priori* social contract, will make provision for collective security. This negative arrangement, prohibiting war, was something less than a complete political organization of the world. But its imperfection was not lamentable. A pacific federation was commanded by pure practical reason. Peace is the appropriate condition for a community of autonomous moral beings who are governed by the same self-legislated law that guarantees to them an equal tranquility and freedom. To Hegel, however, a "perpetual peace" would corrupt the virtue of nations. It was an idea both immoral and impracticable. A moral person does not shrink from the violence that is an inevitable part of the contest between autonomous states. Whenever the call to war rings in his ears, a patriot responds. Despising the vanity of temporal things, he gathers with others in the common pursuit of the universal ideal that is represented by the nation to which he owes allegiance.

Equality was not the ideal for Hegel that it had been for Kant. To Hegel, the inequalities of power between states are based upon an immutable hierarchical order. One should no longer refer to a rational law of nations to promote egalitarian sentiments. Nor may one effectively invoke principles of distributive justice to promote the interests

44. Hegel, *Philosophy of Right,* paras. 334–38. In *The Search for Order,* vol. 5, chap. 2, Voegelin asserts that Hegel uses the symbol *Geist,* in opposition to the Platonic *Nous,* in order to make substance essentially subjective.

of the less fortunate states in the international system. The imperfection of the claims that could be made on behalf of weaker states was reinforced by a belief in the immanent and disparate purposes of temporal development. Impotent states must submit to the forces of history that give pride of place to the strong and aggressive. Temporal success allows states which are in the ascendant to treat others with contempt.[45]

As the nineteenth century progressed, there was a growing movement within Germany for that nation to take its place among the other leading powers. It would join them in a global expansion which would assure the dominance of this minority of states over the rest of the non-European world. Ancient states, which had once been part of a loosely related international community, were now being overcome by a predominantly Eurocentric *Weltgeist*. A new universal order was emerging which showed little respect for Kant's principles of cosmopolitan right. Less developed societies were either reduced to colonies or subjected to an odious regime of capitulations that restricted their territorial sovereignty and imposed upon them unequal and nonreciprocal commercial privileges.[46]

The development of consciousness promoted by Hegelianism was eliminating the tension between transcendence and immanence that had been a distinctive feature of Western Christian culture. *Geist,* the absolute object which gradually revealed itself in history, was very different from that comprehensive reason which had inspired Dante's universalism. Reason was now the essence of man—and it was manifest in the substantiality of the state. On the international plane, that same spirit was at work through the continuous confrontation of sovereign states. Each, as it matured, was convinced that it had become the unique incarnation of a supramundane reality.

These conflicts between absolute entities occurred with the under-

45. Von Treitske, *Politics.*

46. Antonio Cassese, *International Law in a Divided World* (Oxford: The Clarendon Press, 1986), chap. 2.

standing that force was the ultimate measure of their resolution. War was now, more than ever, the final sanction. But, in spite of its being the supreme expression of sovereign will, war was not thought of as having a terminal significance. Custom and the law of nations had a residual influence within this refined state of nature. It was generally understood that each state persisted as something absolute. This guaranteed that a state defeated by force of arms should not disappear from the international community.[47]

As the nineteenth century drew to a close, many jurists were alarmed by the destructive logic of Hegelian internationalism. The contrast between the security within states and the insecurity between states was becoming intolerable. Bluntschi, the most prominent international lawyer in Bismarck's Germany, recognized the value of the Concert of Europe. But he also insisted that the legitimacy of the collaborative system required the recognition of the right of states of lesser stature to participate in international decisions. Only then could a universal order be based upon a common humanity. Bluntschi also saw that it was political, rather than legal, disputes that threatened the general security. He called for the establishment of some machinery of governance that, by combining the authority of large and small states, could effectively adjust controversies which engaged the vital interests of competing states and which, if not resolved, could lead to armed conflict.[48]

In Great Britain, the Scottish legal philosopher James Lorimer was frustrated by the collapse of the ethical aspect of international jurisprudence. While he agreed with Vattel's rejection of a *Civitas Maxima,* Lorimer was also convinced that Vattel's insistence upon the absolute independence of states made it impossible to effectively regulate inter-

47. Hegel, *Philosophy of Right,* paras. 338–39.
48. J. C. Bluntschli, "The Organization of a European Federation," in W. Evans Darby, *International Tribunals,* 4th ed. (1904), 194. There are biographical references to Bluntschli in Holbraad, *The Concert of Europe,* and Arthur Nussbaum, *A Concise History of the Law of Nations,* rev. ed. (1958), 236. Bluntschli's plan called for an independent international judiciary but he was more interested in the settlement of political rather than legal disputes.

national relations. For Lorimer, the only hope for the improvement of world order was the abandonment of the fiction of absolute independence. He also believed that the principle of absolute equality impeded the development of effective international organization. To be a full participant in international governance a state must be able, as well as willing, to carry out the requisite responsibilities.[49]

Lorimer was of the opinion that the peaceful international relations which had characterized the greater part of his century would not continue into the next without the establishment of some form of international government. The dissimilarities between municipal order, where legislation, adjudication, and enforcement created an integrated legal system, and the anarchical situation beyond state boundaries, were too grave to be tolerated. Treaties and custom were useful to normal international intercourse but they were no match for the deeper disorder and potential catastrophe which lurked beneath the surface of conventional diplomacy.

Europe had experienced a prolonged but fragile peace which would continue into the early part of the next century. Yet there was a perpetual danger of destruction. The risk was generally ignored, as one tends to ignore any peril which is a permanent aspect of one's environment. After 1871 there was universal conscription and standing armies were being prepared to go to war.

There was also a substantial peace movement. It was hoped that as economic progress increased the international standard of living, the resulting prosperity would be followed by the peaceful adjustment of disputes among nations.[50] There were hopes for general disarmament. But thinkers such as Lorimer were wise enough to see that while dis-

49. James Lorimer, *The Institutes of the Law of Nations: A Treatise on the Jural Relations of Separate Political Communities,* 2 vols (Edinburgh: W. Blackwood & Sons, 1883–84). In 1865 Lorimer had been appointed to the chair of the Law of Nature and of Nations at the University of Edinburgh. For a biographical summary of his life and work see *Dictionary of National Biography,* (1917 ed.), s.v. "Lorimer, James.". His philosophy of international relations is criticized in Nussbaum, *A Concise History of the Law of Nations,* rev. ed. (1958), 238–39.

50. E. g., John Stuart Mill, *Principles of Political Economy* (1848), bk. III, chap. xvii, 5; William E. H. Lecky, *Rationalism in Europe* (London: Longmans, Green & Co., 1866).

armament was a noble idea, standing armies would never be reduced unless there was some alternative to the prevailing "armed" peace. True disarmament would require the establishment of an international government with necessary military forces. In addition to being empowered to maintain the peace, such a government would also have to provide for the nonviolent vindication of the rights of states.[51]

Given the temper of the times, neither Lorimer nor Bluntschli were taken seriously. Their views were not only inimical to the established international system; they were also not congruent with the general outlook within progressive circles. Influential Americans sought the establishment an international tribunal based upon the model of the United States Supreme Court.[52] There was also an expectation that the peoples of the world would act in a reasonable manner if they only were given the opportunity to do so. Once enlightened, they would act to relieve those subject to unjust oppression and do whatever was necessary to promote the universal enjoyment of liberty.

This pacific vision was essentially nonpolitical. The natural interests of states were assumed to be compatible. Progressives also believed that the potential for general harmony would be impaired by any form of international politics whether plans for world government, or the continuation of traditional balances of power. Struggles for power and authority make no sense to those who are convinced that they themselves are already reasonable.[53]

51. Lorimer, *The Institutes,* bk. 5.

52. An example is Nicholas Murray Butler, *The International Mind: An Argument for the Judicial Settlement of International Disputes* (New York: Scribners, 1913). The origins of such sentiments can be traced to James Wilson's lectures on jurisprudence, which were given in Philadelphia in 1791. Wilson was a signer of the Declaration of Independence and the Constitutional Convention of 1787. Wilson saw the establishment of an independent judiciary in the Federal Constitution, empowered to resolve disputes among the states, as a model for the world. *Works of James Wilson,* edited by R. J. McCloskey (1967), pt. 1, lecs. 8, 10. See also the proposal for international government made by William Ladd, *An Essay on a Congress of Nations for the Adjustment of International Disputes without a Resort to Arms* (1840) (Washington, D.C.: Carnegie Endowment, 1916).

53. W. Schiffer, *The Legal Community of Mankind: A Critical Analysis of the Modern Conception of World Organization* (New York: Columbia University Press, 1954). Compare the observations of Nicolas Murray Butler on the eve of the First World War: "The

On the plane of historical reality, however, the rivalries of expanding empires overcame ideals of order grounded upon economic
theories of free trade. A heightened sense of patriotism was encourag-
ing propensities toward violence. Peace conferences at the Hague had
some successes, but hopes for the compulsory settlement of international disputes were dashed by those who believed that the state, being
an end in itself, could not be a means toward any higher purpose.[54]

Hopes for peace and general well-being were destroyed in the Great
War of 1914–1918. Following that calamity, there were plans for the
restoration of international order to correct the conditions that had led
to so much death and ruin. The imperfections of these efforts would
be reflected in the inevitable failure of the League of Nations. A new
total war would bring the vanquished to the brink of destruction.

Following the Second World War, new initiatives of global organization and aid would try to create a nonviolent, stable, and prosperous
future for all humanity. As we shall see, these practical projects—such
as the establishment of the United Nations—would be matched by
new theoretical approaches to the problem of universal order. These
would seek to justify existing international arrangements by recasting
the international state of nature in a more sociologically attractive
form. More audacious reflections would try to replace the nation-state
system as a whole. These speculations would draw out of the resources
of the collective consciousness of humanity an inclusive communal
ideal of world order. The unity of humanity would be, in theory, secured by an abstractly understood international legal system.

---

civilized world is at peace and there is no ruler and no party bent on disturbing that
peace. The more powerful nations are presided over by governments or monarchs whose
faces are turned toward the light . . . The German Emperor, against whom criticisms
are sometimes leveled, is, I dare assert with confidence, a convinced believer in the
policies of peace . . ." Butler, *The International Mind* (New York: Scribners, 1913), 17–18.

54. See my *The Search for World Order,* chap. 4.

CHAPTER 3

THE SEARCH FOR ULTIMATE AUTHORITY

I

As the nineteenth century progressed, the mind of the West drew further away from its participation in transcendent reality. This increasing inwardness had important implications for international theory. From the time of Dante the universalizing powers of the intellect had been applied to international relations, with the hope of drawing the separate existence of states into a relationship with a higher form of order—cosmic or humanistic. After Hegel, reflection moved in the opposite direction. It was now assumed that humankind could only flourish within the isolated boundaries of absolutely independent nation-states.

The anarchic potential of this shift in outlook was profound. Practically-minded international jurists tried to unify the disintegrating international community by refining and extending the basic principles of international law. Customary rules and treaty obligations were more precisely identified. These rules were also thought of as having an intrinsic validity. The jurists' hope was to accentuate the reality of legal rules in order to restrain the political ambitions of powerful states. Their expectations of establishing a positive international legal order were, ironically, undermined by a critique of international law by a leading legal positivist, the English jurist, John Austin.

Austin sharply separated *positive law* from morality. He defined positive law as an order that exists within a vertical structure of coercive authority. Law was the command of a superior to a subject coupled with a threat of sanction in case of disobedience. The hierarchical municipal legal systems within the developed states conformed to this definition but, beyond the state, there was no positive law. Since so-called international law concerned relations among sovereigns, each of whom recognized no higher human authority, it lacked the indispensable element of subjection to supreme power. According to Austin, the body of rules which the international lawyers were so patiently developing was not, strictly speaking, law. At best, they were a species of morality that was tenuously sustained by an imprecise public opinion.[1]

Austin's analysis provoked some legal philosophers to reconsider the entire foundations of the international system. Vattel's principle of absolute state independence was seen as a basic flaw which made the effective regulation of international existence impossible. Having confined the rule of enforceable law to relations within their borders, modern insubmissive states had left all encounters beyond their frontiers to the perpetual insecurity of a Hobbesian state of nature.

Some felt that the situation called for the development of a form of international government. James Lorimer of Edinburgh proposed the establishment of an international organization which would be authorized to create, apply, and enforce laws enacted by representatives of states for the exclusive purpose of preserving the existence of those states as separate communities. But the prevailing opinion in the late nineteenth century was that an international order could be achieved without the establishment of any permanent authority above the autonomous states.[2]

Since the Congress of Vienna of 1815 a type of quasi-governance had emerged in the form of the Concert of Europe, and other progressive forces were at work that gave reason to hope for the peaceful and lawful development of the existing international community. Reci-

1. John Austin, *Lectures on Jurisprudence, Or The Philosophy of Positive Law,* ed. Robert Campbell (Jersey City: F. D. Linn, 1875), lec. 6, sec. 199. The expression "international law" was used by Jeremy Bentham in the late eighteenth century, and soon began to replace the idea of the Law of Nations.

2. James Lorimer, *The Institutes of the Law of Nations,* discussed in Chapter 2 of the present work.

procities of obligation could be developed without compromising the fundamental independence of the members of the international community. On the eve of the First World War, these possibilities of inherent development were outlined by a distinguished international lawyer, Lassa Oppenheim. To Oppenheim the world was a society of states. Independence is a necessary feature of such a society, but he believed that it can be reconciled with the common interest of the whole human community. He conceded that if law presupposes an enforcing superior power, the society of states is anarchical. But if law is simply understood as a form of *order,* the existence of international law can be proven.

Horizontal regulation establishes order within a society without government. Rules arise out of the interaction between its members, and they are generally considered to be obligatory. These rules affirm the basic principles of the international society by recognizing the independence, equality, and jurisdictional authority of its members. In both peace and war, the more extensive relations of states are regulated by custom and treaty in ways that delimit mutual legal responsibility. International law exists, even thought it lacks the perfection which obtains within states where Austinian principles are fully operative.[3]

Oppenheim believed that the society of states was not lawless, even though its objectives could be more securely achieved if it was transformed into a universal political society. He thought that such a basic change was theoretically possible but morally undesirable. If the world were organized, all the rich variety of human life would be compressed into a single state and the separate states would be reduced to provinces. Unity would bring death. Since each nation makes a distinctive contribution to the universal goal of human happiness, it is only through the separate development of independent states that the vitality of the international community can be sustained.

3. Lassa Oppenheim, *Die Zukunft des Volkerrechts* (1911). The work was published in English in 1921 under the title *The Future of International Law* (London: The Clarendon Press, 1921) (Washington, D.C.: Pamph. Series, Carnegie Endowment for International Peace, Division of International Law, No. 39).

Oppenheim's vision of the future was that of a decentralized society of independent states with sufficient collaborative practices to assure the general progress of the whole human community. The law of nations would flourish as soon as the principle of equality was more fully recognized. When international conferences become more multilateral, a larger number of states would be able to participate in the formation of general international law. If the principle of "one state, one vote" became operative, the traditional predominance of a minority of powerful states could be gradually superseded. No state could be bound by any convention without its consent; however, unanimity was not a condition to the formation of customary international law. Legal development through majority consensus could be reconciled with the basic values of the society of states. The elimination of international violence was also a rational prospect. Oppenheim thought that great possibilities for the administration of justice had been signaled by the Hague Peace Conference of 1899, which had recommended the arbitration of international disputes and had established a Permanent Court to promote that pacific objective.

These hopes were sustained by an optimistic view of the moral character of states. While there are always individuals within states who will only do what is right under threat of compulsion, Oppenheim believed that states have a more elevated nature. They can adjust themselves to a self-imposed order. Over time, the international interests of individual states should become stronger than their national interests. Whoever believes in unlimited progress must also believe that eventually states will freely commit themselves to submit all the controversies between them to judicial or to arbitral decision.[4]

Oppenheim's convictions concerning the development of order within the self-contained society of states illustrates one of the basic limitations of a legalistic understanding of international life. Drawing

4. Oppenheim, *Die Zukunft des Völkerrechts,* chap. 1, secs. 17–26. See also W. Evans Darby, "The Question of Sanctions," in *International Arbitration; International Tribunals, A Collection of the various schemes which have been propounded; and of instances in the nineteenth century.* 4th ed. (London: J. M. Dent and Co., 1904).

inspiration from the Hague Peace Conferences, he was ignoring the political theory of the state that had been vigorously defended at those meetings. Diplomats emphasized the supremacy of the nation rather than the general interests in peace and disarmament. International relations were understood as a continuous struggle between powers—both established and emerging—and these autonomous entities were conceived as being ends in themselves. Lip service was given to pacific ideals. But while states, through their representatives, were posing as moral entities, they were reinforcing their separate military power and increasing their capacity for unilateral action.

From the perspective of political theory, the state had no higher purpose than the protection of its own interests. At the time of Oppenheim's optimistic prognosis neither disarmament, nor the pacific adjustment of differences, were of paramount importance to the leading European powers. There was a movement towards the expansion of arbitral or judicial settlement of international disputes, but it took place with the general understanding that matters of vital national interest were always reserved by the disputing states. A sharp distinction was drawn between legal and political disputes. In matters of essential security or interest, the powers of the self-sufficient state could not be subject to any objective measure of justice. There were no superior principles to which one could refer to adjust states' conflicting claims. At this elementary level of international coordination, the rights of each state were subjective, inalienable, and absolute.[5]

The autonomy of modern states was also not being corrected by other, more hopeful humanistic developments. Oppenheim echoed Kant's belief that states based upon popular will would be more disposed towards peace than the rapacious monarchies that were now being deposed in the name of democratic values. The classical ideal of popular sovereignty was revived, but it became subject to forces of nationalism, which only exacerbated international tensions. The will

5. See Charles De Visscher, *Theory and Reality in Public International Law*, trans. P. E. Corbett (Princeton: Princeton University Press, 1957); R. B. Mowat, *The Concert of Europe* (London: Macmillan, 1930), chap. 13.

of the people was understood as a possession of unlimited power, and
the public expressions of that will did not need to be just in order to
be valid. In matters of international friction, national loyalties were
decisive. Speaking to a world peace conference, the philosopher William James noted that, as a matter of plain truth, "the people want
war."[6]

The prophetic nature of James's comment would soon become
painfully evident. On the eve of the First World War, the distance
between political realities and forces of idealism was accentuated.
Marxist theories of international worker solidarity were proclaimed in
the hope that workers' common interests would lead the industrial
proletariat to transcend the bonds of nationalism and restrain the impulse to warfare. From this ideological perspective, Europe's vacillation between peace and war did not reflect the real relations between
states; rather, insecurity was caused by the distortions of international
capitalism. However, Marxist idealism could not prevent the outbreak
of war. Lenin and his followers did not realize that interstate conflict
was a social phenomenon which had its own noneconomic dynamic.[7]

The essential impotence of the existing forms of international governance was revealed by the events of July and August 1914. It had
been thought that Great Power peacemaking through the Concert system would be an effective means of assuring the primacy of the general
interest in order. What began as a European system had the prospect,
with the rise of the United States and Japan, of becoming a World
Concert with potential supervisory authority over all global conflicts.
But this expectation would be overtaken by the forces of history.

Since the last quarter of the nineteenth century the Concert system
had become increasingly ineffective and collaboration was being reduced in favor of increasing national security. To statesmen such as
Gladstone, the Concert was an institution which reflected a moral soli-

6. William James, "Remarks at the Peace Banquet," *Atlantic Monthly* 94:845 (1904).
See also De Visscher, *Theory and Reality in Public International Law,* chap. 2., sec. 1.

7. W. B. Gallie, *Philosophers of Peace and War* (London: Cambridge University Press,
1978), chap. 4.

darity among Christian states; to Bismarck, the interests of Germany were the measure of his country's participation in any form of international collaboration. With the decline of the Concert, there were no authoritative institutions to which one could appeal in order to prevent the outbreak of war. Following the assassinations at Sarajevo, individual rulers did not have the capacity to control the events which would plunge Europe and the world into a violent catastrophe.[8]

Responsibility for the sufferings of the First World War were properly attributed to the German and Austrian leaders. But mature reflection led to an awareness of a deeper causation. The ultimate explanation for that extraordinary calamity was to be found in the general system of international relations that had developed since the Westphalian settlement in the seventeenth century. The Concert system had a moderating influence and it made some contributions to stability, but its constructive actions were overshadowed by the understanding that no informal diplomatic process, however well-intentioned, could have prevented the outbreak of war. The futility of an "armed peace," with its dependence upon national armaments and fragile alliances, was painfully evident. Statesmen planning a postwar settlement tried to devise an organizational structure which would correct these basic deficiencies and establish the conditions for a durable international peace. But in spite of the obvious need for basic reform, the reformers would not abandon the principle of sovereign independence which was the hallmark of the inherited system.

At the Paris Conference of 1919 the precipitous actions of those immediately involved were identified as one of the major causes of the outbreak of war. As statesmen and emperors lost control of events in the fateful summer of 1914, military staffs, who were committed to inflexible strategic plans, took control of the situation. All hopes of

8. Carsten Holbraad, *The Concert of Europe: A Study in German and British International Theory* (London: Longmans, 1970); R. B. Mowat, *The Concert of Europe,* chap. 26. See also W. N. Medlicott, *Bismarck, Gladstone, and The Concert of Europe* (London: Althone Press, 1956), and E. Lipson, *Europe in the Nineteenth Century 1815–1914* (New York: Collier Books, 1962).

peaceful resolution were then lost. These facts were in the minds of those responsible for the organizational plans of the postwar world.

Under the Covenant of the new League of Nations it was provided that member states would be obliged to pursue modalities of peaceful settlement before resorting to the use of force to remedy an injury to their interests. The Council of the League was also authorized to employ methods of conciliation. These powers were to be used with reference to intractable political disputes that were not amenable to legal resolution. The organization thus hoped to insure the pacific adjustment of serious international differences that implicated the vital interests of states. The Covenant also reflected the influence of Kantian ideals of common security by providing, under Article 10, that each member was obliged to preserve the territorial integrity of all members of the League against external aggression. The Council was empowered to advise how this obligation should be fulfilled.

The failure of the League to realize these values in the period between the two World Wars can be attributed to many contingent factors, including the refusal of the United States to become a member. But the essential collapse was traceable to basic difficulties of a more theoretical nature. Those who devised the League of Nations underestimated the inherent power, as well as the symbolic importance, of the nation-state. They failed to realize that as long as the world was politically arranged as a society of states, the practical logic of sovereignty would be inconsistent with the ideals of the League.

The principles of sovereignty are both explanatory and prescriptive. They bestow powers and authoritatively determine what states may, or may not, do in their relations with the rest of international society. These foundational principles are automatically attributed to every political community which satisfies the criteria for statehood. Sovereignty is also self-generating. The repetition of the recognition that a group of people have become a state, and the conferring of the requisite privileges and obligations upon such an entity, gives the international community a social uniformity which is essential to its preservation and development.

As a particular state becomes a participant in the society of states, it is assimilated into the original archetype. Without regard to its size or resources, each separate society gains automatic access to the advantages as well as the restraints of state sovereignty. Independence, equality, territorial integrity, jurisdictional competence—all these autonomous properties are commonly shared and make the system as a whole intelligible.

State sovereignty also justifies actions done under the aegis of its principles. These can take precedence over moral or legal considerations which, on their own terms, are of greater value. At critical junctures in international relations, the superlative symbols of sovereignty can be decisive. The principles which, to Vattel, constituted the necessary law of nations give a coherence to a society composed of states; they also provide every member of that society with a marginal justification for unreasonable decisions from which there is no effective appeal.[9]

Like an unchanging myth, the entitlements of state sovereignty have an ultimate regulative authority. So it was that the principle of sovereign discretion was used to weaken the security provisions of the League Covenant. As soon as the new organization began to seriously conduct its affairs it was decided that each state member of the League should determine for itself whether the circumstances triggering their security obligations under the Covenant had occurred.

The attempt to close the "gap" in the Covenant, which allowed states to have recourse to force after exhausting the prescribed modalities of judicial or arbitral settlement, suffered a similar fate. The attempt to give decisive peacemaking power to the Council, by way of the Geneva Protocol of 1924, was unsuccessful because the attempt

9. "A mythology is an hypothesis of society's transcendental existence beyond its existence as a constitutional structure system." Philip Allott, *Eunomia: A New Order for a New World*, sec. 1, chap.6.36 (Oxford: Oxford University Press, 1990) (referring to the biological function of myth). Compare John G. Gunnell, *Political Philosophy and Time* (Middletown, Conn.: Wesleyan University Press, 1968). See also Michael Ross Fowler and Julie Marie Bunck, *Law, Power, and the Sovereign State* (University Park: The Pennsylvania State University Press, 1995).

to cover all contingencies which might lead to war was seen as an infringement upon sovereign discretion. This defeat of transnational authority at the hand of political principle was followed by a reversion to the procedures of Great Power diplomacy. The dominant states would make an effort to attain on their own authority the pacific policies which could not be realized within the institutional structure of the League of Nations.[10]

In any social experience there is an inevitable development of some form of controlling authority. No community can persist unless it develops some legitimate means of resolving its basic problems, especially if quarrels between its members reach the irreducible alternatives of war or peace. The Council of the League of Nations was an attempt to give organizational expression to that fundamental need. But as an institutional innovation superimposed upon an established system of state sovereignty, the emergence of the League and its Council created an irresolvable tension between the elementary polarities of anarchy and order.

After the Corfu incident, in which Italy tried to reject the competence of the Council, the major states of Europe asserted their right to resolve among themselves political issues that directly concerned national and continental security. This was done through the Treaties of Locarno of 1925. Locarno reflected the diplomatic conviction that the political problems of Europe were too complex to be adjusted through the procedures of unanimity which prevailed within the Council of the League. Locarno also made the authority of the Council remote and residual. This consequence adversely affected the general morale within the League, and the ideal of corporate responsibility for peace declined.[11]

10. For an appraisal of these developments see S. De Madariga, *Disarmament* (Port Washington, N.Y.: Kennikat Press, 1929), pt. 2, and my *The Search for World Order*, chap. 4.

11. On Locarno, see James Brierly, "The General Act of Geneva," 11 *British Yearbook of International Law* 119–33 (1930); Comment, "The Legal Significance of the Locarno Agreements," 20 *American Journal of International Law* 108–11 (1926). For a similar attitude in the period of the United Nations see Eugene. V. Rostow, *Law, Power and the Pursuit of Peace* (Lincoln: University of Nebraska Press, 1968).

In one sense, the Locarno grouping was an attempt to revive the Concert of Europe. It also revealed the basic practical orientation of the entire international system. Dominant states exercise a hegemonic function on the world stage similar to that of ancient kings within their own domains. Like monarchs, leading states assume a responsibility to look after the good of the whole *as they see it* and provide the leadership necessary for the continuance of the plan of order that originally constituted the community. By their power and influence the preeminent powers uphold the basic organizing principles and apply them to all the circumstances to which they have a potential relevance. The major states also try to coordinate their diplomatic practices in a way that will moderate their own more intractable conflicts as well as pacify the broader society of states.

With the League, as during the Concert period, attempts to legitimize their minority governance were made by the leading European states. In neither instance were the powers of the day able to prevent the outbreak of general war. Yet these Great Power initiatives established a tension between diplomatic practice and the institutionalization of authority that would become an integral aspect of international relations for the remainder of the century.[12]

The interwar period was one of relative stability. During this tranquil time efforts were made to strengthen other forms of order. The role of international law was enhanced. Positive international law had steadily developed during the course of the preceding centuries, and its capacity for providing a basis of order among independent sovereign states was becoming more widely appreciated. At the same time, the importance of general principles of reason and justice to the develop-

12. On the quest for authority as an aspect of practical reasonableness, see John Finnis, *Natural Law and Natural Right,* chap. 9.

During the period of the Concert it was also argued that Great Power peacemaking was incompatible with the principle of equality. Compare John Westlake, *Principles of International Law* (Cambridge: Cambridge University Press, 1894), chap. 7, with Alfred Chretien, *Principes de Droit International Publique* (Paris: Chevalier Marescq. et. cie. 1893). See also Edward Dewitt Dickerson, *The Equality of States in International Law* (Cambridge, Mass.: Harvard University Press, 1920), chap. 4.

ment of an international civilization were being recognized. Hidden sources of international law were becoming influential. Will or consent, expressed in custom and treaties, manifested only the subjective element of international law; the objective aspect of that law was increasingly derived from wider and deeper humanistic values.

It was also becoming evident that positive international rules were amenable to interpretation. Jural understanding could not be completely determined by texts. The basic datum for the discretion of the interpreter was the natural human society as it was divided into sovereign states. In giving meaning to the positive rules, there was a felt need to safeguard the existence and interests of the states within a larger social context. It was also becoming necessary to protect the individual human being, as national or alien, to the extent that such protection was feasible within the overall legal structure.[13]

As a matter of jurisprudence, the problem of international order restates the persistent question whether law must be understood in terms of reason as well as will. In an imperfect international society, principles of justice can influence the interpretation of custom and treaties, and, at times, supplement these positive sources. Jurists were anxious to encourage the more humanistic process, yet they also were aware of the constant danger that the will of states will contradict what rationality would command.

International lawyers struggled with the tension throughout this period, but those who hoped to elevate the quality of international relations felt that moral reform of state conduct was of even greater importance. The foreign policy of the United States exemplified the desire to place international relations on a higher plane. The United States was now a Great Power and in the decade following its military victory in the First World War it began to develop its own idealistic conception of world order. Having refused to join in the collaborative procedures of the League, it began to assert a solitary mission of world moral

13. Hersch Lauterpacht, *The Sources of International Law* (1930). See also Phillip C. Jessup, *A Modern Law of Nations* (New York: Macmillan,1948), and J. L. Brierly, *The Law of Nations,* 6th ed. (Oxford: The Clarendon Press, 1963).

leadership. Emphasizing the sanctity of treaties, the United States expressed its conviction that a continuing peace could be assured by the fulfillment of international promises and by strict adherence to other obligations rather than through devious legalism or the balancing of power with diplomacy.[14]

The external idealism of the United States had its roots in the origins of the Republic. The Founding Fathers believed that the nation had a universal redemptive mission. America was a new Jerusalem. As a modern chosen people, Americans would bear within their hands the destiny of the world. After the First World War, the role of global lawgiver was beginning to assert itself, but this moralistic strain in international relations was not uniquely American. Its immediate antecedents lay in the Enlightenment and especially in Kant's cosmopolitanism.

At a deeper level, the ethical tendency of international idealism manifests the whole Hebraic dimension of Western culture. While Judaic in origin, Hebraism has developed throughout Western history in Christian and secular, as well as in Jewish forms. As a civilizing force, Hebraism can be contrasted with Hellenism. With Hellenism, the tendency is to see things as they essentially are, in all their subtlety and diversity. In Hebraism, the emphasis is upon conduct and obedience. With the one, flexibility and spontaneity predominate; in the other, moral concentration and strictness of conscience are primary.

In whatever form Hebraism makes its appearance, the preference is always for doing over knowing. From this perspective, political philosophy is nothing more than ethics applied to society. For justice and right to prevail throughout the world, it is enough to know how

14. Selig Adler, *The Uncertain Giant 1921–1941: American Foreign Policy between the Wars* (New York: Macmillan, 1965); P. E. Corbett, *Morals, Law, and Power in International Relations* (Los Angeles: John Randolph & Dora Haynes Foundation, 1956), chap. 1; E. H. Carr, *The Twenty Years Crisis, 1919–1939* (London: Macmillan, 1939), chap. 5; Charles Evans Hughes, *The Pathway of Peace* (New York: Harper & Bros., 1925). See also Graebner, "America's Search for World Order," 53 Virginia Quarterly Review 161 (1975); Denis Donoghue, "The True Sentiment of America," in *America in Theory,* edited by Leslie Berlovitz, Denis Donoghue, and Louis Menard (New York: Oxford University Press, 1988).

human beings should treat each other, for that is, ultimately, how one should live.[15]

In a Hebraic internationalism basic precepts that determine how individuals should treat one another at home are extended to embrace the relations between nation-states and the entire world community. One's neighbor is both far and near. This instinct is ennobling, but it has its limitations. All moralism, whether particular or universal, engenders a selective disposition which, in turn, rigorously limits the range of personal responsibility. With respect to international matters, moralism leads to an intense concentration upon certain values, such as *pacta sunt servanda,* (agreements are to be kept) which are deemed to be indispensable to individual honorable behavior.

Such convictions are of immense importance, but they tend to exclude other important matters which also deserve serious attention. Problems which permeate the international system as a whole tend to be ignored. Since the good is understood as a matter of individual righteousness, there is little awareness of collective responsibilities for the general problems of global order. These wider, less personal matters implicate the universal common good and, if they are not taken into account, they will eventually undermine the stability of the entire system.

As a moral disposition, Hebraism has become an essential part of international thought and action. With the termination of the Second World War, a fresh sense of universal mission began to make its appearance, generating hopes for the advance of human rights as well as an end to interstate violence. But other intellectual forces were being brought to bear upon the emerging world society. An abstract positive jurisprudence offered competition to the reforming power of cosmopolitan ethics. Cosmopolitan moralism would also have to share the global stage with sociological understandings of the nature of universal authority.

15. Matthew Arnold, *Culture and Anarchy,* edited by J. Dover Wilson (Cambridge: Cambridge University Press, 1960); John G. Gunnell, *Political Philosophy and Time,* chap. 2. See also Isaiah Berlin "On the Pursuit of the Ideal," *New York Review of Books,* 17 March 1988, 11.

II

During the Second World War the Allied powers decided that upon the conclusion of the hostilities a new world body should be established which would have as its paramount objective the maintenance of international peace and security. The right to the offensive use of military force would be extinguished and the members of this United Nations Organization would be obliged to settle their disputes by peaceful means. A new International Court of Justice would replace the Permanent Court which had functioned in the interwar period. In addition to a General Assembly, Economic and Social Council, Trusteeship Council, and Secretariat, the United Nations would have a Security Council as its executive authority. The victorious powers would have permanent seats on the new Council as well as a veto over substantive decisions. With the exception of those autocratic powers, the organization was based upon the principle of the sovereign equality of all of its members.[16]

Basic flaws in this organizational plan were evident from the beginning. The obligation to settle disputes by peaceful means was qualified by the provision in Article 33 of the United Nations Charter that the parties to an international dispute could themselves decide upon the appropriate means of settlement. The International Court of Justice was a principal organ of the United Nations but it had no compulsory power of adjudication. Under the Optional Clause of the Court's statute states could reciprocally declare an advance acceptance of the court's jurisdiction, but this antecedent submission could be withdrawn upon appropriate notice. And while the Security Council was expected to exercise a supervisory authority over disputes subject to its jurisdiction, it was not empowered to compel the resolution of the underlying controversies.

The Security Council was given authority to deal with threats to or breaches of the peace, or acts of aggression, and member states were obligated to carry out any sanctions imposed for such unlawful con-

16. Charter of the United Nations, art. 2, para. 1.

duct. But the Council was an international executive without its own powers of enforcement. Charter provisions for making armed forces of the member nations available for United Nations service were never developed. More importantly, the plan for Great Power collaboration within the Council would be obstructed by antagonisms between the United States and the Soviet Union.

Agreement among the major powers was essential to the effectiveness of the United Nations Security Council. While this expectation was an improvement over the practical need for unanimity that had paralyzed the League Council, the ideological warfare between the two Council superpowers made the entire United Nations system hostage to their contentiousness. Collaboration within the Council was further impaired by the fact that any permanent member could use its veto to protect the interests of a "client" state.

As prospects for collective security within the United Nations declined, there was a rebirth of the principles and practices of international politics. Tensions between institutional authority and traditional diplomacy which had first arisen during the period of the League of Nations began to reappear. The United States, in addition to its efforts to contain Communism, was seeking to encourage new balances of power throughout the world. It was determined to deploy its military and economic power around the globe in order to relieve international tensions and to promote Western ideals of freedom and prosperity. To promote those ends, the principles and practices of the Organization would be interpreted in a manner that would maximize the freedom of action of the major member states.[17]

These assertions of national strength and leadership were inevitable. It would not been possible, even under more favorable conditions, to assign full responsibility to the United Nations Organization for the maintenance of international order in the volatile postwar period. The United Nations registered some significant accomplishments, such as

17. Henry A. Kissinger, *American Foreign Policy,* 3rd ed. (New York: Norton & Co., 1977). See also E. V. Rostow, *Law, Power and the Pursuit of Peace.*

bringing the odious system of colonialism to an end, but its capacity to promote change was limited by the fact that it is based upon the principle of the sovereign equality of its members. With a few exceptions, such as the duty to accept and carry out the decisions of the Security Council, the Charter left it to the states to find order for themselves.

The United Nations is an organization, but it is not part of an organized society. There is no way for it to assure that in the ongoing business of international relations the private interest of independent states will give way to the public interest of the world community. Under these circumstances, international politics have been haunted by a fear that the relations between states are governed by the principles of a Hobbesian state of nature.

In the increasing chaos, reflective minds have been compelled to face the possibility that beneath the surface of diplomatic practice and legal rhetoric there is a permanent enmity between autonomous states and the peoples that these states represent. There is, undoubtedly, an international *system*. One can observe a factual coordination of the interactions among states and the international institutions that those states have created. The question is whether this mix of law, diplomacy, and institutional innovation constitutes an *order*.

One way of dealing with these anarchical possibilities was to continue the rehabilitation of international law which had begun at the beginning of the century. Austin's judgment that there is no positive international law because of the absence of a superior-subject relation in the decentralized system continued to be a serious challenge to the ideal of the rule of law in the relations between states. Austin, it will be recalled, defined law as a command coupled with the threat of sanction. He believed that there was no positive international law because there was no supreme monopoly of force. Sovereign states were not subject to any higher temporal power. Powerful states might episodically impose sanctions upon wrongful actions and public opinion had some restraining influence, but there was no predictable threat of coercion in case of disobedience.

Earlier reactions to Austin had emphasized the distinction between order and force. Legal criteria are evident within state practice. International claims are commonly asserted as legal rights and state responsibilities are normally characterized as legal duties. Principles of reciprocity, which are elements of any order, are operative, and stability is promoted because mutual expectations are usually honored. These systematic jural realities justified a description of the international rules as law, in spite of the absence of any higher political authority with powers of enforcement. Therefore, the Austinian dogma that legal rules consist of externally coerced measures of conduct was contradicted by international experience.[18]

Horizontal regularities were given deeper confirmation by new developments in humanistic anthropology which revealed an inwardness to the nature of order. Within any group, no matter how primitive or undeveloped, those who constitute the community can by their own actions and deferences express their subjective acceptance of a minimal regime of rules. The order to which they adhere is not imposed from without. Stable rules grow out of the practices of individuals or groups without any intrinsic dependence upon, or fear of, centralized authority.

These insights, with suitable qualifications, were used to strengthen the regulative authority of international law. The structure of the international community is rudimentary. Unlike participants in other, more cohesive, primitive societies, the sovereign states who make up the society of states are presumed to be self-sufficient. The society of states is also culturally heterogeneous, since there is not a shared belief system among its members. But in spite of those differences, it is argued that the members of the society of states, like any other undeveloped

18. E. g., T. J. Lawrence, *The Principles of International Law,* 5th ed. (Boston: D.C. Heath, 1910), chap. 2, secs. 9–11; J. L. Brierly, *The Outlook for International Law* (Oxford: The Clarendon Press, 1944); R. R. Baxter, "International Law in Her Infinite Variety," 29 *International and Comparative Law Quarterly* 549–66 (1980); Richard Falk, *The Role of Domestic Courts in the International Legal Order* (Syracuse: Syracuse University Press, 1964). See also my "Some Reflections on Theories of International Law," 70 *Columbia Law Review* 447–63 (1970).

community, possess a sufficient degree of common interest to sustain the order of the society as a whole.[19]

The proof that sovereign states are governed by international legal rules lies in the fact that they generally obey the rules even when compliance contradicts their short-term interests. States, like individuals, have a sense of long-range utility. Membership in the society of states includes duties as well as privileges, and the desire to be considered a good member of the society has a powerful restraining influence upon international conduct. There is a practical conformity to established rules which are generally considered to be legitimate. Whether the rules are made by states or by international institutions, they are complied with, provided that they are made according to accepted procedures of right process, are adequately communicated, and are usually followed by the community as a whole.[20]

The international community of states is a society having its own order. It has a set of legal rules of custom and convention which prescribe the general conditions of coexistence and provide the means for regulating more specific modes of behavior. The rules are not constantly effective, but they are obeyed most of the time by a sufficiently large number of states to give them the authentic attributes of law. The regime of rules is inescapable; rules enter into the deliberations of all, even those who contemplate breaking them.[21]

The rules of international law are made, communicated, interpreted, and administered by the member states within the formal and informal institutions which they have created to promote and protect their common interests. The rules bring order to pacific intercourse; they also limit the use of force. War has been abolished as a means to

19. H. L. A. Hart, *The Concept of Law* (Oxford: Oxford University Press, 1960); Hedley Bull, *The Anarchical Society* (New York: Columbia University Press, 1977).

20. Bull, *The Anarchical Society;* Thomas M. Franck, *The Power of Legitimacy among Nations* (New York: Oxford University Press, 1990).

21. For a study of the subtle interactions among power, interest, and the restraints of international law, see Oscar Schachter, "International Law in Theory and Practice," General Course in International Law, 178 *Recueil des Cours*(Collected Courses of the Hague Academy of International Law), vol. 5 (1982).

political ends and force must only be used to promote the purposes of the community. International law restricts the use of violence even though some of the relevant norms, such as those concerning self-defense, have an elastic nature. And while each state is ultimately the judge of its own cause, recourse to armed force can not escape the evaluation of the international community.[22]

Modern international jurisprudence assumes that international law exists in the sanctionless world community. However, under the criteria of international politics, international law is not thought of as being the decisive ordering mechanism. Legal principles are of central importance: they encourage reciprocity, restrict the use of violence, allocate jurisdictional competencies, and promote the performance of international agreements. But from a political perspective, legal norms can never be the final measure of order. In addition to the obvious problems of imprecision, deconstructive reinterpretation, and naked defiance, the rules, while describable as law, lack the critical element of enforcement by effective power. When an international crisis arises, the collaborative actions of powerful states provide the ultimate protection from chaos. Even in normal times, actual political hegemony is ultimately controlling. The leading states have a managerial responsibility for the overall stability of the world community, and this practical authority can take precedence over the principle of the rule of law.[23]

The international community lacks a general government, but it is arguably something more than a Hobbesian state of nature. States do not act with complete disregard of legal rules or moral considerations, nor do the interests of one state necessarily exclude the interests of others. The society of states is not cosmopolitan, since the interests of all are not identical; but it is contended that there is a sufficient convergence of interests to provide a minimal order of mutual coexistence. However, even if the international community may legitimately be described as an ordered society, it cannot completely escape the uncertainties and insecurities of a state of nature.

---

22. Id. See also Schachter "The Right of States to Use Armed Force," 82 *Michigan Law Review* 1620–46 (1984).

23. Bull, *The Anarchical Society*.

In global politics, authority is elusive. The order of the society of states is sustained by political, economic and military power rather than by objective criteria of political legitimacy. Universal well-being is maintained by an elite minority of powerful states whose status was not acquired by a conscious delegation of governing authority. Their predominance also offends the foundational principle of sovereign equality. Factual inequality cancels ideals of moral equivalence.

The international political system is also inherently unstable. When states gain a dominant position in international politics they acquire a *de facto* status as leaders. Such is now the case with the United States and the major states of the European Community. But practical supremacy always faces a potentially destabilizing challenge.

Other states also aspire to rule. As the excluded develop their economic, military, or demographic power, they begin to demand the same right as the established powers to a preeminent international position. This was the case in nineteenth-century Europe when Bismarck's Germany challenged British dominance, and it is the case today when rising powers in Asia, Africa, and Latin America seek a restructuring of the Security Council of the United Nations and a greater voice in all the important international decisions.

The prevailing political arrangements are under constant pressure. The quest for supremacy is incessant and the best that can be expected from a reconfiguration of power is a new, but provisional, equilibrium. The entire global process is dangerously fragile because, unlike a domestic political system, international realignments do not occur within a constitutional framework or by way of shared allegiance to a unifying standard of order.[24]

There are deeper instabilities. The international system remains in a state of nature for reasons which were beyond the imagining of earlier theorists. Hobbes did not consider the international state of nature to be as precarious as a similar state among individuals because states could, in his time, provide its citizens with a measure of security from

24. See the collection of essays in *The International System,* ed. K. Knorr and Sidney Verba (Princeton: Princeton University Press, 1961).

external attack much greater than an individual without government could provide for himself. But the development of nuclear weapons changes that comparison. The major nuclear states are like individual Hobbesian men possessing an equal power to destroy one another. The monopoly of nuclear weapons in the hands of a minority also increases the capacity of these states to direct the general course of international relations.

This strategic predominance is maintained by policies of nonproliferation which, while valuable in themselves, do not gain unqualified assent from non-nuclear states. The principle of reciprocity is breached because while these states are expected to refrain from developing such weapons, those who already have them are unwilling to fulfill the corresponding obligation of nuclear disarmament. When this situation is combined with the emergence of chemical and biological weapons of mass destruction, and the virtually unrestricted commerce in conventional arms, one comes to appreciate what Hobbes had in mind when he described a state of nature, with its constant disposition toward violence, as an ultimately tragic condition.[25]

The primitive international community, or society of states, also lacks a positive idea of universal good. The rules, procedures, and political arrangements are matters more of process than of substance. They provide, at best, a negative coordination of the interactions of the separate states. There is order because there are unifying relationships. But the mutualities are self-serving. The general interest is a

25. D. P. Gauthier, *The Logic of Leviathan: The Moral and Political Theory of Thomas Hobbes* (Oxford: The Clarendon Press, 1969), 207; M. Wight, *Power Politics,* edited by Hedley. Bull and Carsten Holbraad (New York: Holmes & Meier, 1978). According to Innis Claude, "The competition of states for power, coupled with their capacity and inclination to make use of power against each other, is perpetually dangerous, sporadically disastrous, and potentially catastrophic . . ." The United Nations, 27th Session Introduction: "The Central Challenge for the United Nations: Weakening the Strong or Strengthening the Weak?" 14 *Harvard International Law Journal* 517–29, 519 (1973).

In its Advisory Opinion on the Legality of the Threat or Use of Nuclear Weapons of July 8, 1996, the International Court of Justice held unanimously that there exists an obligation to pursue in good faith and bring to a conclusion negotiations leading to nuclear disarmament in all its aspects under strict and effective international control. 35 I.L.M. 809–938 (1996).

matter of "playing by the rules" so that each state can, in relative autonomy, work out its own internal destiny. There is no genuine common good because the well-being of all states and peoples is not a shared objective of the community as a whole. Beyond the requirements of minimal order, the community is not based upon any shared purposes. Since the society of states is nothing more than a practical association, the authority of its laws and institutions is not independent of the particular ends of each of its members.[26]

Moral pressures also encroach upon the controlling authority of the existing order. To the degree that the international rules are perceived to be legitimate, compliance can be anticipated; if they are thought to be unjust, those who are disadvantaged will refuse to obey. Like any other community, the society of states is subject to the classical tension between order and justice. It is subject to further strain because it is a developing social organism which lacks effective instruments of change.

Whenever the minimal purposes of global association are considered to be incompatible with the broader aspirations for fulfillment of its diverse members, the possibilities of continuing stability within existing arrangements becomes problematic. Rising demands can to some extent be accommodated within existing multilateral procedures, but fundamental distributive appeals, such as those concerning a new economic order, have run aground on the shoals of sovereign principle. The developing states have been able to articulate their demands for the reform of international trade and finance within the established fora, but implementation of these plans has been blocked by the assertion of state discretion by the prosperous states. In Vattelian terminology, the poorer states are admittedly harmed by the established economic inequities but they do not suffer any legal injury.

International human rights covenants have been adopted with solemn promises of implementation, but accountability has been impeded by the principle of domestic jurisdiction. There have been some

---

26. Terry Nardin, *Law, Morality and the Relations of States* (Princeton, N.J.: Princeton University Press, 1983). On the importance of shared ends, see Finnis, *Natural Law and Natural Rights,* chap. 6.

notable accomplishments in other areas, such as the Convention on the Law of the Sea; nevertheless, the understanding of the international community as a practical association of self-seeking autonomous states is increasingly difficult to reconcile with a growing awareness that the world is in the process of becoming an interconnected society.[27]

The postwar ordering potentials of international law and politics have been ably defended, but an increased understanding of the tentative nature of the established order has also provoked new forms of speculation comprehensive enough to elevate the study of international relations above the minimalist model of mutual coexistence. The prevailing model of the world as a society of states has proven, however, be difficult to dislodge.

When international relations are understood as a regime of rules, it may seem best to just keep the process going so that the independent states can continue to experience a reasonable degree of mutual security and separate self-determination. Within these limited objectives, a certain finality prevails. All progress is to be accomplished through the use of the existing structures and in accordance with established procedures. But this confinement of action paralyzes the powers of thought. Cosmopolitan idealism can protest the restriction with little hope of success. Yet more palatable reforms are conceivable which do not completely abandon all the given realities.

Expectations of improvement were aroused when international legal theory came under the influence of a sociological form of Pragmatism. Pragmatism is a protest against a rule-bound universe. Looking upon all social worlds as essentially unfinished, it subjects them to a reconstruction which will make them more satisfying to the needs of the human spirit. For the Pragmatist, every society is an open-ended field of action. Rejecting determinism, it pursues social actualities in all their subtle empirical interrelations. Pragmatism demands freedom from external authority because it takes emotion seriously. Since man

---

27. Julius Stone, *Visions of World Order* (Baltimore: Johns Hopkins University Press, 1984), chap. 10.

is by nature passionate, he can only conform to what he desires, or to what, by some reasonable procedure, is generally determined to be desirable.[28]

In pragmatism, truth does not reside in abstraction. Solitary reflection leads to a dualism between thought and action which can only be corrected through an immersion in the flow of social experience. Within that experience, the resources of practical intelligence can remove the obstructions to fulfillment and bring existing reality into a more satisfying state of affairs.

The recognition of a problematic situation is of critical importance. A problem activates thought. In a pragmatic endeavor, the will begins to move from hypothesis to action. An inquiry is initiated which starts the process of moving an existing situation closer to conformity with our valued ends. In the pursuit of such ideals it is important to distinguish private truth from public authority. What is desired must be desirable according to some common criteria. This requires collaboration. The emphasis which science places on shared procedures of hypotheses and verification was suitable to the objectives of Pragmatism. Instrumental Pragmatism promotes cooperation in the resolving of practical social problems and, at the same time, reduces the distortions of isolated action. Disciplined inquiry also tempers the partisanship of those who believe they alone know what constitutes the public good.[29]

As a philosophy of community, Pragmatism looks upon the social as the ultimate ground of both practical meaning and public authority.

28. William James, *Pragmatism: A New Name for Old Ways of Thinking* (New York: Longmans Green, 1907); John Dewey, *The Quest for Certainty: A Study of the Relation of Knowledge and Action* (New York: Minton Balsh, 1929); Richard Rorty, *The Consequences of Pragmatism, Essays, 1972–1980* (Minneapolis: University of Minnesota Press, 1982); John Diggins, *The Promise of Pragmatism: Modernism and the Crisis of Knowledge and Authority* (Chicago: University of Chicago Press, 1994).

29. In the instrumentalism of John Dewey, philosophy is a way of dealing with the problems of mankind in community. We adjust ourselves to the environment through the provocation which it offers. The reconstruction that we effect constitutes the career of thinking, and by participating in nature we recreate it and ourselves. T. V. Smith, *The Philosophical Way of Life in America* (New York: The Kennikat Press, 1943), chap. 4.

The living law of any community is the sovereign source of its unity and order. Through inquiry into social relations the self comes to understand, and reach agreement with, that generalized "other" which constitutes the whole community. The sociological school of modern Pragmatism insists that the public order of society has priority over the spurious autonomy of the legal or the political spheres. It boldly asserts that both law and politics are eventually dependent upon the normative superiority of social legitimation.[30]

Sociological Pragmatism has had a profound influence upon jurisprudence and political theory. It has also been used in the search for the ultimate sources of international order. The policy-science jurisprudence developed by Lasswell and McDougal at Yale is, in effect, an application of the principal themes of a pragmatic sociology to the study of world order.

The founders of an internationalized policy-science did not think of the world as being nothing more than a society of states. For them, and their collaborators, the planet was an interdependent earth-space community which had its own distinctive patterns of value. These values are distributed in global processes of effective and authoritative power which constitute the substance of a world public order. This public order is formed in various arenas by the actions of states, international organizations, and transnational corporations as well as by private parties and interest groups. States are not completely autonomous because they are part of this more comprehensive interactive process.[31]

All the participants in global social processes seek to define and apply the fundamental values which make up the humanistic dimension of international experience. The specific objective of policy-science jurisprudence is to influence the decisions toward preferred public policies which maximize the value of human dignity. The com-

30. On the general development of a sociology of law, see my *Modern Legal Philosophy* (Pittsburgh: Duquesne University Press, 1978), chap. 2.

31. Basic works include *Studies in World Public Order* (New Haven: Yale University Press, 1960); *Law and World Minimum Public Order: The Legal Regulation of International Coercion* (New Haven: Yale University Press, 1961). See also "The Writings of Myres S. McDougal," 84 *Yale Law Journal* 965–68 (1975).

mitted scholar or advocate must discern all the values embedded in a particular international conflict and try to promote a resolution that will be both authoritative and controlling. To avoid partiality, the inquiry must be directed towards the aggregate consequences of choice. The community policies at stake must be clarified, the values sought in related decisions must be identified, and all of the contingencies affecting such decisions understood. Policy science also requires a projection, and assessment, of alternative outcomes with respect to any problematic situation. In this disciplined application of thought in action, it is hoped that individuals who are in positions of power can be persuaded to integrate their parochial policies with the values of the whole global society.

Through its refinements of practical intelligence, policy-science jurisprudence hopes to bring a improved sense of reasonableness to the international legal process. In the absence of formal sanctions, as we have noted, international norms are upheld by the voluntary compliance of states. The ordering potentials of these rules depends upon the perception that they are the legitimate expression of established legal procedures and are basically fair. Their binding quality also depends upon their relative degree of precision. When rules of any social group are excessively indeterminate they do not adequately communicate what is permitted and what is forbidden. Their rationality is obscured. This is a particularly difficult problem in the unorganized international society.

Some of the norms of international law are, strictly speaking, rules because they are precepts which of themselves dictate a particular result. The laws concerning the passage of vessels on the high seas are of this character, as are the basic privileges and immunities surrounding the ambassadorial function. And some laws—such as those prohibiting aggression—have been sufficiently defined to make their meaning reasonably clear. However, like any legal culture, international law contains standards and principles which have an open texture. The inherent right of individual or collective self-defense reserved under Article 51 of the United Nations Charter is the standard example. Moreover, incompatible principles can legitimately be brought to bear upon a particular legal issue.[32]

In the absence of official organs to resolve the ambiguities of the international legal process, the comprehensive inquiries of policy-science improve the prospects of authoritative decision. The range of reasonable choice among competing legal arguments is widened and an understanding of all the specific variables which bear upon an important international issue are clarified. Moreover, explicit focus upon purpose can expose the real interests of those who cloak their actions in rhetorical legal terminology.

These expansive objectives are not easily reconciled with established legal practice. A pragmatic global sociology identifies all the subtle interactions which give vitality and direction to international social experience but in doing so it does not always make clear distinctions between social and legal data. Within the method, no part of the world order process has a privileged position. For example, when dealing with the interpretation of treaties, policy-science jurisprudence seeks to elicit the shared expectations of the parties through a complete contextual analysis of their communications. To that end, all indices of meaning, prior to and after the completion of a text, are taken into account. The formal legal expression of the agreement has no special significance. International lawyers were alarmed by this indiscriminate approach because it diminishes the stabilizing function of traditional canons of interpretation and reduces the possibility of objectively ascertaining the intentions of the parties. Jurists also resist the preference

32. For international rules, principles and standards, see Oscar Schachter, "The Right of States to Use Armed Force."

From a sociological perspective, the purpose of reason is to confront the irrational in action. "Reason teased out the constituents of actual situations and the value problems associated with them. Reason thus resolved conflicts. . . ." Donald Macrae, *Max Weber* (New York: Viking Press, 1974), 95. One objection to the policy-science jurisprudence is that its ideal of rational conduct in context tends to make reasonableness the test of legality. See Roger Fisher, review of *Studies in World Public Order* by Myres S. McDougal, *Science* 658 (1962). See also the measured criticism in Julius Stone, *Visions of World Order* (Baltimore: Johns Hopkins Press, 1984), chap. 4. For a qualified defense of the method see Rosalyn Higgins, *International Law and How We Use It* (Oxford: The Clarendon Press, 1994), chap. 1.

that policy-science gives to policies over rules. Community goals cannot be allowed to override the predictive advantages of specific legal prescriptions.[33]

Defenders of the international legal order also insist that the lawfulness of the actions of states can not be validated by reference to the imagined major purposes of an inclusive world community. In a pluralistic international society, the purposes of states are often incompatible. Under such circumstances, common rules of accommodation may be the only reasonable basis for sustaining their mutual coexistence.[34]

The Lasswell-McDougal approach to world public order has been further criticized for not giving sufficient attention to the central position of sovereign states in the political structure of the international community. The desire to persuade individuals who inhabit diverse territorial societies to promote an inclusive world order overlooks the allegiance which an official actually owes to his own government. A related difficulty is that the preferred public order values are postulated. Unexamined value assumptions lend a spurious universality to what are subjectively desired ideals.

Policy-science assumes that the promotion of values associated with human dignity is a shared objective of the whole world society; yet the qualities assigned to that dignity by its practitioners are mainly drawn from a culture-bound western individualism. Other societies either do not agree with these liberal values or they prefer to define them by operational meanings which arise out of their own experi-

33. McDougal, Harold D. Lasswell, and James Miller, *The Interpretation of Agreements and World Public Order* (New Haven: Yale University Press, 1967). Critical reactions can be found in "Panel on Treaty Interpretation," *Proceedings of the American Society of International Law* 108–40 (1967), and in Fitzmauric, "*Vae Victis,* or Woe to the Negotiators! Your Treaty or Our Interpretation of It," 67 *American Journal of International Law* 358–73 (1971).

34. Thomas M. Franck, *The Power of Legitimacy among Nations;* Oscar Schachter, *International Law in Theory and Practice.* See also Richard Falk, "McDougal and Feliciano on Law and Minimum World Public Order," in *Legal Order in a Violent World* (Princeton: Princeton University Press, 1968), 80; Philip Allott, "Language, Method and the Nature of International Law," 45 *British Yearbook of International Law* 79–135 (1971).

ence. In a state-centered world with incompatible cultures, it is impossible to determine whether a particular policy position is authoritative for the whole human society.[35]

Although policy-oriented world public order jurisprudence may be incompatible with the minimal goals of sovereign coexistence, it has revealed the essential impermanence of the existing international arrangements. Sociological insight, coupled with a pragmatic methodology, has shown that a rule-bound international society is not a feasible long-term objective. The school begun by Lasswell and McDougal has seen that rules have a value dimension which cannot consistently be ignored. To do so is ultimately offensive to reason. Policy-science has also proven that the tension between power and authority is pervasive. When other anarchical features of the international system are taken into account, the instabilities multiply exponentially.

In the struggle to understand the world as something more than a society of states, speculative thought goes beyond Pragmatism in search of higher, more hierarchical, forms of universal order. There is a continuing quest for some comprehensive conception which might bring unity, justice, and peace to all of humankind. However, like all the other global theories since the time of Dante, the novel constructs which we will now consider lack an essential element of durable order. They all avoid any serious consideration of fundamental change from a pre-political to a political form of world society.

III

The international policy-science developed by Lasswell and McDougal was a Pragmatic methodology. Practical intelligence was applied to conflicts whose resolution was to be guided by the public values of the world community. But the high hopes for this globalization of sociological jurisprudence were never realized either in academic circles or in international legal practice. The transitory influence

35. See the exchange: Dorsey, "The McDougal-Lasswell Proposal to Build a World Public Order," 82 *American Journal of International Law* 41–51 (1988); McDougal, "The Dorsey Comment: A Modest Retrogression," 82 *American Journal of International Law* 51–57 (1988). See also Julius Stone, *Visions of World Order,* chap. 4.

of this reconstructive method suggests that no form of Pragmatism satisfies the more comprehensive needs of rational reflection.

In the Pragmatic mind methods become mentalities. Beyond practices, there are no independent intellectual criteria to guide future inquiry. One becomes resigned to working with what one has, and what is given too easily becomes what ought to be. Thinking and doing become practically indistinguishable. Reason becomes frustrated when intense concentration upon the nuances of proximate causation leaves no room for the mind's inclination towards more complete understanding. Pragmatism also offends standards of coherence. Equal worth is attributed to each part of the dissected social process, and the discrete fragments are not held together by any connective principle. There are no hierarchical priorities except for a limited number of postulated values.[36]

In spite of its commendable commitment to human dignity, international policy-science was unable to transcend its bondage to experience. Those desirous of deeper reform were attracted to more abstract theories. The ethical regulation of international relations first initiated by Kant was renewed by the revival of contractarian idealism. Moral philosophy was ascendant and with it new prospects for realizing an equal liberty and correcting social and economic inequities. First applied to the constitutional protection of human rights within states, the potential extension of ethics to relations between sovereign states opened up loftier possibilities. But as its practitioners tried to apply *a priori* principles to interstate relations, their unconditional ambitions could not effectively compete with the practical instincts of an international realism. Furthermore, the intrusion of moral values into international law was incompatible with the desire of legal philosophers to impose an elevated juridical order upon the disorderly society of states.[37]

---

36. For a discussion of the intellectual inadequacies of Pragmatism see Alfred North Whitehead, *The Function of Reason* (Boston: Beacon Press, 1962), chap. 1.

37. On modern contractarianism see John Rawls, *A Theory of Justice* (Cambridge: Harvard University Press, 1971). For a qualified application of moral principles to international relations see Terry Nardin and David R. Mapel, *Traditions of International Ethics* (Cambridge: Cambridge University Press, 1993); C. R. Beitz, *Political Theory and International Relations* (Princeton: Princeton University Press, 1979). See also Chaumont,

International law needed to distance itself from empirical theories of order, including the legal positivism of John Austin, which was inductively grounded upon legal experience. As we have seen, Austin held that international law did not exist because there was no superior enforcing power. The new hope for a philosophy of international law was to transcend Austin's negative conclusion through the positive power of abstract thought.

In the Pure Theory of Law developed by Hans Kelsen, all empirical dependencies would be overcome, whether such enslavement to experience was jural or sociological in origin. In this abstract form of legal positivism, both the national and the international legal orders were logically derived from *a priori* categories of thought. Law was known in relation to a pure form which had been purged of all moral or sociological considerations. Through the productive powers of the human mind the experienced world would become subject to the dominion of rational cognition.

Pure understanding was the key to juridical supremacy. Once the power relations within any society are stabilized, Pure Positive Law institutes its own order by a process of logical progression. A foundational *grund* norm authorizes a subsequent norm-creating and norm-applying process, which constitutes the inclusive legal system. Being abstractly conceived, law is able to preserve its autonomous existence throughout time and above experience.[38]

Pure Positive Law is a coercive order. It creates an opposition between what is and what ought to be. Whenever behavior contradicts

---

"Cours General de Droit Internationale Publique" 129 *Recueil des Cours* (Collected Courses of the Hague Academy of International Law)(1971).

38. Hans Kelsen, *The Pure Theory of Law,* translated by M. Knight (Berkeley: University of California Press, 1967); *General Theory of Law and the State* (Cambridge, Mass.: Harvard University Press, 1945). Shorter statements appear in Kelsen, "The Pure Theory of Law and Analytical Jurisprudence," 55 *Harvard Law Review* 44 (1941), and Kelsen, "The Pure Theory of Law," 50 *Law Quarterly Review* 474 (1934). See also Kelsen's *Essays in Legal and Moral Philosophy,* edited by O. Weinberger (1970), and *What Is Justice? Justice, Law and Politics in the Mirror of Science* (Berkeley: University of California Press, 1971).

For general studies of Kelsen's thought see my *Modern Legal Philosophy,* chap. 3, and W. Ebenstein, *The Pure Theory of Law* (Madison: University of Wisconsin Press, 1945).

the normative order created by the law, or exceeds its permissions, an invalidating sanction is, theoretically, imposed. Validity has priority over effectiveness. Normative and causal explanations of legal phenomenon are sharply distinguished. What is given in experience, in all its subtle interactions, does not, as the Pragmatists assumed, govern the quest for understanding. The legal significance of any action is determined by reference to the norm which regulates the act. The extent of inquiry into cause and effect is also more limited than in any explanation that is dependent upon the variations of experience. Imputation determines jural responsibility, and accountability is restricted to an identification of the specific conduct which, according to the relevant legal norms, is the condition of the consequence determined by the positive law.

The Pure Theory of Law also corrects emotional dispositions which can distort the objective comprehension of any legal order. Personal convictions about the substantive purposes of law are idiosyncratic; they lack that universality which can only be achieved by an abstract jural formalism. Reliance upon natural law, ethical cosmopolitanism, or sociological value postulates are all projections of emotion into external realities. Any attempt to find an ideal order of values or normative principles "above" or "behind" the positive legal order betrays a lack of confidence in the ordering powers of independent human thought.[39]

The state is a juridical community. It is nothing other than the unity of its legal order. In Pure Theory, supreme political power is subordinated to law. Acts of sovereign will are comprehended by a valid legal order which legitimizes all law-creating acts. The same logic applies to the international sphere.

Austin had concluded that since there was no sovereign political authority within the world community, international rules were not, strictly speaking, positive law. For Kelsen, this difficulty is removed once the problem was viewed in light of the evolution of legal orders.

39. Kelsen, *What Is Justice?*

Both national and international legal orders are coercive. The differences between them are based upon contingencies which do not impair the logical continuities between the two regimes. International law simply lacks centralized organs for the enactment and the enforcement of law. For Kelsen, this is not an essential flaw. Wrongs in defiance of norms can be corrected by the authorized actions of states either acting alone or in some form of collective security.

In the light of Pure Theory, international law is similar to primitive legal orders which rely upon self-help for the enforcement of their laws. But, from an intellectual perspective, the international system as a whole is far from primitive. Within its rich intellectual complexity there is a wide range of interdependencies and subordinations which make it a supreme cultural achievement. International law is a dynamic system of norms created by the customary practices of states, by international agreements, and by organs created by those agreements. Together, these form a relation of higher and lower authority within an overall hierarchy.[40]

The more difficult question for Pure Theory is that of justifying its prescriptive authority within an international society composed of sovereign states. In the nineteenth century, most jurists assumed that the national and international legal orders were distinct. National law was the law of a state and international law was constituted by the common will of states. Furthermore, on Hegelian premises of state absolutism, a state could always withdraw its consent to be bound by an international rule. These dualisms frustrate the logical mind's desire for universal unity. For legal philosophers such as Kelsen, the bifurcation would be overcome by comprehending the two legal orders as one, and by affirming the validity of each by some controlling principles of reason.[41]

Unity can be achieved by a qualified deference to the principle of

40. Kelsen, *The Pure Theory of Law,* chap. 7; *General Theory of Law and the State,* pt. 2. See also Kelsen, *Law and Peace in International Relations* (1948).
41. For the general background see Hersch Lauterpacht, *The Function of Law in the International Community* (1933), chap. 6.

state autonomy. Positivism can allow that international law only becomes valid for a state when, expressly or by implication, the state recognizes international law as binding. But once recognized, the authority of the law is absolute. The international legal order is delegated by the national legal order, but once the delegation has been made, it cannot be withdrawn. As a *system,* international law can only be defined by the manner in which its norms are created. An alternative, and preferable, monistic construct would understand the national legal order as being subordinate to the supranational international legal order. This position, which was favored by Kelsen, has some empirical validation. Both the spatiotemporal conditions of statehood and the range of legitimate state jurisdiction are determined by international legal rules. Whenever national legal orders impinge upon the world beyond their borders, their authority and competence are potentially subject to the international legal order.

Whichever approach is taken, the conclusion of Pure Theory is that the international and national legal orders form a hierarchical totality. The higher norms of international law determine what ought to be, or can be, done within its own sphere. The national legal order is authorized to decide who shall perform the required or permitted act. Thus, a desired wholeness is achieved throughout the entire system.

Potential conflicts between the two orders is governed by the logical principle of noncontradiction. When a state acts in a way that is inconsistent with its international obligations it does not undermine the validity of the relevant international norms. From the standpoint of Pure Theory, the conflict is more apparent than real. The repugnant lower norm may appear to prevail, but it is *potentially* invalid. If it is not actually annulled, the reason is factual, not logical. Therefore, the integrity of the positive theory remains undisturbed.[42]

International society has not yet developed the institutions that are needed to practically affirm the supremacy of the international norms. But the absence of the necessary enforcement organs is a mere contin-

---

42. See my *Modern Legal Philosophy,* chap. 3, and accompanying notes.

gency which does not affect the intellectual supremacy of the international legal order. Pure Theory is indifferent to consequences of the violation of international law, no matter how disastrous they may be for the human condition. Being speculative in nature, formal legal positivism is detached from the moral dimensions of practical life. The harms caused by the absence of effective institutions of lawmaking and law enforcement is of no meaningful consequence because the problem of international order is comprehended at the level of abstract understanding.

Since Pure Theory of Law is an abstract system of juridical relationships, it pursues no good other than the value of the rational coherence and consistency of the order as a whole. Pure Theory reifies the international order. It treats international law *as if it were* a superior substantial reality. With the aid of logic, it imagines that there exists a supreme legal order which delegates law-making authority and imposes its norms throughout a self-sustaining system of legal relations.[43]

As an imaginary personification, Pure Theory constructs in the world of the mind a harmonious juridical system which cannot be found in the extra-mental real world. This mental attitude is similar to that of modern abstract painting. Mondrian's ambition was to redesign the world of art by the imposition of geometric form; Kelsen's aspiration was to create an impersonal international normative order that could be imposed upon the recalcitrant instabilities and conflicts of an anarchical society of states.[44]

The Pure Theory of Law reflects modern developments which emphasize the creative nature of abstraction. This logical positivism also bears an interesting resemblance to Dante's theory of world govern-

43. For a philosophical critique of the ambitions of systemic logic see Wilhem Dilthey, *The Essence of Philosophy*, trans. Stephen A. and William T. Emery (Chapel Hill: University of North Carolina Press, 1954). For a jurisprudential criticism see Recasens-Siches, "The Logic of the Reasonable as Differentiated from the Logic of the Rational," in *Essays in Jurisprudence in Honor of Roscoe Pound*, ed. R. Neuman (Westport, Conn.: Greenwood Press, 1962), 192.

44. Hilton Kramer, "Mondrian and Mysticism: My Long Search Is Over," *The New Criterion*, Sept. 1995.

ment. For the great Italian humanist, the order of the whole temporal world, as represented by the figure of the Holy Roman Emperor, was an imaginative reproduction of the pattern of Divine Providence. The cosmological integration of time and eternity was speculatively understood to be a supreme good. Within this imaginative edifice, the unity symbolized by the will of the Emperor would benefit the whole human race. For Kelsen, a similar intellectual order is achieved by the logical power of an autonomous reason. Peace is to be achieved by the imposition of a humanly devised juridical will which organizes and enforces a comprehensive legal regime. But in this secular theory of ultimate order, neither mind nor will has a capacity for the infinite. Hermetically closed, Pure Theory does not draw upon anything of substance beyond itself.[45]

The Pure Theory of Law is a part of a modern humanism which recognizes neither higher nor lower authority. The guardians of the international legal system are not accountable to anyone below, or above, for the exercise of their juridical authority. They are not the possessors of any actually delegated power. Yet it would be an intolerable form of deification if those who administered the abstract international legal order did so solely at their own will and pleasure.[46]

The ultimate question—which Pure Theory itself does not address—is, on whose authority does this legal order impose itself on states and individuals? Surely it cannot be as agents of the states, for they are the subjects of the law. Nor can it be sustained by a moral sentiment favoring the rule of law, since all moral considerations are excluded by stipulation. The law is also not administered on behalf of a supreme political authority, because the possible transition to world

45. For the interest in Dante see Hans Kelsen, *La Teoria Dello Stato in Dante* (Bologna: Massimiliano Boni Editore, 1974).

46. An accusation that juridical formalism constitutes a new religion is made in Mohammed Bedjaoui, *International Law—Achievements and Prospects* (Dordrecht: Martinus Nijhoff, 1991). It has also been noted that the imprecision of the idea of an international community means that normative power can be assumed by a directorate, or oligarch, that can impose its understanding of order upon others. P. Weil, "Toward Relative Normativity in International Law?" 77 *American Journal of International Law* 413 (1983).

government has been dismissed, as it were, *a priori*. Juridical sovereignty therefore has no legitimizing source.

A Pure Theory of International Law cannot, of itself, satisfy the quest for the foundations of world order. Yet the search must continue. From a pragmatic perspective, either legal or sociological, global harmony and justice must be concretely pursued within existing realities, however broadly, or narrowly, these actualities are perceived. But there remains the hope that the abstract comprehension of the international legal order can be vindicated by an equally abstract understanding of a humanistic universal authority. We shall momentarily consider that line of thought; but, before doing so, we should first place the modern quest for the abstract knowledge of world order within the context of its philosophical antecedents.

The Pure Theory of Law is neo-Kantian. For Kant, universal laws of moral understanding were discoverable by the autonomous subject. "Ought" implied necessities which did not exist in empirical nature. Where Kant based his theory of law upon his ethics, Kelsen developed a juridical order, purged of morality, by way of a similar *a priori* form of abstract comprehension.

The search for inner certitudes begun by Kant was carried forward by Hegel. Hegel's ambition was to develop a complete science of the experience of consciousness. We have already pointed out how Hegelian idealism made the state the incarnation of a spiritual force. But idealism could also be used for more inclusive ends which, in the international sphere, would transcend the absolutism of the State. The source of this development would be a new intellectual discipline, Theoretical Sociology. Here the social is given priority over the political. This speculative elevation of the social has not only affected the direction of national life; it has also created the possibility of subordinating the anarchic society of states to the order of a universal human society. Hegel's idealism would be generalized as Sociology articulates for itself a potentially universal and all-embracing human society. It would think of that society of societies as a revelation of the collective self-consciousness of the whole human race.

Auguste Comte was a seminal figure in these innovations. The focus of Comte's mind was upon the idea of humanity. To him, humanity was not simply the fragmented human species; it was a collective whole which ought to become a supreme object of love and devotion, an indivisible social community that is irresistibly unified as it passes through the travails of temporal history. In Comte's theory, this unification would be directed by intelligence inspired by feeling. A dictatorship of sociocrats would exercise spiritual authority over the rest of mankind. They would be empowered to organize, regulate, and discipline the peoples of the world and instruct them on their obligations to the whole.[47]

Sociology was a new science. Modern science discovers an ever-extending network of invariable relations throughout the physical world and unifies these diverse phenomena by the power of abstract thought. Comte would extrapolate this reasoning to the social sphere in order to articulate a unified conception of the human world. The social world was an immanent reality. Its meaning was not derived from any sources beyond itself. To Hegel, man was himself *Geist;* present to himself, within the dialectic of consciousness, as the absolute object which is his essence. This universal whole was found in the absolute state which is an incarnation of the Ideal. In the mundane eschatology of Comte, only the social whole is real. The social is antecedent to the political. In its ideal form, society is a reality which lies beyond the state.

The supremacy of the social is now being extended to the international plane. State-societies are the basic datum. They are thought of as subordinate societies within that society of societies that is the authentic world community. Order implies superior-inferior relations. The order of international existence is part of a transcendental totality which embraces all of humanity. Order arises out of a communal con-

47. Auguste Comte, *Positive Philosophy,* 2 vols., trans. Harriet Martineau (New York: W. Gowans, 1868); Jacques Maritain, *Moral Philosophy: An Historical and Critical Survey of the Great Systems* (New York: Scribners, 1964), pt. 2, chap. 2; Eric Voegelin, *From Enlightenment to Revolution,* ed. John H. Hallowell (Durham, N.C.: Duke University Press, 1975), chap. 6. See generally Raymond Aron, *Main Currents in Sociological Thought,* trans. R. Howard and H. Weaver (1965).

sciousness which creates an endlessly developing ideal reality for itself. As physical necessity constitutes the order discovered by the sciences, the ordered reality of the society of societies is composed of obligations which, in turn, constitute the necessities consciousness makes for itself so that it can act as a social system.[48]

As any society forms itself, it assumes the unity of a person. It subsumes, and fulfills, the individual. The individual is part of the human multiplicity which must be gathered together in order to constitute a society. A socionomy, which reflects the values of society, imposes the obligations of order. By this order society, as a totality, determines the willing and acting of each of its members. As the individual is socialized, and society is individualized, society gradually becomes a reality for itself.[49]

The present international community is unsocial. The distinct societies which comprise the peoples of the world are confined within states and these states, in their mutual encounters, treat each other as competitors for power and influence. Those who control the separate state-societies manipulate their citizens to believe that other human beings do not constitute part of their own humanity. Separate national societies are closed units of power. Within them, singular energies are applied for self-interested purposes. International diplomacy is the external projection of this sovereign power, and international law, in its practical forms, ratifies these unsocial conditions.

Law and diplomacy expend their authority in adjusting the conflicting interests of territorial, limited states, rather than in enforcing the social interests of humanity as a whole. International law is also impotent, since it has no mastery over economic forces. The global economy is dominated by multinational corporations which operate outside the effective control of national legal orders and are not subject

48. For the connection between Hegel and Comte, see Voegelin, *From Enlightenment to Revolution,* chap. 6. The extension of these ideas to the international realm can be found in the preface to Philip Allott, *Eunomia: A New Order for a New World* (Oxford: Oxford University Press, 1990), although without explicit acknowledgement. See *Eunomia,* preface, xx–xi.

49. Philip Allott, *Eunomia,* pt. 1, chaps. 3–4.

to any universal juridical authority. Under present conditions, the ultimate authority of the peoples of the world cannot fully express itself as a society of societies. There is, therefore, a need for a comprehensive social theory within which the well-being of each can be reconciled with the well-being of all.[50]

The British lawyer and academician, Philip Allott, has developed a theory of social idealism that provides a model for the good order of a self-ordering international society. Allott believes that the policy-science jurisprudence of Lasswell and McDougal was a progressive force because it explicitly made social values an integral part of international law. But it was ineffective. Having a pragmatic spirit, it could not articulate a general social theory that transcended cultural differences. This practical sociology did not provide an appropriate form for the development of a universal human consciousness. Kelsen's Pure Theory of Law gave a transcendent status to international law, but, as we have observed, it had no higher authorization. Allott believes that the detached logical formalism of the Pure Theory of Law would possess universal legitimacy if it were integrated with a philosophically coherent concept of a supreme world society.

Allott's pure theory of social idealism is grounded upon the principle of the self-creation of societies. Social self-creation determines the identity of any society. This collective consciousness ascertains the nature of its relationship to what is beyond itself as well as its relation to the subordinate societies and individuals that it contains within itself.

Self-creation becomes self-ordering as the social ideal moves from theory to practice. Hypothetical order becomes prescriptive as each society struggles with the essential dilemmas of order and seeks to resolve them in a manner which is satisfying to itself. Society establishes the identity of self and others, reconciles the one and the many, balances stability with change, and adjusts a plurality of values to a unified social ideal. It also seeks the comprehensive realization of justice and tries to adjust the continued existence of society to the fungibility of

50. *Eunomia,* preface.

its members. Societies acquire form through structures and they create systems to defeat the aimlessness which arises when the membership of society is atomized.[51]

The constitution of any society is a work of reason and imagination, operating within consciousness. Collective self-consciousness is the fruit of a society's contemplation of itself in time and space. This awareness is given constitutional expression in the social constitution. As an ideal, the social constitution presents to society a conception of what the society might be; as a reality, it is the here and now of that society's fundamental struggle of self-creation as it actualizes itself throughout the total social process.

The legal constitution of society is the social constitution manifesting itself as law. Through legal relations the willing and acting of the members of society—and of subordinate societies—are integrated with the willing and acting of society as a whole. Allott imaginatively integrates the Pure Theory of Law into an Hegelian form of Pure Social Theory. Consciousness is the master of the self-ordering system that the society of all humanity has created for itself. Every particular legal relation, in any part of the global environment, is part of a integral network of legal relations which move up to, and include, the total system of the society of societies. As part of an entire social process, a positive, but abstract, international law enforces the generic principles of the constitution, and its juridical logic assures the operation of the global legal order as a coherent and comprehensive system.[52]

The law releases the dynamic forces of international society as the society struggles to transform its past into the future. By its permissions, law recognizes the impulse of life, which is expressed in desire; by its imposition of legal obligations, it enforces the necessity which the human world shares with the physical universe. Legal and social theory are reconciled as international law brings its order into the order of the social whole which constitutes humanity. Delegating legal power, and limiting such power to social purposes, the law also main-

51. Id., pt. 1, chap. 4–6.
52. *Eunomia*, pt. 2, chaps. 10–11.

tains the supremacy of the social interest and makes those holding any legal power accountable for its use.[53]

According to Allott, if one wishes to understand the problem of order in international society one must first understand the history of state societies. That history manifests a prolonged quest by the human race for some supersocial embodiment of sovereignty. Kingship, democracy, and state sovereignty are all aspects of the search for some definitive supreme authority. In societies influenced by reformers as diverse as Kant and Marx, the process of political organization has been followed by a supersocialization of society in the name of some compelling ideal of justice. In all modern societies, ordered well-being demands that the will of each be united with the will of all. As the harmonization advances, sovereignty as authority is transformed into sovereignty as the self-willed order of the social whole.[54]

Comprehensive and inclusive, supersocialization is one with the idea of Being. It conforms to the nature of the individual, of society, and of all that is. Supersocialization elevates the standards of state societies as they strive for the perfection of justice and harmony. This quest for ultimate social authority also provides a standard for the reformation of international society.

Allott posits that, until now, self-enclosed state-societies have operated upon Vattelian premises. They encounter each other as independent units within a barren global arena through the interaction of their separate public realms. States have made a world which is fit only for governments. The international authority of these governments is spurious because it was not derived from the totality of international soci-

53. Weil, "Toward Relative Normativity in International Law?" Thinkers such as Charles Foucault have noted that in the modern world power is less a matter of overt, brutal coercion as it is an unseen force that follows the logic of organization and the use of authoritative symbols to enforce obedience. Foucault, *The Order of Things: An Archaeology of the Human Sciences* (New York: Pantheon Books, 1971). These approaches to authority are supported by biological interpretations of human nature. For example, Allott claims that "The human animal, like the chimpanzee and the termite, is a social animal. To be a social animal is to be law-abiding. The human being, endowed with consciousness, is able to present its socializing to itself as law." *Eunomia*, pt. 2, chap. 14.2.

54. *Eunomia*, pt. 2, chaps. 12–13, esp. 13.27 and 13.35.

ety and it was not conferred upon them by the peoples of the world. The external authority of isolated governments was established by the intermediate state system which these states created for themselves. This interstatal community is an unsociety which arrogantly calls itself a society of states.[55]

The ordered well-being of all is the objective of all modern societies except the international. Because of this, global disorder is more pervasive than is usually understood. Violence and arbitrary actions are not just occasional deviations from a normal tranquility. The basic dilemmas of war and peace are unresolved because the use of force, even in self-defense, is unsocialized.

Social power under law has not yet replaced the unilateral use of coercion. The search for balances of power, and appeals to principles of reciprocity, demonstrate that the self-creating of the separate state societies is not completely isolated from the self-creating of all the others. But others, if not enemies, are considered to be rivals. Under these fragile conditions successful diplomacy is usually nothing more than the "fortuitous aggregation of unilateral calculations."[56]

State sovereignty is a substantial obstacle to the realization of an authentic international society. Entitlements such as independence, territorial integrity, and domestic jurisdiction breed indifference to the well-being or fate of others. Social progress within state-societies proceeds—at an uneven pace—while, simultaneously, the existing international arrangements remain essentially unsocialized. The amoral tendencies of states are not counteracted by a reality-forming morality which emanates from the whole of humanity.

---

55. Id., chaps. 12.13 and 13.105–9.

56. Id. "Diplomacy is the dialogue of a stunted society, the dignifying of human desolation . . . Elegant diplomacy, and espionage, its half-witted underworld crony, play the grown-up game which begins in whispering and ends in suffering; which begins in deception and ends in war." Pt. 3, chap. 15.24. Allott makes some important observations on the idea of peace as being nothing more than the absence of war. He argues that this conception is hypocritical ". . . because it assumes that all that people deeply desire is a greater interval between wars . . . what the people of the world long for is an end to the self-inflicted terminal insecurity of their lives and possessions . . ." *Eunomia*, pt. 3, chap. 15.17.

The existing global arrangements are generally viewed as natural, inevitable, and permanent. Yet there are signs of change. In the modern world the material and moral interdependence of peoples has become increasingly apparent to the universal consciousness. Through the creation of international organizations and other multilateral institutions the state-societies, acting collectively, have begun to positively organize their international intercourse. Governmental activity is being conducted internally and externally in a single continuum. Sovereign states were once sealed in their mutual isolation. Now they are becoming more like cellular societies, permeable to systemic innovations which originate beyond themselves. We are at the dawning of a new age, "rising from the graves and ashes of an exhausted world."[57]

The outlines of the future are beginning to appear. Human rights have been introduced and, as elements of Pure Social and Legal Theories, they are placed above the variances of culture. Beyond the partial reality-forming of states there are further horizons of social comprehension. Human consciousness will continue to pursue these insights as it seeks to understand the ultimate authority of the whole of humanity. The peoples of the world are now imprisoned within states, but, as the enhancement of consciousness moderates all forms of external authority, state sovereignty will cease to be the dominant social reality. The freedom that inheres in the moral core of consciousness will begin to express itself at the intersection of desire and obligation. A global social power will coalesce as international society's own reality.

57. *Eunomia*, pt. 3, chap. 15.23. The emergence of an international public realm is a distinct advance in the understanding of international relations. Traditionally, the objective had been only to coordinate the actions of separate states; the new public authority acts, to some extent, on behalf of the international society itself. See *Eunomia*, pt. 3, chap. 15.56. Allott was instrumental in the development of the European Community. He sees the development of that community as being of importance to the international society. The EC, a "socializing by state activity," is already a state society, and it is an "international public realm, integrating and superceding to an ever-increasing extent the public realm of all statally organized subordinate societies" (*Eunomia*, pt. 2, chap. 13.78–79). See also "Mare Nostrum: A New Law of the Sea," 86 *American Journal of International Law* 764 (1992). The usefulness of the European analogy will be discussed in Chapter 4 of the present work.

A supreme social authority will confer new possibilities upon sub-societies and individuals, in exchange for the subordination of particular aims to the normative purposes of the society of societies. The legal constitution of the world society will fulfill the objectives of the ideal constitution. States will be seen in their limited role as subordinate societies. Their legal powers will be delegated. The international legal process will no longer originate with the will of states; all legal relations, in every society, will be connected to the legal relations in every other society through the mediation of the society of all societies from which every legal authority is ultimately derived.[58]

58. *Eunomia,* pt. 2 chap. 14; pt. 3 chap. 19.

CHAPTER 4

꜒

FROM A SOCIETY OF STATES TO A WORLD

POLITICAL SOCIETY

I

The Social Idealism of Allott represents a refinement of the movement toward immanence which has characterized much of modern
international theorizing. This development has been influenced by the
philosophy of the German Enlightenment. As we saw in Chapter 2,
the inward turn begins with the speculations of Leibniz and culminates
with the philosophy of Hegel, who absorbed what had previously
been thought of as existing outside the mind into the immanence of
self-consciousness.[1]

Hegel's metaphysics influenced his conception of the state and his
understanding of international relations. The state was Mind objectified. As a self-contained entity, it was an autonomous sovereign power.
The status of the state in the order of existence was no longer derived
from natural law or from considerations of divine providence. There
was no higher authority than that of *Geist,* or Absolute Mind. International society was essentially anarchic because autonomous states were
in a state of nature in their mutual relations.[2]

This philosophical justification of international disorder was challenged by Hans Kelsen's Pure Theory of Law. In Pure Theory, the state

1. Eric Voegelin, *In Search of Order,* vol. 5 (Baton Rouge: Louisiana State University
Press, 1987), chap. 2; Jacques Maritain, *Three Reformers: Luther, Descartes, Rousseau* (London: Sheed & Ward, 1936), sec. 5.

2. See the discussion in Chapter 2, section III, of the present work and accompanying notes.

is nothing other than the unity of its legal order. It is subject to the abstract hierarchy of international norms that determine what it ought to do in its relations with other states. But Kelsen's legal formalism was a logical order which lacked any authoritative foundations. Allott's Social Idealism provides such a basis. He postulates a society of societies that imaginatively encompasses all of humanity and through its supremacy legitimizes the enforcement of a universal legal order.

The origins of the imagined international society are to be found in the sociology of Comte. Comte announced the advent of a new universal history. In his Messianic positivism the social whole, rather than the state, would have exclusive authority over human destiny. All social and political institutions were to be reorganized first in the West, then among all civilized peoples, according to the new humanistic ideal. Universal humanity would be regenerated and its prophets would discipline the world. Comte believed that the disorder of states and individuals could be corrected by the application of the principle of unity. Harmony could be achieved when *Homo gregarius,* prone to chaotic separation, is made to conform to a order appropriate to a scientific age. Intelligence, inspired by a sentimental altruism, would be the instrument of that integration.[3]

Allott's thought centers on the idea of an international society which is gradually becoming the definitive representative of humanity. His conception is indirectly drawn from Comte, even though Allott attributes an authority to international law that Comte, who favored the rule of technocrats, would not have approved. Allott does not recognize his indebtedness to Comte, but he does acknowledge the influence of the priest-scientist, Pierre Teilhard de Chardin. Through this connection to scientific anthropology we can grasp the significance of Allott's *Eunomia* in the ongoing effort to establish a basis for universal human governance.

Chardin believed that social order was derived from the collective

3. Auguste Comte, *Positive Philosophy.* See also Jacques Maritain, *Moral Philosophy,* pt. 2, chap. 2; Eric Voegelin, *From Enlightenment to Revolution,* chap. 6; and John Stuart Mill, *Auguste Comte and Positivism* (Ann Arbor: University of Michigan Press, 1961).

movement of thought. Progressive anthropogenesis is rooted in a collective consciousness. Like Comte, Chardin was convinced that the evolution of man is a process of organic becoming which has made possible new forms of total organization. Evolution does not lead up to man; it surrounds him. Humankind has a unique self-consciousness which distinguishes it from the rest of the universe, but its mental structure has been developed in a way that makes humanity an unfinished product of past evolution. Man is evolution conscious of itself. Scientific epistemology has transformed and expanded the powers of human thought. Now time and space are joined and the illusion of proximity is overcome. Chardin realized that we can think continuously of past, present, and future and, by so doing, grasp the unity of the biosphere that lies beyond our own limited existence. For him, the mind had its own *noosphere* which can see those deeper connections of existence that exist in spite of the discrete proliferations that tend toward disintegration. In the ascent of thought, reflective consciousness is enabled to understand the totality that subsists above the ongoing cosmogenesis.[4]

This Jesuit philosopher was sure that humanity, as well as matter, was undergoing a maturity of organization. The biosphere begins its formation as the organic emerges from its chemical components. A new order of life begins. Within restricted space, cellular organisms multiply, but their expansion is held together inexperientially from above. There is a forward-looking centricity to life which preserves the particulars within an overall order. At the summit of speculation

4. Pierre Teilhard de Chardin, *The Phenomenon of Man,* trans. Bernard Wall (New York: Harper Bros., 1959); *The Future of Man,* trans. Norman Denny (New York: Harper & Row, 1964); *The Divine Milieu* (New York: Harper & Row, 1968). Chardin's work has been criticized by other Christian thinkers as being a form of pantheistic naturalism. See, e.g., Maritain, *The Peasant of the Garonne,* trans. M. Cuddihy and Elizabeth Hughes (New York: Holt, Rinehart & Winston, 1968).

An earlier Catholic work which achieves a better balance between faith and evolution is E. I. Watkin, *The Bow in the Clouds* (New York: Macmillan, 1932). See also Hans Ur von Balthasar, *The God Question and Modern Man* (New York: The Seabury Press, 1967). For a more recent Anglican perspective on religion and science see John Polkinghorne, *The Faith of a Physicist* (Princeton: Princeton University Press, 1994).

the organizational phenomenon appears in all its complex grandeur. Looking down from the peak, one sees the pattern of the whole laid out in an immense but perfect harmony. An evolving "noosystem" draws the whole human species into a mindful union. Within a single, self-developing framework of thought the order of the whole is revealed. From top to bottom a cosmic process of unification begins to become intelligible. There is now hope for the collective advance of all.[5]

In the thought of Chardin the evolutionary process of organization culminates in societies. Aggregations are formed through collective reflection as the mind articulates stable and coherent unities. Such an integration reconciles the individual with the group. The individual is no longer the center of existence. Now caught up in something greater than himself, he becomes subject to the laws of controlled maturation.

The need for total organization arises out of the experience of compression. The explosion of human reproduction over the restricted surface of the globe has created a crisis of embryogenesis. In earlier ages, the expansion of the masses was a discrete phenomenon, limited to the social environment of particular states and empires. But it is now planetary in scope. Being global, it can only be controlled by some systematic form of universal order. Chardin concedes that the collective regulation which such an order demands poses a threat to human dignity and freedom. Like Comte, he believed that such dangers could be moderated by the power of love. Through the development of a mutual internal affinity, human beings can learn to love one another even as they draw closer together.[6]

The previous phases of human socialization occurred within divergent cultural units organized as nation-states. Enclosed within themselves, they could not think beyond themselves. According to Chardin, this process of dispersal is at a dead end. Only the power of

5. Chardin, *The Phenomenon of Man,* bk. 3, chap. 3.
6. Chardin, *The Future of Man,* chap. 15. Compare the critique of Comte's altruism in Voegelin, *From Enlightenment to Revolution.*

consciousness can save the world from folding in upon itself. Collective reflection embraces all the individual units of humankind within a single center. Situated within a continuum of past, present, and future, reason and imagination will design a hyperpersonal organization of humanity. The collective will preserve the diversity of existence while holding everything together from above.[7]

Allott's social idealism continues the conceptions of universal order that are found in scientific anthropology. Like Chardin, Allott believes that the social world of the future will be coercively ordered by structures and systems devised by collective consciousness for the purpose of assuring human survival and prosperity. This order will be differentiated from the order of the whole physical universe, but it will be integrated with the material cosmos. The two are mentally integrated. Together, they constitute the "system of order of all that is . . ."[8]

In Allott's conception, the self-creation of the peoples of the world will be directed by international law. That law will no longer be the servant of the governments of states; it will regain its dignity by becoming the instrument for the universalizing of social purpose. Functioning on a global scale, the law will delegate all jural authority and bring all the powers of the world to account. As imagined by Allott, the law will insert the universal into the particular and draw the particular into the universal. International law will aggregate the energies of all as it directs the process by which humanity takes control of its becoming.

As the idea of universal order flows out of pure into practical theory, order becomes prescriptive. Coercive authority must reconcile desire with obligation. Awakening from its Vattelian nightmare, international society will begin to develop a public realm which will be of, and for,

7. *The Future of Man,* chap. 14.
8. Philip Allott, *Eunomia,* pt. 3, chap. 19.6. The society of the human race is the proximate unifying standard; the ultimate standard is consciousness deified. "Ultimately, it is not society but human consciousness that is God; human consciousness projects all that is, including space and time . . ." Martti Koskenniemi, review of *Eunomia,* 87 American Journal of International Law 160–64 (1993).

the whole human society. The existing state-societies will act as agents of the whole in the overall process of creative renewal.[9]

A union of ideal social and legal theory provides an alternative to the chaotic incoherence of the existing nation-state system. But when viewed as part of the history of ideas of world order, Allott's project becomes more problematic. From the time of Dante there has been, as we have seen, a general aversion to any philosophical plan of universal organization. Such prearrangements are seen as impositions on the freedom of action of sovereign states.

In Allott's construct there is a rationalism at work which bears comparison with Wolff's *Civitas Maxima*. Both assume that the concrete problems of international disorder can be resolved when the unifying power of abstract reason is imposed upon the complexities of actual experience. In considering the value of Allott's conception one is also reminded of Oppenheim, who opposed any further world authority because he believed that it would destroy the rich variety of human life which is being developed within the pluralistic nation-state system.[10]

This criticism, which we shall consider further, has relevance to Allott's demand that in the coming age all particularities be subject to an idealized society of societies. But the deeper meaning of these objections can be seen by evaluating the way that scientific sociology deals with the distinctiveness of the human person.

Like Chardin, Allott is convinced that all unities are formed by a collective consciousness. The individual consciousness will presumably integrate itself into the structure and system of the whole. The collective consciousness, which determines the nature of society, is also the unique identity of each individual human being. To form the global association of all, one must come to understand, within one's own

9. Allott, *Eunomia*, pt. 3, chaps. 15.6–8; 15.56; 16.18–19. According to Comte, the "supreme direction of intelligence should cease to appertain to lawyers." *System of Positive Polity* (1875) (New York: Ben Franklin Press, 1968), 543.

10. Allott's theory also reminds one of an earlier model: ". . . There is a touch of Dante's *De Monarchia* here." Anthony Black, review of *Eunomia*, 62 *Political Quarterly* 303 (April 1991). See also the discussion of Oppenheim's views on the dangers of world government in chap. 3, sec. I of the present work.

consciousness, that the universal and the individual are ascending together in the same direction. They are jointly moving toward that *Omega point* that confirms each as it draws them into itself. Once the whole is organized, the parts will fulfill and perfect themselves. "Steeped in Omega," they will have found within the depths of their unique consciousnesses that centeredness from which all emerge and to which all must return. As all are knitted together, each will become more itself. In an anthropology grounded in scientific sociology, the individual self becomes more distinguishable from others the closer it gets to them.[11]

It is also assumed that if individuals, and the governments which represent them, continue to separate themselves from the emerging society of societies, they will be acting contrary to an objective understanding of human nature. Within the universal frame of consciousness, the isolation of one from the many is no longer feasible. Anthropogenesis requires coalescence; there is no other evolutionary future. That future will be humanistically sound because in a centered universe the All and the Singular are personalized. The egoism which resists such a reconciliation is essentially retrograde.[12]

11. "To grasp the power of synthesis and organization we must look *beyond* our souls. Rather than being mutually exclusive, the Universal and the Personal (that is to say the 'centered') grow in the same direction and culminate simultaneously in each other . . ." Chardin, *The Phenomenon of Man,* bk. 4, chap. 2. Compare Allott, *Eunomia,* pt. 3, chap. 19. See also the comment by Koskenniemi, supra, note 8.

According to Allott, consciousness transforms the physical world into itself and collective consciousness makes the social world. As for individual consciousness, it ". . . orders itself into the structure and system which is the unique identity of each human being, as each human being seeks survival and prospering—as individual, as a member of societies, as self-differentiated part of an undifferentiated universe." *Eunomia,* pt. 3, chap. 19.2.

Voegelin traces the understandings of humanity that concentrate upon the data of consciousness back to Hegel, for whom the subject was the substance of being. This fusion of transcendence and immanence within consciousness was also related by Voegelin to the speculations of the Upanishads on the identity of the *Atman* (the self as conscious subject) with Brahma, the superpersonal, supermundane reality. Voegelin, *Order and History,* vol. 2, *The World of the Polis,* introduction. The influence of Hegel upon Allott is evident in Allott's treatment of the self-transcending spirit in international culture. See *Eunomia,* pt. 3, chap. 18.

12. Chardin, *The Phenomenon of Man,* bk. 3, chap. 1.

Scientific social theory raises to a higher level the ideological conflicts between liberalism and communitarianism which permeate modern political theory. The basic antagonism can be found in Hegel. Under his influence, modern social theory—including that of Allott—has developed a hostility to individualistic interpretations of any form of social life. Whether manifest in the separate individual or the isolated state, singularity is understood as being a primary source of social disorder. All separate self-assertion is destructive and aimless; it must become subject to a systematic order that enforces the values of a group. This attitude, which can also be found in Marx and Comte, exaggerates the dependence of the human being upon society. Social theory is prone to this error because it fails to make any distinction between the individual and the person.

As an individual, the human being is a part of the physical universe. He, or she, shares what is common to all entities, whether animal, plant, microbe or atom. But as a person, the human being is unique. The person subsists in itself, having an existence and perfection which is its own. Its being is not caused by any universal energy. The exceptional dignity of the human person exists because it is a relative whole standing under the transcendent whole that is God.

Because the person is relatively, rather than absolutely, independent, it is oriented toward society. Indeed, by its nature, personality tends toward communion with others. But there is no separate social substance which draws persons together. All human societies are societies of persons; there is no higher reality within which they coexist. As persons associate they become something different from what they were in isolation. Nevertheless, the basic foundation of community is the person and not the social whole.[13]

13. "The word *person* is reserved for substances which, choosing their own end, are capable of themselves of deciding upon the means, and of introducing series of events into the universe by their liberty . . ." Jacques Maritain, *Three Reformers*, 8. See also *The Person and the Common Good*, trans. John F. Fitzgerald (New York: Scribners, 1947), chap. 3; *Moral Philosophy*, chap. 8. See further Charles Taylor, *The Ethics of Authenticity* (Cambridge, Mass.: Harvard University Press, 1992).

The primacy of the social over the individual is evaluated in Robert Nisbet, *The*

These philosophical distinctions are indispensable to international, as well as domestic, political theory. The capacity of human beings to live together in some form of public association is not limited to modes of coexistence that may arise within the state. The propensity towards political life which inheres in human nature cannot be antecedently confined within such a restricted space. But broader forms of association must be realized in freedom. As persons, human beings cannot be compelled to enter into higher forms of organized life. Persons have a need to interact with others in a way that enlarges, as well as enriches, community; but they must do so without restraint. Scientific naturalism does not recognize such liberty. Its excursions into international theory are grounded in a metabiology which considers man to be simply the last of the animals. Thus, for Allott, the ordinary human is a sociable being in the same sense as "the chimpanzee and the termite."[14]

Such abstract theorizing does not understand what might motivate a reconsideration of existing global arrangements. Individuals may be inert, but persons are not passive phenomena to be universally regulated on behalf of some imagined collective consciousness. Those having the appropriate responsibilities must be persuaded that there are sufficient reasons for change. A person develops reasons for acting through reflection and communication with others. An adequate reason for acting is not an event in consciousness which the person somehow discovers. By dialogue with oneself—and others—one deter-

---

Sociology of Emile Durkheim (New York: Oxford University Press, 1974). For the transformations of the individual as a result of social association see Benjamin Cardozo, *The Paradoxes of Legal Science* (New York: Columbia University Press, 1928). For a critique of radical social theory, see my *Descent into Subjectivity,* chap. 3.

14. Allott's scientific naturalism leads him to say that "The human animal, like the chimpanzee and the termite, is a social animal. To be a social animal is to be law-abiding . . ." *Eunomia,* pt. 2, chap. 14.2. Compare Edmund O. Wilson, *Consilience* (New York: Knopf, 1998).

The dangers of transposing scientific concepts into the study of human relations was perceived by the distinguished historian, Herbert Butterfield. He protested the view of social scientists that history should be the study of great collectivities and who considered history as being nothing more than a branch of biology. Butterfield, by contrast, placed the human person at the heart of the historical process. *Masters of International Thought,* ed. Kenneth W. Thompson (Baton Rouge: Louisiana State University Press, 1980).

mines that certain proposals are, or are not, good reasons for moving
beyond the existing state of affairs. To be conscious, at this level, is not
the same as being absorbed into a totality.[15]

From a Hobbesian perspective, any change in the nation-state system would be motivated by fear of mutual destruction. But the nobility of the human lies in the use of reason to choose some good. By
the use of reason the person becomes the master of his or her destiny.
Persons use their reason to choose their social, as well as their individual, ends. They can decide among themselves upon the appropriate
means of fulfilling their common political objectives, whether these
be national, transnational, or global in scope.

Because of the dialectic of ends and means which engages its powers, reason has an inherently practical character. It is not, as idealism
imagines, essentially disposed toward the comprehension of transcendental unities. The persistence of the pragmatic spirit in philosophical
circles is an indication of the fact that practical reason resists being
absorbed into a theoretical construct that would determine in advance
any goal of personal or social action.[16]

Abstract global theories are built upon the assumption that the creation of a world community is reducible to a simple choice between
the existing international arrangements and an ideal universal order
held together in some predetermined structure. The inhuman quality
of such speculation is revealed by the way that they terminate in imperatives addressed to the will. Reducing reason to the comprehension
of the universal, they leave no room for any further concrete reflection
on the essentials of a good common life. Kant believed that states
should submit to a cosmopolitan moral law that terminates in injunctions. In Kelsen's Pure Theory, international law is an order of juridical
relations which command obedience under threat of sanction. And for

15. Here, and in the immediately preceding reflections, I am indebted to Stuart
Hampshire, *Thought and Action* (Notre Dame, Ind.: University of Notre Dame Press,
1983).

16. On the central importance of practical reasonableness see John Finnis, *Natural
Law and Natural Rights*. See also Gregory Bruce Smith, "The End of History as a Portal
to the Future: Does Anything Lie beyond Late Modernity?" in Timothy Burns, ed.,
After History?

Allott, the universal society imposes its values upon the masses in the name of the whole of humanity.

The central mistake of these speculative abstractions is their supposition that a teleology of human flourishing can be derived from timeless symmetries. They fail to see that the future good of the world will depend upon a more concrete understanding of the power and range of human reason. As the proximate measure of human acts, reason has the capacity to pass beyond ideal preferences and reach aspects of the good that are embedded in the more mundane and fragmentary aspects of incarnate existence. The exercise of these abilities requires an awareness of extramental realities which is incompatible with the premises of idealism. By concentrating upon the immanent development of consciousness, pure thought limits the mind to a conversation with itself. It assumes that nothing further is to be discovered because all has already been conceived. Thus it misses the meanings which can be discovered outside the self within the workings of experience.[17]

Idealism is also alienated from the ontological aspects of human nature. Since it fuses transcendence and immanence within consciousness, it will not recognize any order of being outside of the mind which could have normative authority over the processes of social evolution. It thus ignores the most important aspects of human personality and the levels of fulfillment, under the guidance of practical reasonableness, to which the person is dynamically attracted.

Ideal theory is ultimately vacuous. Its insubstantial nature can be seen in the approach which Allott takes toward the controversial

---

17. Some of these idealistic tendencies can be seen in the philosophical poetry of Coleridge, who thought that "by a strange and dim similitude/Infinite myriads of self-conscious minds/Are one all-conscious Spirit . . ." In his study of Thoreau, Denis Donoghue identifies the transcendentalism of early New England as expressing the desire of the mind to pass through the senses and reach a unity which, it is felt, constitutes a soul. *Reading America: Essays on American Literature* (New York: Alfred A. Knopf, 1987), 59–65.

In Allott's social theory the importance of ends or purposes is stressed, but they are always seen as elements of a system, rather than as an expression of personal liberty. See, e.g., *Eunomia*, pt. 3, chap. 16.19–21. It has been observed that "[T]hinking in terms of systems lies at the bottom of illiberty in all its varieties." Ralf Dahrendorf, *Reflections on the Revolution in Europe* (London: Chatto & Windus, 1990), 55.

subject of universal human rights. Rights are an aspect of justice, but in pure social theory justice is itself simply "the relationship of its own order to all that is."[18] Human rights are thought of as having their origin in a supersocialized international society which is itself part of that transcendental and abstract totality.

There are, admittedly, advantages to this approach. Abstraction accentuates the tenacity of mind; once thought, the idea of human rights cannot be unthought. Moreover, ideal comprehension transcends ideological attempts to divide the Universal Declaration into specific preferences. Western democracies emphasize civil and political rights; socialist regimes stress economic, cultural, and social entitlements. When theoretically conceived, however, all these different values are seen as parts of a unified humanistic ideal. But the meaning of specific rights is otherwise unintelligible. Ideal comprehension is too far removed from either concrete understanding derived from the dictates of conscience or any sense of obligation that could be connected to a positive law of fundamental entitlements.

Pure Social Theory is not morally compelling because it treats questions concerning the *content* of human rights, as well as their enforcement, as matters of secondary importance. It thus cannot grasp either the essentials or the nuances of meaning concerning the discrete value of specific human rights. It does not understand why rights are fundamental, or how they may be fundamental without being absolute.[19]

Universal human rights are better understood as a contemporary expression of the classical ideal of the *jus gentium*. Traditionally, natural law was a reflection of Creative Wisdom. The *jus gentium,* by contrast, was a human creation, positive in nature, but subject to the influence

18. *Eunomia*, pt. 1, chap. 5.40.

19. On the distinction between fundamental and absolute rights see *Whitney v. California*, 274 U.S. 357, 373 (1927)(Justice Brandeis, concurring). Compare *Eunomia*, pt. 3, 15.60–68.

The idea of inherent human rights is based in the understanding that such entitlements are grounded in the ontological perfections that inhere in the immediate human being. Neither Hegel nor Comte could see that rights are specifically personal, and exist in the subject as an other, because for both, humanity was always some form of a social whole. See Maritain, *Moral Philosophy,* 14–21.

of natural law. The law of nations developed in the interstices between immutable principles and the contingencies of experience. It is the same with universal human rights. They are dependent upon the growth of common principles of civilization which must arise out of authentic divergences of cultural experience. The particular is not fully universalized.[20]

The pragmatic principle that how one understands the world is a function of the community to which one belongs has some relevance here. This does not mean that there are no noncontextual truths to which one can refer to evaluate particular situations. The position of the *jus gentium* between the normative and the contingent is incompatible with absolute relativism. Basic human rights are grounded upon truths which are superior to time; nonetheless, our knowledge of fundamental freedoms cannot be completely separated from the field of experience.

There is no unifying transcendence sweeping through history which cancels the significance of varied understandings of human rights. As a "common language," human rights discourse implicates a temporal, as well as an ideal, order of values, and in the articulation of universal rights there is, of necessity, some mixture of local and cosmopolitan understanding. As Pope John Paul II has said, "The truth about man is the unchangeable standard by which all cultures are judged; but every culture has something to teach us about one or another dimension of that complex truth."[21]

20. See the discussion in my *Modern Legal Philosophy* , chap. 4.

21. Pope John Paul II, "Address to the General Assembly of the United Nations," Oct. 5, 1995, in *Origins* 18, 294–99 (19 October 1995). See also the statement "Human Rights: The Common Language of Humanity" by United Nations Secretary-General Boutros Boutros-Ghali at the opening of the World Conference on Human Rights, held at Vienna, Austria, on June 14, 1993. In *World Conference on Human Rights* (New York: UN DPI/ 1394-39399, Aug. 1993).

The recognition of variations in the authentic understanding of the content of human rights reflects, to some degree, the pragmatic principle that the way one sees the world is a function of the community to which one belongs. However, the position defended here must be distinguished from the radical pragmatic view that there are no noncontextual truths to which one can refer to evaluate particular situations. That view is espoused by Richard Rorty. See, e.g., *Consequences of Pragmatism*. Compare Tibor Machan "Inde-

The dependence of the human good upon contrasting modes of social experience is also relevant to the larger questions of future global governance. The sociojuridical organization of the world advocated by Allott would subject the pluralistic community of nation-states to the superior authority of an imagined society of societies. This power would liberate the peoples who are now trapped within the boundaries of existing state societies and tyrannized by ruling elites. As a self-creating structure, the global society will make state-societies subsocieties of the totality. The nature and jurisdiction of the separate states will be determined by international law, acting on behalf of the entire human community. Like the physical universe, the human species will then be constituted as a network of extensive, invariable relations held together from above as a coherent whole.[22]

The idea of a progression of the human race from the existing nation-state system to a collective form of universal order is undoubtedly attractive. Like other reformers, Allott has demonstrated that the present international arrangements cannot be reconciled with the common good of the whole. The recurring cycles of violence, the deceptions of diplomacy, and endemic economic injustice expose great masses of people to a global "theater of the absurd." But like the abstract analysis of human rights, the atemporal quality of theories of global integration is too far removed from the world of experience to move men and women of good will to transformative action.[23]

---

fatigable Alchemist: Richard Rorty's Radical Pragmatism," *American Scholar* 65, no. 3 (Summer 1996): 417–424.

Differences of understanding also reflect moral complexity. The heterogeneous quality of value judgments in practical life is recognized by many contemporary philosophers. See, e.g., Martha Nussbaum, *Love's Knowledge: Essays on Philosophy and Literature* (New York: Oxford University Press, 1991), chap. 2; Charles E. Larmore, *Patterns of Moral Complexity* (New York: Cambridge University Press, 1987), chap. 1; Nicholas Rescher, *Ethical Idealism: An Inquiry into the Nature and Function of Ideals* (Berkeley: University of California Press, 1987); E. F. Schumaker, *A Guide for the Perplexed,* and Edmund Pincoffs, *Quandaries and Virtues.*

22. *Eunomia,* pt. 3, chap. 15.40. Compare the observation of Maritain: "Positivism never admits anything but duties of all to all . . . as a consequence of functions." *Moral Philosophy,* chap. 12, sec. 2.

23. *Eunomia,* pt. 3, chap. 15.25. Compare Richard Falk, *On Humane Governance* (University Park: The Pennsylvania State University Press, 1996).

Universal utopianism does not adequately account for the human good which can be realized within the present fragmented form of international association. It fears that dispersed humanity will turn against itself unless it is held together systematically by a central authority. This overlooks the values which arise through personal attachment to a particular community. All the members of the human family live within a historically determined social group. Within these provincial societies, with all their unique qualities, humanity achieves its highest forms of creativity.[24]

The values of familiar density are political as well as cultural. Every state, therefore, has the right to develop the good of its members, in the light of its traditions and according to the tempo of its own innovations. At the same time, it must respect the rights of all within its borders and fulfill its responsibilities for peace, justice, and mutual collaboration in its relations with all other peoples of the world. This requires a subtle balance between the universal and the particular.[25]

At this stage of human history, the United Nations is a corporate

24. The political common good is not just the good of the nation. All persons should strive for the universal common good of the world as a whole. However, it is within the nation that the common good of humanity achieves its greatest density. Maritain, *The Person and the Common Good,* chap. 4. There are similar balances of particular and universal in the arts. "Art depends upon what history and tradition, time and country, transmits to mind and body . . . the most universal, the most human works of art, are those which clearly bear the mark of their country." Maritain, *Art and Scholasticism,* chap. 9, sec. 3.

25. Pope John Paul II, *Address to the United Nations:* "Every nation therefore has also the right to shape its life according to its own traditions, excluding of course every abuse of basic human rights and in particular the oppression of minorities . . ."

The Holy Father does not identify the nation with the state. He also asserts that the common human right of groups to exist as nations does not entail a right to exist as a state. Language and culture are a form of "spiritual sovereignty" because each culture is ". . . a way of giving expression to the transcendent dimensions of human life. The heart of every culture is its approach to the greatest of all mysteries; the mystery of God." Ibid. The pontiff says further that "The exercise of the rights of nations, balanced by the acknowledgment and the practice of duties, promotes a fruitful 'exchange of gifts' which strengthens the unity of all mankind" Id. It is the hope of the Holy Father that this century of violence will give way to a new century of dialogue and persuasion. For a fuller discussion of the Church's view see the Encyclical Letter of His Holiness Pope John XXIII, *Pacem In Terris* (Peace on Earth) (1963); see also Second Vatican Council, *The Pastoral Constitution on the Church in the Modern World* (1965), chap. 5.2.

attempt to reconcile the local and the cosmopolitan demands of human sociability. Within the framework established by its members, the UN provides various fora within which each member state can advance its own interests in a manner which is expected to be reasonably compatible with the interests of all. The good of others is implicit in this process. However, as we saw in the previous chapter, prevailing interpretations of international association are minimalist in nature. They do not require anything more than the negative coordination of the self-serving policies of separate independent states.

Social idealism goes to the opposite extreme. Considering the world as an indivisible social community, it would compel a love for humanity that devalues more immediate bonds of state-centered attachment and allegiance. This attitude is consistent with the origins and development of social theory. Since the time of Comte, all forms of altruistic humanism have presupposed that love for one's own society is incompatible with a universal love for all. But it is a mistake to believe that concern for the welfare of others, and a genuine regard for the well-being of the state to which one belongs, are essentially irreconcilable.

Separate allegiances do not necessarily preclude higher unities. The formation of these complex bonds is, of course, extremely difficult. Something more demanding than a shared adherence to common principle is required. But it is possible for states, as discrete human communities, to develop a form of international friendship which is morally superior to an interconnectedness based upon transitory alliances. The pursuit of such an inclusive amity engages the powers of moral reason as well as sentiments of affection. The vital interests of the state must be subject to a discipline that prevents foreign policy from being nothing more than a sophisticated self-centeredness. At the same time, however, transnational collaboration can leave ample room for the advancement of legitimate national interests. The affirmation of the independent good of other states, whether they be weak or strong, does not eliminate all self-regarding actions.[26]

26. On the importance of friendship to every form of community life see Finnis, *Natural Law and Natural Right,* chap. 6. 4. On the theme of more positive collaboration

When a state recognizes that other states are also authentic human communities, it must acknowledge their right not simply to exist, but to flourish, even at the expense of its own primacy. Nonetheless, these broad obligations do not require any state to abandon the proper pursuit of its own well-being. In a humanistic internationalism, friendly relations require cooperation, which must be, in part, for the sake of others. But when reasonableness prevails, foreign policy is not made exclusively from the point of view of one state or the other. The common good of friendship is inclusive. The welfare of one's own nation and the well-being of other societies must both taken into account in any decisions that may have multilateral consequences.

Scientific anthropology looks upon the communal pluralism of the nation-state system as an obstacle to the creation of higher forms of collective unity. It sees the society of the world as a self-moving cosmos, directed toward a systematic socialization that will subsume multiplicity as it holds all together. A humanistic anthropology, by contrast, recognizes an inherent value in the centrifugal forces of human diversity. Attentive to the temporal, it looks toward richer unities.

---

among nations, the former Secretary-General of the United Nations, Boutros Boutros-Ghali, has written of the need for ". . . a commitment on the part of all states not only to engage in dialogue and debate but also to discourage isolationism, to oppose unilateralism, to accept decisions reached democratically, to refrain from using force illegitimately, to oppose aggression, to promote and respect the rule of law in international relations and to maintain a general spirit of solidarity, cooperation and community. Unless the majority of Member States [of the United Nations] have the political will to pay attention to global affairs as they do to national affairs, the democratization of international relations will not succeed." *An Agenda for Democratization* (New York: United Nations Publication DPI/ 1867, December, 1996), chap. 5.76.

The dangers of extreme nationalism were noted by the poet Rabindranath Tagore earlier in the century in his book *Nationalism* (London: Macmillan, 1917). It is not sufficiently realized, however, how Messianic Utopianism also obstructs the development of international friendship. Utopianism posits an opposition between love of self and love of others which has communal, as well as interpersonal, implications. Comte's conception of love for others was one ". . . from which was excluded all love for the lover's own being and his proper perfection . . . no place in us for the desire for the good of our own person . . . Our life is no longer, under any aspect, *for us* but exclusively for others . . ." Maritain, *Moral Philosophy,* p. 336. See further Joshua Cohen, ed., *For Love of Country: Debating the Limits of Patriotism* (Boston: Beacon Press, 1996).

Such unities will be experientially developed through a proper balance of the rights and duties of independent, but fraternally cooperative, states. Within this deeper understanding, the international community can achieve a greater degree of solidarity then is possible when relations among states are governed by rules and procedures whose only purpose it to allow each to pursue its own interests. But these improvements must be considered as being parts of an interim ethic.

The fundamental instabilities of the nation-state system are so pervasive that no measure of improvement, no matter how well-intentioned, can fully correct them. As we have already observed, the present organization of the world is primitive in nature. Its laws have no regular sanctions. The order of the whole is dependent upon the managerial dominance of the few, and the leading states act under constantly shifting criteria of legitimate power and authority. Developments in weaponry, arms transfers, and terrorism have eroded the limited security which states possessed in an earlier international state of nature. Much can still be done to improve the reasonableness of the current arrangements, but it would be irrational to assume that, in its present form, the international community will naturally evolve into a durable and pacific union.

At some point, in an indefinite future, the basic form of global organization which the world has inherited must be substantially changed. Persons from distinct states and cultures must come together in some public space, and start something new. This will require the establishment of institutions that can balance national and international authority in a way that preserves all the unities and diversities of human experience. To begin to approach that unknown gathering there must be a shift in intellectual, as well as moral, orientation.

The reflective mind must move away from its fascination with science and its metabiological understanding of human nature, together with the conformities it implies. The full potential of human sociability can only be realized when political philosophy regains its rightful place in the articulation of a comprehensive international theory. For the fundamental questions of world order are essentially political, and not sociological, in nature. And they begin with the problem of sovereignty.

II

In the late nineteenth century the Scottish legal philosopher James Lorimer proposed the establishment of a world government. He believed that the essential questions of universal order could not be resolved without establishing on the international plane the institutions which had proven to be necessary to the effective operation of a domestic legal order. But while his plan called for the establishment of legislative and executive organs, as well as courts, the sole purpose of the universal government would be to maintain the separate existence of states. The society of states would continue to be the basic form of international community.[27]

After the First World War, others came to believe that no substantial progress was possible unless the separate states were seen as parts of a larger society. This change can be seen in the reflections of Robert Lansing, the American secretary of state. Lansing was impressed by Austin's argument that since positive law was the command of a sovereign to a subject, international law, did not, strictly speaking, exist among independent states. The need was to transfer the Austinian theory of sovereignty to the global plane. Lansing thought that within societies sovereignty is a power that is antecedent to the powers of the governing state authorities. Individuals who live within any organized political community are, considered separately, subjects; collectively, they constitute the supreme governing authority. Expanding that idea, Lansing argued that although the state was the most highly developed form of political organization, it was, nonetheless, a part of a wider social organism that embraced the entire society of mankind. For genuine global progress to occur, one must first identify that wider power which potentially could express the unwilled will of the whole human race.[28]

---

27. See the discussion of Lorimer's plan in chap. 2, sec. III of the present work.

28. Robert Lansing, *Notes on Sovereignty* (Carnegie Endowment, Pamph. 38, 1921). The text originally appeared in two law review articles: "Notes on Sovereignty in a State," 1 *American Journal of International Law*. 105 (1907); "Notes on World Sovereignty," 15 *American Journal of International Law* 13 (1921). On "unwilled will" see Allott, *Eunomia,*

Lansing's reflections renewed questions about sovereignty which had vexed international theory from its beginnings. Dante, it may be remembered, had claimed that the Holy Roman Emperor had a divine commission to rule the known world. Contesting that view, the Spanish jurist-theologians held that any assertion of universal jurisdiction as a matter of divine right was incompatible with natural law. For them, the only legitimate authority that came from above was the spiritual power of the Church. Political authority was conferred from below, coming from a specific people, at a particular time, as they exercised their collective right of self-governance. A Lord of the World would have to have been designated as such by the people of the whole world, united as a deliberative body politic. Such an event not only had not occurred; it was practically inconceivable.[29]

The Spanish thinkers drew upon principles of classical political theory, as refined by medieval experience. Political sovereignty was understood as a temporal right of a community that had united to establish the conditions of a peaceful common life. Authority resided in a people, which was considered to be more than a simple aggregate or mass. With the coming of the modern world, however, the idea of general social authority began to decline. Beginning with Hobbes, political legitimacy was conceived as being derived from isolated and self-interested individuals who, under the terms of an imagined covenant, had transferred their individual rights of self-governance to a representative power. That supreme authority would enforce the agreement and insure the general peace.

Hobbes's contractarianism complemented earlier theories of political absolutism which were already part of the political literature and which had influenced international reflection. Grotius had held that the supreme authority of established princes was an independent power and not a participation in citizens' rights of governance. An

---

chap. 12.53. See also Hans Kelsen, *Peace through Law* (Chapel Hill: University of North Carolina Press, 1944), 36: ". . . If 'power' means actual power, i.e., the capacity to bring about an effect, 'supreme power' would mean to be a first cause, a *prima causa*. In this sense, only God, as the Creator of the World, is sovereign."

29. See chap. 1, sec. II of the present work.

even deeper influence of absolutist conceptions of sovereignty can be seen in the work of Vattel. Vattel's position is instructive, because while it abandons the classical view it does not ignore it. Vattel affirms that the sovereignty of the nation belongs to the whole society. Every society which is not dependent upon any other nation is self-governing. It is also self-sufficient. When organized as a state, the nation is a perfect moral being, capable of achieving its own ends and lacking nothing necessary to reach those ends. Although sovereign power comes from the nation, the sovereign represents its moral personality, especially in his dealings with other powers. The ruler holds the nation's rights and bears its responsibilities.[30]

Vattel brings explicitly into international relations the idea that the authority of the ruler is independent of general social power of self-governance. Over time, the moral personality of the state gradually eclipsed the personality of the prince. The sovereign state, in its external, as well as its internal, relations was increasing understood as possessing a power that was separate from, and above, that of the people. The state substituted itself for the whole. With Hegel, the state becomes itself a whole.

Like Locke, Vattel held that the grant of governing authority to the state by the people divested the people of power so long as the state was faithful to its duties. Rousseau asserted that sovereignty always resides in the people in spite of any agreement they may have made to alienate their authority. The sovereignty of the *volonté général* is, for Rousseau, as absolute in the people as it had been for Hobbes in the ruler. The general will is an indivisible collective power which can be represented only by itself.[31]

30. Emmerich Vattel, *The Law of Nations*, bk. 1, sec. 4, 26–29, 40–41. See also Francis Ruddy, *International Law in the Enlightenment* (Dobbs Ferry, N.Y.: Oceana Publications, 1975), chap. 5. Pufendorf and Wolff also wrote of the state as if it had a moral personality.

31. Jean-Jacques Rousseau, *The Social Contract*, bk. 2, chap. 1. See also the introduction to Sir Ernest Barker, *Social Contract: Essays by Locke, Hume and Rousseau* (New York: Oxford University Press, 1962); J. W. Gough, *The Social Contract: A Critical Study of Its Development,* 2nd ed. (Oxford: The Clarendon Press, 1952).

In *The Social Contract* Rousseau attacks Grotius, whom he describes as one who "spares no pains to despoil the people of all their rights, and in the most artful manner, bestow them on kings."

Allott's social idealism reflects these changes in the understanding of sovereignty. From his perspective, state sovereignty is the most damaging feature of the existing structure of the world community because it has displaced all other forms of social authority beyond, as well as within, state borders. The task of social theory is to rescue humanity from the encroachments of state power upon the potential of universal sociability. This is done by explicating the way in which the whole of the human race might collectively think of itself as a coherent social structure.

In modern societies democracy has become the authority of all authority. But Allott contends that this advance does not eliminate the need to identify sovereignty as a matter of theoretical understanding. Democratic authority is not self-justifying; it can easily become majoritarian oppression. To save itself, democracy must have some supersocial embodiment. This requires a further search for sovereignty, for the sovereign must be above every social process.

In Allott's speculations, social consciousness supersocializes democracy in the name of social justice. This assures that political and legal manifestations of democracy will reflect the authentic will of society as it reconciles the will of each with the will of all. According to Allott, the redemption of democracy in the name of social justice has already become the policy of mature state-societies. A similar supersocialization will become the measure of international development. International governance will then not be the exercise of any inherent authority. It will only be the ordering aspect of international experience. Sovereignty as authority—which is a central principle of the nation-state system—will have evolved into the self-willed order of the society of societies.[32]

The peoples of the world do not form a political society. Nor, from Allott's perspective, do they need to do so. In his *Eunomia* the world already has a constitutional structure—a becoming composed of ideal, legal, and real forms. The ideal constitution expresses what the society

---

32. Philip Allott, *Eunomia*, pt. 2, chap. 12; pt. 3, chaps. 13; 20.13–34; 15.82.

of humanity might become as it struggles to form a new collective identity. The legal constitution manifests the structure and system of law that reconciles desire and obligation as it addresses the perennial dilemmas of human association. The real constitution is the current social process, reflecting the changing forces at work in the restless energy of the world as humanity tries to recreate itself into a universal form of unification.[33]

Allott's social idealism, like De Chardin's Scientific Anthropology, sees the becoming of the world society as an evolution held together from above. By the intervention of the infinite into the here and now, international society participates in a world of the spirit. This universal *Geist* is a world which is beyond all human societies. This is the world of all—that is, the universe of totality. Within this comprehensive culture, every particular society forms a reality for itself. The spirit also enables humanity to see itself as a self-transcending, self-judging whole as it reveals to consciousness the unfinished, unsocial, and impermanent nature of the existing international society.[34]

Allott's conception transposes the spiritual force which for Hegel constituted the ultimate source of the autonomous state into the cultural foundations of the global structure-system. Allott also incorporates Rousseau's idea of a *volonté général,* making it the supersocialization of the society of societies. As with Rousseau's theory, the general will is not a majority will. It is rather a separate transcendental power which Humanity, by forming a single sovereignty, places over itself. Where once the authority of the people was considered to have been transferred from the people to the state, it now returns, in absolute form, to all the peoples of the world. Ideal logic thus absorbs the Society of States into the Society of Societies.

But the will of all is not to be expressed by all. As a general intention, collective order is legitimately enforced by any who, from a

33. Id., pt. 2, chap. 9; pt. 3 chaps. 14.4; 16.5.
34. Id., pt. 3, chap. 18.2 "Society-as-culture . . . is a society participating in a world of the spirit whose nature is always to be a world beyond society . . . Society-as spirit secretes itself into every pore and fibre of society as process."

position of power, grasp its meaning and who are willing to tell the people what they ought to will. As sociology joins forces with Pure Legal Theory, the function of the "wise legislator," first contemplated by Rousseau, is now fulfilled by international law. The world is to be legally related and unified by a juridical process which draws its authority from ideal public values rather than from the political institutions of a worldwide government.[35]

The theoretical social sovereignty of the world society proposed by Allott is a modern secular counterpart to medieval attempts to unify the world on the basis of a common faith. While admirable in its intention, it is essentially flawed. Social idealism tries to harmonize the world community without reference to the political principles that are indispensable to a sound understanding of the possibilities of universal governance. Allott's central mistake is that he misconceives the nature of ultimate temporal authority.

Sovereignty is a power which is transcendentally supreme and is exercised, from above, without accountability. By its nature it is a quality essentially divine. Strictly speaking, sovereignty cannot be attributed to any earthly power. Neither the state, nor society, is sovereign. As for the body politic: it is not sovereign, but it does have a right to full autonomy. People who have formed the will to live together are entitled to govern themselves. They have a relatively supreme power to determine the manner by which they wish to be ruled. Once established, organs of government participate in the political authority of a people through a fundamental law which designates their competencies and holds them accountable. The people, having exercised their authority, come under the law.[36]

35. In Rousseau's thought the wise legislator holds no office of government. He rules by his genius and gives institutions to the nation. He is also one who "ought to feel himself capable, as it were, of changing human nature; of transforming every individual, who in himself is a complete and independent whole into a greater whole." Gough, *The Social Contract,* chap. 8. In constitutional theory, some theorists would attribute the wise legislator function to the judiciary. See, for example, the ideal of a Herculean Judge proposed by Ronald Dworkin, which I discuss in *Descent into Subjectivity,* chap. 2.

36. Jacques Maritain, *Man and the State,* chap. 5. Compare R. R. Palmer, "The People as Constituent Power," in J. R. Howe, Jr., ed., *The Role of Ideology in the American*

The state is the topmost part of a political society that has conferred a practical "sovereignty" upon the government it has created. State sovereignty is both internal and external. Through the enactment, application, and enforcement of law a political community governs all within its jurisdiction. By this means it assures order and well-being within its own borders. The authoritative power of government is not just a matter of general obedience. At appropriate points the good of organized existence requires the submission of the private interest to the public interest and of private decision to public decision. Moreover, to assure the rights of the individual, the internal order must also effectively provide for due process of law and the equal protection of the laws.[37]

Externally, every state is sovereign. Some see this as a illegitimate extension of a justifiable internal authority. However, at this stage of history states are members of a society of states; they are not parts of a larger political society. For that reason, every state is entitled to relatively supreme independence with respect to all other states within the international community. Every state, as a representative of a distinct body politic, has a right to maintain its separate existence and pursue its own well-being. The range of its discretion in matters of foreign policy is subject to customary international law and treaties and other agreements to which the state has given express consent. It is also morally bound by general principles of order, coordination, and reciprocal justice. But because of its independence, any state can rightfully assert the defense of its vital interests against all others. The right exists

Revolution (New York: Holt, Rinehart & Winston, 1950). On the general need to move away from sociology to political thought see Margaret Canovan, *The Political Thought of Hannah Arendt* (New York and London: Harcourt Brace Jovanovich, 1974). Arendt tried to "redirect our attention away from society, that self-moving cosmos of which we are presumed to be parts, to Politics, that is, to the public actions and interactions of particular individual men, and the events they bring about . . . the defense of politics against sociologism is a defense of human freedom and dignity against determinism and abject submission to fate." Id., chap. 1.

37. Id. See also Mortimer J. Adler, *How to Think about War and Peace* (New York: Fordham University Press, 1996), chap. 8. On the need for both subordination and the protection of individual rights see Joseph Tussman, *Obligation and the Body Politic* (New York: Oxford University Press, 1960).

even if a state, under particular circumstances, may be forced to submit its will to some form of *de facto* coercion. This insubmissiveness of states is the ultimate cause of international anarchy. Each state, at decisive moments, acts in relation to other states as individuals would act among themselves if they were not subject to the power and authority of government.[38]

States interact, but they do not live together under a government that regulates their interaction. States generally abide by customary and conventional rules which they create or recognize; however, in matters of importance, each acts as its own judge in applying the law. Each—acting either alone or in concert with allies—will use its own might to enforce its judgment or to resist what it considers to be an unjust imposition. No external authority can determine for a state what are its vital interests and, short of overt aggression, each state can use whatever means are at its disposal to obtain or preserve what it thinks is necessary to fulfill its right to exist. The situation is essentially unstable because the function of judgment and law application has not been taken away from states and conferred upon judges whose decisions would be uniformly enforced.[39]

The inability of the United Nations to resolve political disputes which engage the vital interests of states is a further indication of the fact that the world is not a political society. The Charter of the United Nations obliges member states to peacefully settle their international disputes but it confers upon them the right to decide upon the means of settlement. Where the continuation of such a dispute might endanger international peace and security, the Security Council is empowered under Chapter Six of the Charter to act as an organ of collective conciliation. But the conflicted states are not required to collaborate with the Council. Because the international community has not taken serious controversies out of the hands of the parties, interminable conflicts such as those in the Middle East, India, and Korea, remain un-

38. Maritain, *Man and the State,* chap. 2. 5. Compare Martin Wight, *Power Politics,* ed. Hedley Bull and Carsten Holbraad (New York: Holmes & Meier, 1978).

39. Adler, *How to Think about War and Peace,* chap. 7.

resolved and susceptible to violent outburst. There is some measure of peacekeeping but there is no decisive peacemaking authority either in the UN, or in the world community as a whole.[40]

A greater willingness on the part of powerful states to submit their legal controversies to the World Court might decrease the degree of unresolved conflict. It is also possible that states which are members of the United Nations Security Council will, in the future, more vigorously exercise the pacific authority which the Charter has conferred upon them. Other agencies of the United Nations, as well as leading states, will continue to play a peacemaking role in situations where they have an influence. But it is not possible for all important legal and political disputes among states to be peacefully resolved so long as the world is not constituted as a political society. Such is the logic of sovereignty. As long as the external sovereignty of states persists the world community cannot develop an internal sovereignty of its own comparable to that which, within states, assures the nonviolent resolution of serious conflict between all subject to its jurisdiction.

The society of states is a primitive legal community. It has legal rules, but there is no higher authority to enforce the rules or to prevent states from taking the law into their own hands in times of crisis.

40. Id. The optional clause under Article 36 of the Statute of the International Court of Justice is best understood as a substitute for the lack of compulsory jurisdiction over legal disputes between states, a jurisdiction which would automatically apply if states were members of an organized political society. In spite of this deficiency, that Court's docket has increased significantly in recent years. See generally Shigeru Oda, "The International Court of Justice from the Bench," 244 *Recueil des Cours* (Collected Courses of the Hague Academy of International Law), vol. 7 (1993).

It has been suggested that member states of the UN should accept the general jurisdiction of the Court without exceptions, or, when this is not possible, to provide lists of the matters which they would be willing to submit to the Court. Boutros Boutros-Ghali, *An Agenda,* chap. 5, sec. 112. However, the strict obligation to resolve their differences nonviolently, as provided in Article 33 of the UN Charter, leaves the member states with complete freedom to choose the means of settlement. See Cassese, *International Law in a Divided World,* chap. 8.

On nonjudicial settlement, see my "The Conciliatory Responsibilities of the United Nations Security Council," 35 *German Yearbook of International Law* 190–204. For the distinction between political and legal disputes see Charles de Visscher, *Theory and Reality in Public International Law;* Milton Katz, *The Relevance of International Adjudication* (1968).

Potentials for armed conflict exist because the society of states is an international state of nature. However, it would be a mistake to limit the analysis of international anarchy to questions of interstate, or even intrastate, violence. Historically, such a concentration has tended to limit the problematic of world order to matters of collective security. Thinking of peace only as the absence of war deflects attention away from other aspects of the pervasive disorder which exists in a world which is not yet a political society.

Consider the global economy. The international market extends across the entire surface of the planet and even intrudes into oceanic and outer space. Fueled by the dynamics of production, exchange, and consumption, worldwide capitalism has enhanced the material conditions of much of the world's population. The development has, however, been accompanied by inequities and exploitation which go uncorrected. And, by its own momentum, the process breeds unresolved conflict. Trade and finance have become the paramount mode of mode of interaction among the nations of the earth and access to world markets has replaced the acquisition of territory as a primary objective of international policy. As competition accelerates, confrontations between states intensify. The total amount of disorder increases in proportion to the dynamic expansion of the world economy.[41]

The principal actors in the international economy are powerful multinational corporations which are not subject to effective international control and are only sporadically regulated by the legal systems of the various states within which they do business. Even though their private purposes have universal consequences, they are not accountable to any general human authority. States and peoples can be engulfed by ubiquitous economic forces, as market calamities in one part of the world have potentially disastrous effects within others.

The mobility of the factors of production and exchange makes terri-

41. Philip Allott, *Eunomia,* pt. 3, chap. 17. See also Julius Stone, *Visions of World Order* (Baltimore: Johns Hopkins University Press, 1984), chaps. 10–12, and Susan Strange, *The Retreat of the State: The Diffusion of Power in the World Economy* (Cambridge: Cambridge University Press, 1996).

torial jurisdiction problematic. Labor-management relations within states, which have traditionally been the source of national prosperity, begin to unravel as the material integration of the world opens up transnational commercial opportunities. The world society is itself paralyzed by this uncontrolled development. As private interest prevails over public good, material well-being occurs unevenly throughout the world. Viewed comprehensively, the whole process offends fundamental principles of distributive justice which the world community is itself powerless to enforce.[42]

The expansion of the international economy has also exacerbated the political tensions among nation-states. At one time quarrels were often influenced by ideological differences between states committed to laissez-faire capitalism and those following a militant socialism. As states began to assert a comprehensive jurisdiction over their natural resources, their legal policies often conflicted with the expectations of foreign investors whose interests reflected absolutist conceptions of private property.[43] But the reduction of ideological warfare in world politics has not diminished the wider economic antagonisms between separate political societies. Investment disputes have become more manageable, but the deeper causes of discord persist. Even among relatively friendly nations, serious tensions arise whenever states design their foreign economic policies to sustain the prosperity of their own peoples and disregard the well-being of those who are not their citizens. Jurisdiction is then extended beyond the limits which reason would impose. The potential for interstate confrontation increases exponentially as major states use economic weapons in order to advance what they consider to be desirable political objectives.[44]

Although the conscience of the world community has condemned economic coercion, moral principle is often trumped by national policy. Embargoes, boycotts, dumping, and trade wars poison the stream

42. *Eunomia*, pt. 3, chap. 18.36–43.
43. See Richard B. Lillich, ed., *The Valuation of Nationalized Property in International Law*, vol. 3 (Charlottesville: University of Virginia Press, 1975).
44. On the criteria for resolving jurisdictional conflicts, see Restatement (Third) Foreign Relations Law of the United States, secs. 401, 403.

of international commerce with the toxins of sanction and retaliation. While more opaque than overt violence, these actions and reactions do substantial harm to the general good of the world community. Hostilities based upon material interests not only obstruct the free flow of goods and services; they also impede the development of those sentiments of solidarity among diverse peoples which would be the normal result of just and peaceful commercial relations.

Allott contends that private as well as public actors should be made legal subjects of public international law so that significant transnational activities can be effectively regulated in the social interest of the world society. However, although corporations do have some legal standing under public international law, it is unrealistic to expect that their activities will be generally subject to the normative prescriptions of a legal regime designed to regulate the relations between states. Distinctions between public and private law are an integral part of any legal culture and these divisions are already in place in the global community. Like conflicts of law in domestic legal systems, private international law is the primary means of reconciling diverse private interests with respect to actions which have transnational consequences. This dichotomy will persist, to some degree, into the foreseeable future.[45]

Allott also suggests that global economic discord could become subject to world public order through the far-reaching authority of multilateral treaties. While such a development has promise, it cannot reach the deeper causes of conflict. Within the framework of its basic agreements the European Community has reached a high degree of economic integration and the laws of the community have a direct effect within the member states. But this is not a plausible model for order within the nation-state system as a whole. Common historical tragedies have left the peoples of Europe with a profound desire for reconciliation and these experiences, coupled with compatible cultural traditions, give the foundational treaties of the European Community

---

45. ". . . There is as much need for legal, as well as social, accountability for the non-state actors as for states and international organizations." *Eunomia,* pt. 3., chap. 17.80.

a quasi-constitutional status which is not universalizable. In addition, uncertainties about further political development of the community reveal the reluctance of the member states to fully relinquish the traditional prerogatives of external sovereignty.[46]

Allott also points to the Convention on the Law of the Sea as a model of economic legislation by multilateral treaty. That agreement includes provisions for regulating the harvesting of oceanic resources, but it does so without regard for principles of distributive justice. These principles should govern any substantial wealth allocation in a well-ordered society. The treaty generally confirms the accidents of geography. It gives to coastal states resource preferences which cannot be justified by wider criteria of need or industry. Furthermore, while important standards of the public interest are incorporated into the treaty, there are no effective instruments of enforcement. And there is no good reason to anticipate in advance that when serious conflicts arise the parties will have recourse to the extensive dispute-settlement provisions of the Convention.[47]

The actual legal effect of any multilateral treaty cannot be determined until the ratification process, reservations, understandings, and subsequent behavior of the parties are fully taken into account. The disparities between legal text and political realities can quickly discount the apparent value of the published agreement. There is also an essential, inherent weakness in all treaties among sovereign nations:

46. See generally Tony Judt, *A Grand Illusion? An Essay on Europe* (New York: Hill & Wang, 1996); John Pinder, *European Community* (New York: Oxford University Press, 1991); Rolf Dahrendorf, *Reflections on the Revolution in Europe.*

47. For an optimistic assessment, see Jonathan Charney, "The Implications of Expanding International Dispute Settlement Systems: The 1982 Convention on the Law of the Sea," 90 *American Journal of International Law* 69–75 (1996). See also Philip Allott, "Mare Nostrum: A New Law of the Sea," 86 *American Journal of International Law* 764–87 (1992).

The dispute-settlement provisions of the World Trade Organization are an improvement over prior practices because domestic laws alleged to be contrary to international economic agreements can be challenged before an international body. However, a member state is not obliged to comply with an adverse ruling. It can make restitution or simply allow itself to suffer an authorized retaliation against its own exports to restore the previous balance. See *Editorial Comment,* 90 *American Journal of International Law* 416–18 (1996).

none are enforceable by the laws of a government which is superior to the parties to these agreements. This deficiency can be moderated by appeals to the principle of good faith, but the basic infirmity is irremediable.[48]

There is a further consideration. Important conflicts have a complexity which makes them impervious to conventional legal regulation. At the heart of these disputes there is a divergence of values which makes them refractory to any process which assumes the existence of shared agreement.

The goals of the parties involved in the international economic process are heterogeneous. Policies of industrial development conflict with values of environmental protection; free trade is resisted by the needs of a domestic economy; the financial interests of the rich are incompatible with the need of the poor—especially for debt relief. On a more fundamental level, the formal equality of states is contradicted by vast material inequities. To make matters worse, the established international institutions which enforce trade and monetary policies are organized to protect the economic interests of the states which hold the superior power.[49]

There are those who believe that these endemic difficulties, which affect the distributions of economic, military, and political power, will be alleviated by the growth of an international civil society. Committed private groups acting in the public interest bring a subtle range of values to bear upon the deliberations of existing world institutions and this influence can relieve the existing tensions. The growing prestige

48. "States are most unlikely to find that they have been robbed unawares of their sovereign virtue by the disarming blandishments of draftsmen of lawmaking conventions." Stone, *Visions of World Order*, at 16. Stone also points out that the operative content of any treaty can only be determined after practice before and after the agreement, and all reservations, have been taken into account. For a record of reservations see *Multilateral Treaties Deposited with the Secretary-General*, U. N. Doc. St/Leg/ Ser. E/(1994). Adler characterizes international agreements as being like private contracts without public remedies in *How to Think about War and Peace*, chap. 12.5.

49. On the essentially divergent nature of important moral, social, and legal conflicts see E. F. Schumaker, *A Guide for the Perplexed*, and other authorities cited at note 21, supra.

of nongovernmental organizations within the United Nations, and at world conferences sponsored by the UN, is a further manifestation of this activity. The emergence of an active international civil society encourages the hope that the basic quarrels within the global village will eventually be resolved in a way that transcends the differences which now divide the peoples of the world. But civil and political authority are distinguishable. The UN Charter formally recognizes the value of collaboration with NGOs, but the UN is itself ultimately responsible for promoting, within the limits of its powers, stable solutions to the daunting problems of economic and social development which now fragment the international community.[50]

There is a sense in which we must work with what we have. As has been demonstrated, the principles which legitimize the external sovereignty of states are essential impediments to the securing of a worldwide order of justice and peace. However, it would be irresponsible to abandon the traditional framework of world order and simply contemplate, or insist upon, ideal alternatives. The obligation to strive for the good with what one has been given is indispensable to the experience of being human, and this basic truth applies to all forms of social, as well as personal, existence.

There are practical moral implications. In their bilateral, multilateral, and institutional relations, states must give meaning and substance to the formal policies of friendly relations. Each state has an obligation to promote the progress of all as well as to secure its own prosperity.

50. Article 71 of the Charter of the United Nations provides that the "[E]conomic and Social Council may make suitable arrangements for consultation with nongovernmental organizations which are concerned with matters within its competence . . ." The number of international nongovernmental organizations has risen from approximately 1,300 in 1960 to over 36,000. As private groups acting for public purposes outside the state, their future importance is noted by Boutros Boutros-Ghali in chapter 5 of *An Agenda for Democratization.* See also Susan Strange, *The Retreat of the State.* For a reflection upon the general value of private associational activity see Alejandro Llano, *The New Sensibility,* trans. Alban d'Entremont (Pamplona: University of Navarra, 1991), and Francis Fukuyama, *The End of History and the Last Man* (New York: The Free Press, 1992), chap. 30.

At the same time, all whose vocations draw them to international affairs are bound to realize, through these same experiences, the outer limits of their goodwill. At some point, universal generosity comes into irresolvable tension with particular responsibility. In any world of action, a mature person eventually comes to understand the bounds, as well as the value, of his or her constructive pursuits. What is true for individuals is also true for nations. When the outer reaches of positive international action are realized, we shall be in a better position to think of how the world can be delivered from its international state of nature and become, in freedom, a fully formed political society.

III

By the close of the Middle Ages the supreme political authority of the Holy Roman Emperor was being effectively challenged by the rulers of separate, autonomous communities. As these new powers gradually centralized their control over their subjects, they also began to develop an international society which was based, in principle, upon the sovereign independence and equality of its members. Following the Westphalian settlement of the seventeenth century, the international association which had originated in Europe began to be extended into a global society of states. The future of that worldwide system has now become problematic.

Social, economic, and technological developments have drawn the innumerable interdependencies of the world into a novel form of universal integration which lacks any discernible form of central direction. Novel forces of planetary unification are threatening to make the nation-state an anachronism. As humanity is being irresistibly drawn together it hovers precariously between an obsolete form of universal association and a nascent world civilization. If this situation is not to lead to unmanageable chaos the whole must be sustained by reasonable forms of interim order which will be acceptable to all.[51]

51. Jean-Marie Guehenno, *The End of the Nation-State,* trans. Victoria Elliott (Minneapolis: The University of Minnesota Press, 1995). See also Richard Rosecrance, "The Rise of the Virtual State," *Foreign Affairs,* July/Aug. 1996, 45–61. These socioeconomic

The authority of international law must be strengthened. Rules of customary international law, based upon practices widely considered to be obligatory, need to be continuously developed. Multilateral and bilateral agreements based upon shared understanding and, as far as possible, upon precise expression, will help to stabilize what would otherwise be an anarchic social evolution. Jurists must further refine the distinctions between the legitimate and illegal uses of force. They must continue articulating principles of attribution with respect to both individual and state responsibility. Greater use of the World Court by all states, as well as an increase in arbitration and other modes of peaceful settlement, will be of great value. And within all of these processes there will be room for cautious innovations which help the system accommodate the forces of change. At the same time, it will be necessary to recognize the imperfections of these elements of a legal conception of world order. As we have already noted, the international legal process cannot reach the deeper sources of discord which pervade the planetary state of nature. Under these conditions, the maxim that equity never does a vain thing takes on a special relevance.

As we move towards the future, jurists must prudently decide what international legal projects are really worth undertaking by making a realistic appraisal of potential effectiveness. Continuing lawmaking can be usefully directed towards the regulation of the prosaic reciprocities which are an inherent part of the interaction between sovereign political communities. Matters such as the adjustment of overlapping jurisdiction, cooperation in the administration of criminal justice, and the promotion of the mutual recognition of judgments illustrate the types of problems which can reasonably be subject to legal regulation in a sanctionless world.

The degree of constructive lawmaking cannot be determined in advance; however, it would be unwise to exaggerate the potential scope of international jurisprudence. The tradition of the rule of law in inter-

---

developments were anticipated by Hannah Arendt in her seminal work *The Human Condition* (Chicago: University of Chicago Press, 1958) and by Karl Jaspers in *Man in the Modern Age* (London: Routledge & Kegan Paul Ltd., 1933).

national relations is an indispensable part of any rational conception of universal order. However, the possibilities must be kept in perspective. It should not be imagined that the law, on its own authority, can be developed into a virtual legislative competence that can resolve the most complex problems of corrective or distributive justice which arise in the normal course of international existence. Lawyers who insist that sovereign states are subject to law are prone to forget that law is dependent for its effectiveness upon the existence of government.[52]

It would be equally injudicious to expect a legitimate lawmaking competence to naturally evolve out of existing multilateral venues such as the General Assembly of the United Nations. The quasi-legislative process of the Assembly has some of the same features of general lawmaking as are found in domestic legal systems. Whenever rules and policies are clearly declared by large numbers of state representatives to the General Assembly, their actions do have juridical consequences. Resolutions and declarations of international bodies can accurately reflect and clarify existing law; in some circumstances, they can create a normative framework for future lawmaking. However, there is a crucial difference between the international and national forms of general, explicit lawmaking. In the General Assembly each state has a vote regardless of its population or status. Within states, legislative bodies are organized upon the basis of representative criteria, which make more reasonable distributions of power and authority among those who are ultimately expected to obey. These distinctions affect both the legitimacy of, and expectations of compliance with, any form of enacted legislation.[53]

52. For an example of inordinate expectations with respect to the international legal process see Jonathan I. Charney, "Universal International Law," 87 *American Journal of International Law* 529–51 (1993). Compare Martti Koskenniemi, *From Apology to Utopia* (1989).

53. On the legal significance of Resolutions of the United Nations General Assembly see Rosalyn Higgins, *International Law and How We Use It.* See also Mohammed Bedjaoui, *International Law: Achievements and Prospects* (Dordrecht: Martinus Nijhoff, 1991); Cassese, *International Law in a Divided World,* sec. 107. On the practical question of whether a policy declared by a majority is consonant with geopolitical realities, see Stanley Hoffman, *Duties beyond Borders: On the Limits and Possibilities of Ethical International Policy* (Syracuse, N.Y.: Syracuse University Press, 1981).

Difficulties of substance must also be taken into account in considering the prospects for the authoritative growth of global law. The universal problems of the world community, such as security, development, and environmental integrity, engage divergent conceptions of value and purpose among the various states whose interests would be affected by any attempted resolution of these issues through a quasi-legislative process. The antinomies which lie at the heart of such conflicts cannot be reconciled by the statement of abstract principles, no matter how much bargaining precedes the final articulation of a textual declaration. Meaningful adjustment of such difficult questions can only occur within representative political institutions which are authorized to harmonize divergent interests through a process of give and take, ultimately leading to binding legislation.

An unorganized society might last for a long time without having legislative institutions. But in order to survive, it must have some form of effective executive authority. During the extended pre-political phase of international experience which we must contemplate, it will be necessary to improve the institutional expression of common action. The most pressing problems of peace, security, and humanitarian assistance cannot be managed by isolated discretion. They require swift and coordinated solutions. And those who act on behalf of the decentralized world community must have some effective authority within that community.

In these matters of international concern there are difficult balances to be struck between power and authority. In world politics a small number of states posses superior military, economic, or social power, and these realities are not properly reflected in the executive competencies of international organization. The United Nations Charter gave the five victorious states of the Second World War a position of permanent membership in the Security Council and a veto over its substantive decisions. These competencies reflect the discrepancy between historical memory and political reality. Pressures for reform are mounting. If the membership on the Security Council was changed so that the present leading powers were properly represented, the situation would be improved, even though the Security Council would still lack the degree of universality a worldwide organization should possess. It would still be necessary to determine the degree to which a realigned Security Council can legitimately exercise a global executive authority, especially since it probably would continue to be based upon representative criteria that are more oligarchic than democratic.[54]

Compliance with the executive orders of the Security Council can reasonably be expected even if the decisions it takes on behalf of the whole United Nations also benefit those who have made the decisions. Such judgments can create reasons for common action which exclude alternatives that states which are not members of the Council might rationally have preferred. Recognition of these obligations will promote a greater unity of purpose within the UN as well as among the member states. But the tentative nature of such arrangements must not be ignored. So long as controlling executive authority of the world community is dominated by a minority of states, coordination of the actions of all in matters of importance will be increasingly difficult to sustain. In the United Nations—and in other international organizations where decisive authority is based upon unequal distributions of power—it will become increasingly evident that such arrangements are incompatible with the common good of the world community as a whole.[55]

While much can be done to improve existing global institutions and procedures, the imperfections of structure and objectives will endure. Progress toward greater solidarity, order, and justice will remain the responsibility of those who formulate and execute the foreign policies of independent states. Within international politics, the representatives of states need to move toward a greater degree of friendship with all the peoples of the world. Self-centered policies which are oblivious to obligations beyond borders will have to be replaced by more construc-

54. The emphasis on the importance of international executive authority should be compared with the belief that the judiciary is the only indispensable organ of international order. See, e.g., Kelsen, *Peace through Law.* See also Adler, *How to Think about War and Peace,* chap. 10.

55. Compare John Finnis, *Natural Law and Natural Rights,* chaps. 6.3–4; 9.

tive forms of positive collaboration and deeper respect for the common humanity. These prospects will, however, be tempered by the conflicting obligations of those who hold specific positions within the geopolitical milieu.

At the level of international action there is an ethical ambivalence which inevitably hampers all who struggle, in good faith, to reconcile their primary allegiances with more inclusive global responsibilities. The statesman and the diplomat must live with the disproportion between the ideal and the real. Unlike the prophet or the philosopher, those who exercise leadership in world affairs have their vocations forged in the furnace of contingency. And, to be effective, they must become masters of complexity. They hope to adjust conflicting claims by negotiation rather than by unconditional demand; yet their freedom of action is circumscribed by imperious domestic pressures. All who serve in foreign affairs know that they act in a competitive environment which has ambiguous and elastic purposes. There is cooperation; there is also deceit. In this "war-like peace" they live a life of moral ambiguity, torn between longings for peace and the necessities of force.[56]

The moral dilemmas of the conscientious diplomat dramatically illustrate the limitations of the existing international system. The inherent quandaries verify for men and women of action what others have known as a matter of thought: that a humanistically satisfying measure of peace, justice, and sustainable development can not be achieved throughout the world by the foreign policies of sovereign states. An essential imperfection runs through the entire arrangement, a deformity which has personal as well as structural implications. Whenever power is fragmented into separate autonomous units, decisive allegiance is ultimately to the parts rather than the whole. The logic of global politics subordinates personal virtue to the demands of the competition just as it makes the social structure increasingly anarchic.

56. Henry Kissinger, *A World Restored* (Gloucester, Mass.: Peter Smith, 1973), chap. 10; Raymond Aron, *Peace and War, A Theory of International Relations*, pt. 4. The moral responsibilities of diplomats are detailed in pt. 3 of Pope John XXIII's 1963 encyclical *Pacem in Terris* (Peace on Earth).

The impasse in the development of world society raises the question of what, if anything, is be done. Some, fascinated by the unifying effects of technology, counsel passivity. They see the archaic nation-state system being replaced by a new global empire which is sociological, rather than political, in nature. A new, indefinite, nonhierarchical *Monarchia* seems to be spreading throughout the planet. Lacking any discernible form of central direction, the ubiquitous power of the totality unifies the innumerable interdependencies of the world into a vast information network. Within that cybernetic community, an ensemble of bureaucratic institutions tranquilize pliable masses of people and imposes a system of social pacification upon a world having no significant aspirations beyond the primitive struggle to survive. The new order imitates the science of meteorology: perfectly rational at its core; unpredictable at the margins. Whatever disruptions occur are healed by its self-correcting mechanism.[57]

Functional ordering lacks the grandeur of Dante's vision. An insidious socioeconomic imperialism does not look to the heavens for inspiration, nor does it seek its justification in transcendental values. And, notably, it does not invoke the unwilled will of a universal sovereignty to legitimize its ascendancy. The peoples of the world are treated as an amorphous mass, nothing more than interchangeable parts of a huge impersonal operation. Without their knowledge or consent, they are being governed by the imperceptible force of a vast transnational social system.

Such a dismal comprehension marks the degree to which the social sciences have replaced political thought in the field of international studies. One response is the attempt to awaken aspirations for universal reform at a grassroots level with an activism which places pressure upon the existing state system. However, while increasing an awareness of universal bondage, such efforts can also destabilize an already precarious order of global politics.[58]

---

57. Guehenno, *The End of the Nation-State.*

58. The main source of international activism has been the World Order Models Project (WOMP) of Professor Richard Falk and his associates at Princeton University.

Preoccupation with the material forces of unification can obscure comprehension of those substantial political changes that are a matter of immediate experience. In the contemporary world, the prospects for communal self-governance have been severely weakened by civil strife as well as by other influences, but the natural human inclination toward the formation of political societies has not been extinguished. The constitutional transformation of South Africa is a paramount example of a people forming a will to live together as a body politic in spite of profound racial differences and the memories of past injustices. In other volatile communities the right of peoples to freely determine their own political destiny is rising out of the ashes of war. A broader measure of the resurgence of the political can be seen in the efforts being made by the United Nations to build viable participatory communities in societies whose governing institutions have collapsed. The fact that there have been failures as well as successes in these endeavors does not detract from the essential soundness of what is being attempted. As we shall see, these experiences have considerable relevance to the prospects for the eventual establishment of a world political society.

Recognition and affirmation of the right of peoples to govern themselves within the communities they inhabit is of profound importance to the historical development of the human race. For centuries, the generation of political communities has been more by way of conquest than by consent, and the legitimacy of controlling power has been

---

The seminal work is Falk's "A New Paradigm for World Order Studies: Prospects and Proposals," 84 *Yale Law Journal* 969 (1975). A more recent modified expression is Professor Falk's *On Humane Governance: Toward a New Global Politics* (University Park: The Pennsylvania State University Press, 1995). See also R. Kothari, *Footsteps into the Future* (New York: The Free Press, 1975), and Saul H. Mendlovitz, ed., *On the Creation of a Just World Order* (New York: The Free Press, 1975). For a basic criticism see Hedley Bull, *The Anarchical Society*, chaps. 11–12. Maritain also observes that ". . . It would not be good, either for cause of the idea or for the cause of peace, to use the idea of World Government as a weapon against the limited and precarious international agencies which for the time being are the only existing practical means at the disposal of men to protract the truce among nations. . ." *Man and the State*, 201.

determined by criteria of *de facto* submission. But the common conscience of humanity now insists that governments must be established
by the deliberate choice of peoples to become subject to authority.[59]

This process should be distinguished from the growth of an international civil society. The mobility of populations in the modern world
and the shifting of sentiments of identity and community have con-
tributed to a denigration of the value of territorial sovereignty. New
polarities are challenging established boundaries. Intrastate pressures
for increased local autonomy are matched by the commitment of ded-
icated individuals to the formation of an international civil society
whose values and aspirations are cosmopolitan in the their range and
cannot be confined by established boundaries or existing allegiances.[60]

There are two difficulties with the use of this paradigm as a standard
of the future. First, insistence upon "local" identities is too often made
in the name of narrow ethnic or tribal sameness; exclusive nationalisms
can lead to idolatry, absolutism, and intolerance. A right to be a nation
does not entail an entitlement to complete independence. As for the
other extreme, the growth of a universal civil society, while a good in
itself, is not a substitute for the development of the discrete political
experiences which are an indispensable prerequisite to the possible
creation of a world political community.

A civil society is not the same as a body politic. Political unity is
marked by the explicit determination of a multitude to live together,
by common agreement, in the orderly pursuit of public ends. A universal body politic would be a manifestation of the right of the peoples
of the world to govern themselves in some appropriate form of common life. But sovereignty is a matter of experience as well as of principle.
Within their own particular state-societies, the many must first learn the
concrete value of freedom and democracy. Without that experience,
they will not be capable of any higher form of political existence.[61]

---

59. Maritain, *Man and the State,* chap. 7, pt. 4.

60. Falk, *On Humane Governance,* 100.

61. Adler, *How to Think about War and Peace,* chap. 5. Compare Suarez, *De Legibus,* 3,
chap. 2.

The complex good of universal human association will not arise out of an immanent anthropological evolution. It will be a matter of history. Human history is not made by inexorable biological laws, nor is it compelled by fate or fortune. History is the result of choices made by those who participate in a mode of being proper to acts of reason and will. The goods they seek are those of civilization both at home and abroad. The pursuit of those goods, which also constitute the political maturation of humanity, should be guided by moral principles which affirm a common human nature and can inspire the formation of pluralistic political communities.[62]

The challenge is both one of growth and of integration. Many modern states embrace heterogeneous populations which coexist within defined borders. The humanistic call is to make these diverse groupings more viable political societies. They must become communities which are free from repression and respectful of the rights of all. Internal pluralism, however, must be reconciled with broader commonalities that permit the larger society to form a public identity of its own and bring tranquillity and justice to all. Complex political communities have to be unified, in freedom, on the basis of shared ideals and within a common political culture which transcends, but does not eliminate, more discrete forms of cultural identity.[63]

---

62. See Josef Pieper, *Hope and History.*

63. On the situation in the United States see Arthur M. Schlesinger Jr., *The Disuniting of America* (New York: W. W. Norton & Co., 1992). While it has already been pointed out that every nation is not entitled to become a state, it is equally true that every state need not be composed of a single nation. According to Lord Acton, the coexistence of several nations within one state is more conducive to liberty and civilization. See William Ebenstein, *Modern Political Thought: The Great Issues,* 2nd ed. (New York: Holt, Rinehart & Winston, 1960), pt. 5. Most of the nearly 200 nation-states in the world consist of more than one ethnic group, and most of these experiments in multiplicity have been successful. "Diversity need not become a cause for division. A challenge to governance is to make it a source of enrichment." *Our Global Neighborhood: The Report of the Commission on Global Governance* (Oxford: Oxford University Press, 1996), 75.

As for the size of political communities, Aristotle believed that constitutional government was not possible within a large territory. *Politics,* 7.4.1326a35–40. Grotius, arguing against Dante, took a position similar to Aristotle. *De Jure Belli ac Pacis,* bk. 2, chaps. 12, 22. These concerns are moderated by technological developments which unify communication and transportation and also by the experience of larger modern democracies

Independent political development must also be guided by reason rather than by ideology. The collapse of Soviet Communism has led to the widespread assumption that the renewal of the nation-state system must be exclusively directed toward the realization of individualist democracy and economic free enterprise. This form of liberal internationalism expects that the spread of liberty and equality, coupled with an expansive material prosperity, will inexorably lead to the homogenization of the whole of humanity. These hopes of immanent and inevitable development are not sufficiently attentive to the cultural differences which constitute the enduring heritage of humankind.

Liberal democracy and market economics express the genius of Western culture, and these values have worldwide significance. But what is particular is never fully universal. As we have already indicated, the flourishing of human nature is expressed in difference and contrast. Cultural diversity reveals the richness of human experience, and any balanced conception of the political future must be open to legitimate divergences in conceptions of the nature and purposes of social life.[64]

A deepening understanding of other traditions has led many in the West to an awareness of the negative aspects of Occidental culture, with its exaggeration of the value of science and technology, and the depressing materialism to which it leads. It is more difficult, however, to comprehend the limitations of the political vision of the West because it is in itself so compelling.

The core of personal rights has become part of a contemporary *jus gentium,* and most societies recognize the need for the public recognition of individual status and equal dignity under the law. But within many societies shared traditions are as important to personal identity

including that of the countries of North America. For a defense of the expansiveness of political societies see Adler, *How to Think about War and Peace,* chap. 17. See also Kenichi Ohmae, "The Rise of the Regional State," 72 *Foreign Affairs* 78 (1993).

64. For a study of the directional history of international relations see Francis Fukuyama, *The End of History and the Last Man,* chaps. 22–25. For a study of the adverse effects of liberal democracy see Theodore H. Von Laue, "From Fukuyama to Reality: A Critical Essay," in Burns, ed., *After History? Francis Fukuyama and His Critics.* See also Arnold Toynbee, *Civilization on Trial* (Oxford: Oxford University Press, 1948), chap. 5.

as is a separate sense of well-being. Moreover, the operative sense of the value of community, in specific historical circumstances, can qualify the degree of deference which will be given to the values associated with liberal individualism. The political culture of some societies which claim to be democracies give social solidarity and the general interest more weight than they receive in communities which see no value in just institutions other than the affirmation of reciprocal liberty.[65]

These contrasting emphases make it extremely difficult to measure authentic political progress. When engaged in evaluation one must respect differences while resolutely upholding essential values. An international realism which accepts without question the legitimacy of controlling power must be renounced; yet, at the same time, one must not try to impose a cosmopolitan ethic upon an authentic multiplicity. In the process of democratization there must be a patient appeal to standards of reasonableness which pass beyond all forms of ideology.

When reason and amity are ascendant, the prospects for unity in spite of difference between nations are enhanced. A common consensus on the criteria of political legitimacy can arise out of divergent philosophies of human nature. In spite of profound heterogeneity, men and women of good will can practically agree upon the indispensable aspects of democratic freedom. Through dialogue all can come to recognize that legitimate power is based upon the consent of the governed, and that every adult citizen has the right to participate, by ballot or candidacy, in the operation of political institutions. Responsible accounting of those who hold office, the primacy of civilian

65. "Democracy is not an affirmation of the individual at the expense of the community; it is through democracy that individual and collective rights, the rights of persons and the rights of peoples, can be reconciled. Many different balances can be struck between the rights of individuals and the rights of the community within the context of democratic politics. Democratic processes are the most reliable ways to assure that these balances are genuinely reflective of a people's broader culture, which, in every society, must itself serve as the ballast for the healthy functioning of democracy." Boutros Boutros-Ghali, *An Agenda for Democratization,* chap. 2, sec. 23. On the general cultural divergencies see Samuel P. Huntington, *The Clash of Civilizations and the Remaking of World Order* (New York: Simon & Schuster, 1996).

over military rule, the effective protection of human rights, freedom of expression, the rule of law, and the independent administration of justice are also among the values which can become the basis of common political understanding among peoples of distinctive cultures.[66]

Over time, the struggle against despotism may substantially eliminate entrenched authoritarian governments over large areas of the globe. Considerable progress may also be made within a variety of states and regions towards the securing of personal liberty and the advancement of social and economic justice. What will then become of the idea of one world society? For political philosophies which are nourished by a neo-Hegelian immanence, the realization of democracy within the divergent state-societies would virtually constitute the end of history. Most of the basic yearnings of the human heart would be satisfied. The mutual recognition of individual liberty and equality, substantially achieved on the national level, would become the governing standard of relations between autonomous states. Within a world society of states a pacific union would arise, based upon the mutual recognition of independent right. The realization of universal human dignity would eliminate the violent propensities which are essential to any master-slave relationship. There will be no more complex order to pursue because there will not be any further, more encompassing, reality drawing human nature to a pursuit of any additional good of temporal civilization. All political purposes will have been realized because the cosmos will finally be concentrated in particularity. Distinct communities would lead separate, parallel existences. Having no meaningful contact with others beyond their frontiers, individual citizens would confine their national identities to the "soft glow of private life."[67]

This image of immanent but fragmented development promises a general happiness but it is in reality a prediction of social disintegra-

66. ". . . [A]greement on any particular philosophy is not necessary to concerted action on political questions. The fact is that united action can and often does rest on divergent perspectives and philosophies." Jerome Hall, *The Living Law of a Democratic Society* (Indianapolis: Bobbs-Merrill, 1949), 90. Compare Boutros Boutros-Ghali, *An Agenda,* chap. 2, sec. 21. See also Maritain, *Man and the State,* chap. 5.

67. Francis Fukuyama, *The End of History,* 272.

tion. The logic is one in which the masses lapse into automatism and conformity while public affairs are manipulated by a dominant minority. The vision also overlooks the degree of international interdependence which is an integral part of modern social existence. Like individuals, states can feel that they are self-sufficient; as with individuals, the sense of autonomy is largely unrealistic. Furthermore, unlike individuals, states coexist in an international state of nature. The propensities toward violent disorder within such an association are only partially the result of desires for prestige which can be cured by mutual recognition of a common dignity. As we have repeatedly pointed out, the international society will remain destabilized so long as there is no effective way of resolving serious international disputes. But the deeper flaw in this perspective of dispersed fulfillment lies in its assumption that the individual citizen who will be living within these separate but equal states will gradually abandoned all interest in the world beyond his, or her, frontier.

The assumption is that as individuals gain the benefits of liberal democracy, the increase in security and affluence they experience will expunge their interest in public life. But consumerism is not a terminal human condition. Meaningful democratization requires the ongoing participation of great numbers of citizens in all the processes of self-government. The sovereignty of the people is a grave responsibility and its exercise will make considerable demands upon personal, as well as collective, maturity. While civic duties are primarily cultivated within the societies to which the person bears primary allegiance, the congeniality they cultivate eventually reaches out to serve the needs of a common humanity.[68]

As we noted above, a global civil society is already being formed by the actions of private individuals and groups who are assuming public responsibility for an ever-increasing transnational well-being. Rich

68. "Once again we deem it opportune to remind Our children of their duty to take an active part in public life, and to contribute towards the attainment of the common good of the entire human family as well as that of their own political community." Pope John XXIII, *Pacem et Terris,* sec. 146; see also pt. 3. The encyclical's objective of separate allegiance and common commitment to universal order is noted in Harvey Wheeler, *Democracy in a Revolutionary Era* (New York: Frederick A. Praeger, 1968), chap. 8.

and poor are forming a larger "we" as they participate in the international community which they share. The world is becoming a society of individual persons as well as a society of states. However, as we have already stated, a global civil society is not the same as a world political community. Although the magnitude of shared interests, values, and purposes is constantly increasing, the international system as a whole remains in a pre-political condition. No matter how deeply the bonds of a transnational solidarity are extended, states will retain the privileges of external sovereignty which prevent the world at large from forming an internal order of its own. An increase in social action will not fundamentally change the situation. Nor is there a planetary sovereignty already in being which a progressive leadership could justly represent. Yet, as others have realized, states are parts of a wider human society, or society of societies, and this deeper authority is the ultimate source of global sovereignty.

World political institutions cannot be created by the governments of existing states. Even if practicable, such a transition would be unacceptable as a matter of principle. If the states which compose the Society of states were to establish universal instruments of governance, the result would be a world-state imposed, from above, upon existing political societies. States cannot delegate such supreme authority because states are not themselves the final repository of the political authority of the people they represent. They are only the topmost agencies of diverse bodies of political communities.[69]

A world state would be illegitimate. And no power on earth has, or will ever have, a rightful claim to a supreme political authority over the whole of human society. A world government, however, remains a rightful possibility. But it would only come into existence when, and if, the peoples realize that their desires for fulfillment—to live well as well as to survive—cannot be satisfied within the imperfections of the nation-state system. They must then freely develop the will to live together under a fundamental law to which they can give consent.

69. Maritain, *Man and the State*, chaps. 1, 7; Adler, *How to Think about War and Peace*, chap. 8.

The community of nations will have become one body politic, having its own supreme authority. States, as parts rather than wholes, will no longer have that absolute independence and external sovereignty which is the fundamental source of international anarchy.

The constitutional order of the world political society must be established in freedom and not out of fear or compulsion. Having rid the world of despotism from below, the peoples will not tolerate it from above. There will have to be a balanced allocation of national and universal authority. Within strict limits, and with full regard for the principle of subsidiarity, the public authority of the world will posses legislative, executive, and judicial powers which are necessary to any effective government. Law will have its sanctions. There will be hierarchy but no absolute unaccountable power. Both universal and particular modes of governance will be parts of the wider political community, which will have begun to govern itself.[70]

The system as a whole will be devoted to the permanent diversity of the particular bodies politic which now exist, or which, by then, will have come into existence. The pluralism of peoples and the rich diversities of cultural experience will be preserved. There will be no renunciation of particular attachments in favor of some unconditional transnational identity. And states, free from the threat of war and the burden of armaments, will be able to devote a greater degree of their resources to internal development and social justice.

The idea of a world political society, having its own governing authority, is not utopian. It corresponds with essential, but unfulfilled, inclinations of human nature toward the goods which can be obtained through varying forms of political existence. The state remains as a political good, but it can no longer be viewed as the highest form of human association. It is time to think of moving beyond it.

But all must be kept in perspective. Hopes for a complete and uni-

70. Adler had criticized the papacy for not acknowledging the need for international government, although the Church's teaching about peace was susceptible of such development. Compare Adler, chap. 9, with Robert Hutchins, *St. Thomas and the World State*. However, *Pacem in Terris* states clearly in pt. 4 that the universal common good requires the establishment, by common consent, of some form of global public authority.

fied order of all humanity may at some time be realized, but such an achievement will not have the status of an absolute good—or of a final good. There will always be an infinite distance between the Kingdom of God and the temporal arrangements of humanity, which, unfortunately, are never free from discord. Still, those who respect the distinction between time and eternity know they have an obligation to do whatever they can to develop those political potentialities that can bring a greater measure of peace, justice, and happiness to all who cherish life on earth.

Adler, Mortimer J. *The Common Sense of Politics*. New York: Holt, Rinehart & Winston, 1971.

————. *How to Think about War and Peace*. New York: Fordham University Press, 1996.

Adler, Selig. *The Uncertain Giant 1921–1941: American Foreign Policy Between the Wars*. New York: Macmillan, 1965.

Advisory Opinion on the Legality of the Threat or Use of Nuclear Weapons of July 8, 1996. The International Court of Justice, 35 International Legal Materials 809–938 (1996).

Alighieri, Dante. *On World Government* (De Monarchia). Translated by Herbert W. Schneider. Indianapolis: Bobbs Merrill, 1957.

Allott, Phillip. *Eunomia: A New Order for a New World*. Oxford: Oxford University Press, 1990.

————. "Language, Method and the Nature of International Law." 45 *British Yearbook of International Law* 79–135 (1971).

————. "*Mare Nostrum*: A New Law of the Sea." 86 *American Journal of International Law* 764–787 (1992).

Althusius. *Politica*. Indianapolis: Liberty Fund, 1995.

Arendt, Hannah. *The Human Condition*. Chicago: University of Chicago Press, 1958.

————. *Lectures on Kant's Political Philosophy*. Edited by Ronald Beiner. Chicago: University of Chicago Press, 1982.

Aristotle. *The Politics*, Book 1. Translated by B. Jowett, edited by Stephen Everson. Cambridge: Cambridge University Press, 1988.

Arnold, Matthew. *Culture and Anarchy*. Edited by J. Dover Wilson. Cambridge: Cambridge University Press, 1960.

Aron, Raymond. *Main Currents in Sociological Thought*. Translated by Richard Howard and Helen Weaver (1965).

————. *Peace and War, A Theory of International Relations*. Edited by Richard Howard and Annette Baker Fox. Garden City, N.Y.: Doubleday and Co., 1966.

Austin, John. *Lectures on Jurisprudence, or The Philosophy of Positive Law*. Edited by Robert Campbell. Jersey City: F. D. Linn, 1875.

Balthasar, Hans Urs von. *The God Question and Modern Man*. New York: The Seabury Press, 1967.

Baltz, A. G. A. *Writings on Political Philosophy by Benedict de Spinoza*. New York: Appleton-Crofts, 1937.

Barker, Sir Ernest. *Social Contract: Essays by Locke, Hume and Rousseau*. New York: Oxford University Press, 1962.

Baxter, R. R. "International Law in Her Infinite Variety." 29 *International and Comparative Law Quarterly* 549–66 (1980).

Becker, Carl C. *The Heavenly City of the Eighteenth Century Philosophers*. New York: Yale University Press, 1932.

Bedjaoui, Mohammed. *International Law: Achievements and Prospects*. Dordrecht: Martinus Nijhoff, 1991.

Beitz, C. R. *Political Theory and International Relations*. Princeton: Princeton University Press, 1979.

Benedict XV, Pope. *Praeclara Summorum*. In vol. 6 of *The Papal Encyclicals*, edited by Claudia Carlen. Ann Arbor: The Pierian Press, 1981.

Bentham, Jeremy. *Plan for an (sic)Universal and Perpetual Peace, Principles of International Law (1786–89)*. In J. Bowering, ed., *The Works of Jeremy Bentham*. Vol. 2. Edinburgh: William Taft, 1843.

Berdyaev, Nicholas. *The End of Our Time*. New York: Sheed and Ward, 1933.

Berlin, Isaiah. "On the Pursuit of the Ideal." *New York Review of Books*, 17 March 1988, 11.

Black, Anthony. Review of *Eunomia: New Order for a New World*, by Philip Allott. 62 *Political Quarterly* 303 (April 1991).

Bluntschli, J. C. "The Organization of a European Federation." In W. Evans Darby, *International Arbitration; International Tribunals, A Collection of the various schemes which have been propounded; and of instances in the nineteenth century*. 4th ed. London: J. M. Dent and Co., 1904.

Bodin, Jean. *Six Books of Commonwealth*. Translated by M. J. Tooley. Oxford: B. Blackwell, 1955.

Boutros-Ghali, Boutros. "Human Rights: The Common Language of Humanity." *World Conference on Human Rights*. New York: United Nations Department of Public Information DPI/ 1394–39399, Aug. 1993.

Boutros-Ghali, Boutros. *An Agenda for Democratization*. New York: United Nations Department of Public Information DPI/ 1867, Dec. 1996.

Brierly, James Leslie. "The General Act of Geneva." 11 *British Yearbook of International Law* 119–33 (1930).

———. *The Outlook for International Law*. Oxford: The Clarendon Press, 1944.

———. *The Basis of Obligation in International Law and Other Papers*. Oxford: The Clarendon Press, 1958.

———. *The Law of Nations*, 6th ed. Oxford: The Clarendon Press, 1963.

Bryce, James. *The Holy Roman Empire*. New York: Macmillan, 1904.

Bull, Hedley. *The Anarchical Society*. New York: Columbia University Press, 1977.

Bull, Hedley, Benedict Kingsbury, and Adam Roberts, eds. *Hugo Grotius and International Relations.* Oxford: The Clarendon Press, 1990.

Burns, Timothy, ed. *After History? Francis Fukuyama and His Critics.* Lanham, Md.: Rowman and Littlefield, 1994.

Butler, Nicholas Murray. *The International Mind: An Argument for the Judicial Settlement of International Disputes.* New York: Scribners, 1913.

Butterfield, Herbert. *Masters of International Thought.* Edited by Kenneth W. Thompson. Baton Rouge: Louisiana State University Press, 1980.

Cairns, Huntington. *Legal Philosophy from Plato to Hegel.* Baltimore: Johns Hopkins University Press, 1949.

Calvin, John. *On God and Political Duty.* Edited by John T. McNeill. New York: Liberal Arts Press, 1956.

Canovan, Margaret. *The Political Thought of Hannah Arendt.* New York: Harcourt Brace Jovanovich, 1974.

Cardozo, Benjamin. *The Paradoxes of Legal Science.* New York: Columbia University Press, 1928.

Carr, Craig L., ed. *The Political Writings of Samuel Pufendorf.* Translated by Michael J. Seidler. New York: Oxford University Press, 1994.

Carr, E. H. *The Twenty Years' Crisis, 1919–1939.* London: Macmillan, 1939.

Carr, Herbert Wildon. *Leibniz.* London: E. Benn, Ltd., 1929.

Cassese, Antonio. *International Law in a Divided World.* Oxford: The Clarendon Press, 1986.

Cassier, Ernst. *The Philosophy of the Enlightenment.* Translated by Fritz C. A. Koelln and James P. Pettegrove. Princeton: Princeton University Press, 1951.

Chardin, Pierre Teilhard de. *The Phenomenon of Man.* Translated by Bernard Wall. New York: Harper Bros., 1959.

———. *The Future of Man.* Translated by Norman Denny. New York: Harper & Row, 1964.

———. *The Divine Milieu.* New York: Harper & Row, 1968.

Charney, Jonathan I. "Universal International Law." 87 *American Journal of International Law* 529–51 (1993).

———. "The Implications of Expanding International Dispute Settlement Systems: The 1982 Convention on the Law of the Sea." 90 *American Journal of International Law* 69–75 (1996).

Charter of the United Nations.

Chaumont, Charles. "Cours General de Droit Internationale Publique" 129 *Recueil des Cours.* (Collected Courses of the Hague Academy of International Law)(1971).

Chretien, Alfred. *Principes de Droit International Public.* Paris: Chevalier Marescq. et. cie. 1893.

Claude, Innis. "The United Nations, 27th Session Introduction: The Central Challenge for the United Nations: Weakening the Strong or Strengthening the Weak?" 14 *Harvard International Law Journal* 517–29 (1973).

Cohen, Joshua, ed. *For Love of Country: Debating the Limits of Patriotism.* Boston: Beacon Press, 1996.

Collins, James. *The Continental Rationalists.* Milwaukee: Bruce Publishing, 1967.

Comment. "The Legal Significance of the Locarno Agreements." 20 *American Journal of International Law* 108–11 (1926).

Comte, Auguste. *Positive Philosophy.* Translated by Harriet Martineau. 2 vols. New York: W. Gowans, 1868.

———. *System of Positive Polity* (1875). New York: Ben Franklin Press, 1968.

Copleston, F. *A History of Philosophy.* Westminster, Md.: Newman Press, 1950. Vol. 6 contains good general summaries and evaluations.

Corbett, Percy Ellwood. *Law and Society in the Relations of States.* New York: Harcourt, Brace & Company, 1951.

———. *Morals, Law, and Power in International Relations.* Los Angeles: John Randolph & Dora Haynes Foundation, 1956.

Dahrendorf, Ralf. *Reflections on the Revolution in Europe.* London: Chatto & Windus, 1990.

Dante Alighieri, see Alighieri, Dante, supra.

Darby, W. Evans. "The Question of Sanctions." In Darby, ed., *International Arbitration; International Tribunals.*

De Madariga, S. *Disarmament.* Port Washington, N.Y.: Kennikat Press, 1929.

De Visscher, Charles. *Theory and Reality in Public International Law.* Translated by P. E. Corbett. Princeton: Princeton University Press, 1957.

D'Entreves, A. P. *Dante as a Political Thinker.* Oxford: The Clarendon Press, 1952.

Dewey, John. *The Quest for Certainty: A Study of the Relation of Knowledge and Action.* New York: Minton Balsh, 1929.

Dickerson, Edward DeWitt. *The Equality of States in International Law.* Cambridge, Mass.: Harvard University Press, 1920.

Diggins, John. *The Promise of Pragmatism: Modernism and the Crisis of Knowledge and Authority.* Chicago: University of Chicago Press, 1994.

Dilthey, Wilhem. *The Essence of Philosophy.* Translated by Stephen A. and William T. Emery. Chapel Hill: University of North Carolina Press, 1954.

Donoghue, Denis. *Reading America: Essays on American Literature.* New York: Alfred A. Knopf, 1987.

———. "The True Sentiment of America." In *America in Theory,* edited by Leslie Berlovitz, Denis Donoghue, and Louis Menard. New York: Oxford University Press, 1988.

Dorsey, "The McDougal-Lasswell Proposal to Build a World Public Order." 82 *American Journal of International Law* 41–51 (1988).

Draper, G. A. D. "Grotius' Place in the Development of Legal Ideas about War." In Bull, Hedley, et al., eds., *Hugo Grotius and International Relations.* Oxford: The Clarendon Press, 1990.

Ebenstein, William. *The Pure Theory of Law.* Madison: University of Wisconsin Press, 1945.

———. *Modern Political Thought: The Great Issues.* 2d ed. New York: Holt, Rinehart & Winston, 1960.

Editorial Comment, 90 *American Journal of International Law* 416–18 (1996).

Edwards, Charles S. *Hugo Grotius: The Miracle of Holland.* Chicago: Nelson Hall, 1981.

Englebrecht, C. *Johann Gottlieb Fichte: The Study of His Political Writings with Special Reference to His Nationalism.* New York: Columbia University Press, 1933.

Falk, Richard. *The Role of Domestic Courts in the International Legal Order.* Syracuse: Syracuse University Press, 1964.

———. "McDougal and Feliciano on Law and Minimum World Public Order." In *Legal Order in a Violent World.* Princeton: Princeton University Press, 1968.

———, "A New Paradigm for World Order Studies: Prospects and Proposals." 84 *Yale Law Journal* 969 (1975).

———. *On Humane Governance: Toward a New Global Politics.* University Park: The Pennsylvania State University Press, 1995.

Ferguson, Adam. *An Essay on the History of Civil Society* (1767). Edited by Fania Oz-Salzberger. Cambridge: Cambridge University Press, 1995.

Figgis, John Neville. *Political Thought from Gerson to Grotius.* New York: Harper & Row, 1960.

———. *Studies of Political Thought from Gerson to Grotius 1414–1625.* New York: Harper, 1907.

Finnis, John. *Natural Law and Natural Right.* Oxford: The Clarendon Press, 1980.

Fischer, Roger. Review of *Studies in World Public Order,* by Myres S. McDougal and Associates. 135 *Science* 658–660 (1962).

Fitzmauric, "Vae Victis, or Woe to the Negotiators! Your Treaty or Our Interpretation of It." 67 *American Journal of International Law* 358–73 (1971).

Foucault, Charles. *The Order of Things: An Archaeology of the Human Sciences.* New York: Pantheon Books, 1971.

Fowler, Michael Ross, and Julie Marie Bunck. *Law, Power, and the Sovereign State.* University Park: The Pennsylvania State University Press, 1995.

Franck, Thomas M. *The Power of Legitimacy among Nations.* New York: Oxford University Press, 1990.

Friedrich, C. J. "Philosophical Reflections of Leibniz on Law, Politics, and the State." In H. G. Frankfurt, ed., *Leibniz: A Collection of Critical Essays.* Garden City, N.Y.: Anchor Books, 1972.

Fukuyama, Francis. *The End of History and the Last Man.* New York: The Free Press, 1992.

Gallie, B. *Philosophers of Peace and War.* London: Cambridge University Press, 1978.

Gauthier, David. *The Logic of Leviathan: The Moral and Political Theory of Thomas Hobbes.* Oxford: The Clarendon Press, 1969.

Gay, Peter. *The Enlightenment: The Rise of Modern Paganism.* New York: Alfred Knopf, 1967.

Gierke, Otto. *Political Theories of the Middle Ages.* Translated by Frederick William Maitland. Cambridge: Cambridge University Press, 1900.

———. *Reason and Revelation in the Middle Ages.* New York: Scribners, 1938.

Gilson, Etienne. *Dante and Philosophy.* Translated by David Moore. New York: Harper & Row, 1963.

Gough, J. W. *The Social Contract: A Critical Study of Its Development,* 2d ed. Oxford: The Clarendon Press, 1952.

Graebner, "America's Search for World Order." 53 *Virginia Quarterly Review* 161 (1975).

Grotius, Hugo. *De Jure Belli ac Pacis.* Translated by Francis W. Kelsey. Indianapolis: Bobbs-Merrill, 1962.

Guardini, Romano. *The End of the Modern World.* Translated by Joseph Theman and Herbert Burke. Chicago: Henry Regnery Company, 1968.

Guehenno, Jean-Marie. *The End of the Nation-State.* Translated by Victoria Elliott. Minneapolis: The University of Minnesota Press, 1995.

Gunnell, John G. *Political Philosophy and Time.* Middletown, Conn.: Wesleyan University Press, 1968.

Hall, Jerome. *The Living Law of a Democratic Society.* Indianapolis: Bobbs-Merrill, 1949.

Hamilton, Bernice. *Political Thought in Sixteenth-Century Spain.* Oxford: The Clarendon Press, 1963.

Hampshire, Stuart. *Spinoza.* Harmondsworth: Penguin Books, 1952.

———. *Thought and Action.* Notre Dame, Ind.: University of Notre Dame Press, 1983.

Hart, L. A. *The Concept of Law.* Oxford: Oxford University Press, 1960.

Hearnshaw, F. J. C., ed. "Dante and World Government." In *The Social and Political Ideas of Some Great Medieval Thinkers.* London: G. G. Harrap, 1923.

———. *The Social and Political Ideas of Some Great Thinkers of the Sixteenth and Seventeenth Centuries.* New York: Barnes & Noble, 1967.

Heer, Frederick. *The Holy Roman Empire.* Translated by Janet Sondheimer. New York: Frederick Praeger, 1968.

Hegel. *Philosophy of Right.* Translated by T. M. Knox. Oxford: The Clarendon Press, 1952.

Hemleben, H. J. *Plans for World Peace through Six Centuries.* Chicago: University of Chicago Press, 1943.

Higgins, Rosalyn. *International Law and How We Use It.* Oxford: The Clarendon Press, 1994.

Hinsley, F. H. *Power and the Pursuit of Peace: Theory and Practice in the History of Relations between States.* Cambridge: Cambridge University Press, 1967.

———. *Sovereignty.* 2d ed. Cambridge: Cambridge University Press, 1986.

Hobbes, Thomas. *Leviathan* (1651). Edited by Michael Oakeshott. New York: Macmillan, 1962.

———. *De Cive* (1658).

Hoffman, Stanley. *The State of War: Essays on the Theory and Practice of International Politics.* New York: Frederick Praeger, 1965.

———. *Duties beyond Borders: On the Limits and Possibilities of Ethical International Policy.* Syracuse, N.Y.: Syracuse University Press, 1981.

Holbraad, Carsten. *The Concert of Europe: A Study in German and British International Theory.* London: Longmans, 1970.

Hughes, Charles Evans. *The Pathway of Peace; representative essays delivered during his term as Secretary of State (1921–1925).* New York: Harper & Bros. 1925.

Hume, David. "Of the Balance of Power" (1752). In *Political Essays.* Edited by Knud Haakonssen. Cambridge: Cambridge University Press, 1994.

Huntington, Samuel P. *The Clash of Civilizations and the Remaking of World Order.* New York: Simon & Schuster, 1996.

Hutchins, Robert. *St. Thomas and the World State.* Milwaukee: Marquette University Press, 1949.

James, William. "Remarks at the Peace Banquet." 94 *Atlantic Monthly* 845 (1904).

———. *Pragmatism: A New Name for Old Ways of Thinking.* New York: Longmans Green, 1907.

Janik, Allan, and Stephen Toulmin. *Wittgenstein's Vienna.* New York: Simon & Schuster, 1973.

Jaspers, Karl. *Man in the Modern Age.* Translated by Eden and Cedar Paul. London: Routledge & Co., 1951.

Jessup, Phillip C. *A Modern Law of Nations.* New York: Macmillan, 1948.

John XXIII, Pope. *Pacem In Terris* (Peace on Earth) (1963).

John Paul II, Pope. "Address to the General Assembly of the United Nations." In *Origins* 19 October 1995: 294–299.

Judt, Tony. *A Grand Illusion? An Essay on Europe.* New York: Hill & Wang, 1996.

Kant, Immanuel. *Critique of Pure Reason* (1781).

———. *Prolegomena to Any Future Metaphysics (1783).*

———. *Perpetual Peace: A Philosophical Sketch* (Zum Ewigen Frieden ein Philosophischer Entwurf.) (1795).

———. *Die Metaphysic der Sitten.* (The Metaphysics of Morals) (1797). In *Political Writings,* edited by Hans Reiss, translated by H. B. Nisbet, 2d enlarged ed. Cambridge: Cambridge University Press, 1990.

Katz, Milton. *The Relevance of International Adjudication.* Cambridge, Mass.: Harvard University Press,1968.

Kelsen, Hans. "The Pure Theory of Law." 50 *Law Quarterly Review* 474–498 (1934); 51 *Law Quarterly Review* 517–535 (1935).

———. "The Pure Theory of Law and Analytic Jurisprudence." 55 *Harvard Law Review* 44–70 (1944).

———. *Peace through Law.* Chapel Hill: University of North Carolina Press, 1944.

———. *General Theory of Law and the State.* Cambridge, Mass.: Harvard University Press, 1945.

———. *The Pure Theory of Law.* Translated by M. Knight. Berkeley: University of California Press, 1967.

———. *What Is Justice? Justice, Law and Politics in the Mirror of Science.* Berkeley: University of California Press, 1971.

———. *Essays in Moral and Political Philosophy.* Edited by Ola Weinberger, translated by Peter Heath. Dordrecht & Boston: Reidel 1973.

———. *La Theoria Dello Stato in Dante.* Bologna: Massimiliano Boni Editore, 1974.

———. *Law and Peace in International Relations: The Oliver Wendell Holmes Lectures 1940–41.* (1948) Buffalo: W. S. Hein & Co., 1997.

Kissinger, Henry A. *A World Restored.* Gloucester, Mass.: Peter Smith, 1973.

———. *American Foreign Policy.* 3d ed. New York: Norton & Co., 1977.

Knight, W. S. M. *The Life and Work of Hugo Grotius.* London: Sweet & Maxwell, 1925.

Knorr, K., and Sidney Verba, eds. *The International System.* Princeton: Princeton University Press, 1961.

Koskenniemi, Martti. Review of *Eunomia, New Order for a New World,* by Philip Allott. 87 *American Journal of International Law* 160–64 (1993).

Koskenniemi, Martti. *From Apology to Utopia: The Structure of International Argument.* Helsinki: Finnish Lawyer's Pub. Co., 1989.

Kothari, R. *Footsteps into the Future.* New York: The Free Press, 1975.

Kramer, Hilton. "Mondrian and Mysticism: My Long Search Is Over." *The New Criterion.* Sept. 1995.

Krieger, Leonard. *The Politics of Discretion: Pufendorf and the Acceptance of Natural Law.* Chicago: University of Chicago Press, 1965.

Krutch, Joseph Wood. *The Modern Temper.* New York: Harcourt Brace & World, 1929.

Ladd, William. *An Essay on a Congress of Nations for the Adjustment of International Disputes without a Resort to Arms* (1840). Washington, D.C.: Carnegie Endowment, 1916.

Lansing, Robert. *Notes on Sovereignty.* Washington, D.C.: Carnegie Endowment, Pamph. 38, 1921. The text originally appeared in two law review articles: "Notes on Sovereignty in a State." 1 *American Journal of International Law* 105 (1907) and "Notes on World Sovereignty." 15 *American Journal of International Law* 13 (1921).

Larmore, Charles E. *Patterns of Moral Complexity.* New York: Cambridge University Press, 1987.

Lauterpacht, Hersch. "Spinoza and International Law." 8 *British Yearbook of International Law* 89 (1927).

———. *International Law and Human Rights.* London: Stevens, 1930.

Lawrence, T. J. *The Principles of International Law.* 5th ed. Boston: D.C. Heath, 1910.

Lecky, William E. H. *Rationalism in Europe.* London: Longmans, Green & Co., 1866.

Leibniz, Gottfried. *Portrait of the Prince* (1679). In Patrick Riley, *The Political Writings of Leibniz.* Cambridge: Cambridge University Press, 1972.

———. *Meditation on the Common Concept of Justice* (c. 1702). In Riley, supra.

———. *Opinion on the Principles of Pufendorf* (1706). In P. Riley, supra.

———. On the Works of the Abbé de St. Pierre" (1715). In Riley, supra.

Lillich, Richard B., ed. *The Valuation of Nationalized Property in International Law.* Charlottesville: University of Virginia Press, 1975.

Lipson, E. *Europe in the Nineteenth Century 1815–1914.* New York: Collier Books, 1962.

Llano, Alejandro. *The New Sensibility.* Translated by Alban d'Entremont. Pamplona: University of Navarra, 1991.

Locke, John. *Second Treatise on Government* (1690). In *Two Treatises of Government,* edited by Pete Laslett. London: Cambridge University Press, 1967.

Lorimer, James. *The Institutes of the Law of Nations: A Treatise on the Jural Relations of Separate Political Communities.* 2 vols. Edinburgh: W. Blackwood & Sons, 1883–84.

MacDonell, J., and E. Manson, eds. "Leibniz." In *Great Jurists of the World.* Vol. 2. *Journal of Continental Legal History* Series 283. South Hackensack, N.J.: Rothman Reprints, 1968.

Machan, Tibor. "Indefatigable Alchemist: Richard Rorty's Radical Pragmatism." *American Scholar* 65, no. 3 (Summer 1996): 417–424.

Machiavelli, Niccolo. *The Prince* (1513). New York: New American Library, 1952.

Macrae, Donald. *Max Weber.* New York: Viking Press, 1974.

Manuel, Frank E. and Fritzie. P. *Utopian Thought in the Western World.* Cambridge, Mass.: The Belknap Press of Harvard University Press, 1979.

Maritain, Jacques. *Three Reformers: Luther, Descartes, Rousseau.* London: Sheed & Ward, 1936.

———. *Art and Scholasticism, with other essays.* Translated by J. F. Scanlan. New York: Scribner's, 1937.

———. *The Person and the Common Good.* Translated by John F. Fitzgerald. New York: Scribners, 1947.

———. *Man and the State.* Chicago: University of Chicago Press, 1951.

———. *Moral Philosophy, An Historical and Critical Survey of the Great Systems.* New York: Scribners, 1964.

———. *The Peasant of the Garrone.* Translated by M. Cuddihy and Elizabeth Hughes. New York: Holt, Rinehart & Winston, 1968.

McDougal, Myres S. and Associates. *Studies in World Public Order.* New Haven: Yale University Press, 1960.

McDougal, Myres S. and Feliciano, Florentino P. *Law and World Minimum Public Order: The Legal Regulation of International Coercion.* New Haven: Yale University Press, 1961.

McDougal, Myres S. "The Dorsey Comment: A Modest Retrogression." 82 *American Journal of International Law* 51–57 (1988).

McDougal, Myres S., Harold D. Lasswell, and James Miller. *The Interpretation of Agreements and World Public Order.* New Haven: Yale University Press, 1967.

McShea, Robert M. *The Political Philosophy of Spinoza.* New York: Columbia University Press, 1968.

Medlicott, W. N. *Bismarck, Gladstone, and the Concert of Europe.* London: Althone Press, 1956.

Mendlovitz, Saul H., ed. *On the Creation of a Just World Order.* New York: The Free Press, 1975.

Mill, John Stuart. *Auguste Comte and Positivism.* Ann Arbor: University of Michigan Press, 1961.

————. *Principles of Political Economy* (1848).

Milosz, Czeslaw. *The Witness of Poetry.* Cambridge, Mass.: Harvard University Press, 1983.

Mowat, R. B. *The Concert of Europe.* London: Macmillan, 1930.

Multilateral Treaties Deposited with the Secretary-General, UN Doc. St/Leg/ Ser. E/(1994).

Murphy Jr., Cornelius F. "Some Reflections on Theories of International Law." 70 *Columbia Law Review* 447–63 (1970).

————. *Modern Legal Philosophy.* Pittsburgh: Duquesne University Press, 1978.

————. *The Search for World Order.* Dordrecht: Martinus Nijhoff, 1985.

————. *Descent into Subjectivity.* Wakefield, N.H.: Longwood Academic, 1990.

————. "The Conciliatory Responsibilities of the United Nations Security Council." 35 *German Yearbook of International Law* 190–204 (1993).

Nardin, Terry. *Law, Morality and the Relations of States.* Princeton: Princeton University Press, 1983.

Nardin, Terry, and David R. Mapel. *Traditions of International Ethics.* Cambridge: Cambridge University Press, 1993.

Nippold, Otfried. See his introduction to vol. 2 of Christian Wolff, *Jus Gentium Methodo Scientifica Pertractatum* (The Law of Nations According to a Scientific Method). Carnegie translation, 1934 for a short biography of Wolff.

Nisbet, Robert. *The Sociology of Emile Durkheim.* New York: Oxford University Press, 1974.

Nussbaum, Arthur. *A Concise History of the Law of Nations.* New York: Macmillan, 1947 and rev. ed. 1958.

Nussbaum, Martha. *Love's Knowledge: Essays on Philosophy and Literature.* New York: Oxford University Press, 1991.

Oda, Shigeru. "The International Court of Justice from the Bench." 244 *Recueil des Cours* (Collected Courses of the Hague Academy of International Law) vol. 7 (1993).

Ohmae, Kenichi. "The Rise of the Regional State." 72 *Foreign Affairs* 78 (1993).

Onuf. "*Civitas Maxima:* Wolff, Vattel, and the Fate of Republicanism." 88 *American Journal of International Law* 280 (1994).

Oppenheim, Lassa. *Die Zukunft des Völkerrechts* (1911). The work was published in English in 1921 under the title *The Future of International Law.* London: The Clarendon Press, 1921; Washington, D.C.: Pamph. Series, Carnegie Endowment for International Peace, Division of International Law, No. 39.

———. *International Law: A Treatise.* London: Longmans, Green & Co., 1906.

Our Global Neighborhood: The Report of the Commission on Global Governance. Oxford: Oxford University Press, 1996.

Palmer, R. R. "The People as Constituent Power." In *The Role of Ideology in the American Revolution,* edited by J. Howe Jr. New York: Holt, Rinehart & Winston, 1950.

"Panel on Treaty Interpretation." *Proceedings of the Annual Meeting of the American Society of International Law* 108–40 (1967).

Panizza, Diego. "Conceptions of International Order in Eighteenth Century Political Thought: A Typology in Context." 17 *Quinnipiac Law Review* 61–98 (1997).

Pieper, Josef. *Hope and History.* Translated by David Kipp. San Francisco: Ignatius Press, 1994.

———. *Leisure: The Basis of Culture.* With an introduction by T. S. Eliot. Translated by Alexander Dru. New York: New American Library, 1963.

Pinckaers, Servais. *The Sources of Christian Ethics.* Translated by Sr. Mary Thomas Noble. Washington, D.C.: The Catholic University of America Press, 1995.

Pincoffs, Edmund L. *Quandaries and Virtues: Against Reductivism in Ethics.* Lawrence: University of Kansas Press, 1986.

Pinder, John. *European Community.* New York: Oxford University Press, 1991.

Polkinghorne, John. *The Faith of a Physicist.* Princeton: Princeton University Press, 1994.

Pufendorf, Samuel. *Elementorum Jurisprudentiae* (Elements of Universal Jurisprudence) (1660). Carnegie trans., 1931.

———. *De Jure Naturae et Gentium* (1672). Carnegie trans., 1934.

Rawls, John. *A Theory of Justice.* Cambridge: Harvard University Press, 1971.

Recasens-Siches. "The Logic of the Reasonable as Differentiated from the Logic of the Rational." In *Essays in Jurisprudence in Honor of Roscoe Pound.* Edited by R. Neuman. Westport, Conn.: Greenwood Press, 1962.

Rescher, Nicholas. *Ethical Idealism: An Inquiry into the Nature and Function of Ideals.* Berkeley: University of California Press, 1987.

———. *The Philosophy of Leibniz.* Englewood Cliffs, N.J.: Prentice-Hall, 1967.

Restatement (Third) Foreign Relations Law of the United States, secs. 401, 403.

Riley, Patrick. *The Political Writings of Leibniz*. Cambridge: Cambridge University Press, 1972.

Rorty, Richard. *Consequences of Pragmatism: Essays, 1972–1980*. Minneapolis: University of Minnesota Press, 1982.

Rosecrance, Richard. "The Rise of the Virtual State." *Foreign Affairs*, July/ Aug. 1996, 45–61.

Rostow, E. V. *Law, Power and the Pursuit of Peace*. Lincoln: University of Nebraska Press, 1968.

Rosvotseff, Michael A. "International Relations in the Ancient World." In *The History and Nature of International Relations*. Edited by Edmund A. Walsh, S. J. New York: Macmillan, 1922.

Rousseau, Jean-Jacques. *A Lasting Peace through the Federation of Europe and the State of War*. Edited by C. E. Vaughan. London: Constable & Co., 1917.

———. *The Social Contract* (1762).

Rubin, Alfred P. *Ethics and Authority in International Law*. Cambridge: Cambridge University Press, 1997.

Ruddy, Francis Stephen. *International Law in the Enlightenment: The Background of Emmerich de Vattel's "Le Droit des Gens."* Dobbs Ferry, N.Y.: Oceana Publications, 1975.

Schachter, Oscar. "The Right of States to Use Armed Force." 82 *Michigan Law Review* 1620–46 (1984).

———. "International Law in Theory and Practice," General Course in International Law, 178 *Recueil des Cours*(Collected Courses of the Hague Academy of International Law) vol. 5 (1982).

Schiffer, Walter. *The Legal Community of Mankind: A Critical Analysis of the Modern Conception of World Organization*. New York: Columbia University Press, 1954.

Schlesinger Jr., Arthur M. *The Disuniting of America*. New York: W. W. Norton & Co., 1992.

Schumaker, E. F. *A Guide for the Perplexed*. New York: Harper & Row, 1987.

Second Vatican Council: *The Pastoral Constitution on the Church in the Modern World*. (1965).

Shell, Susan Meld. *The Rights of Reason: A Study of Kant's Philosophy and Politics*. Toronto: University of Toronto Press, 1980.

Shklar, Judith. *Freedom and Independence: A Study of the Political Ideas of Hegel's Phenomenology*. Cambridge: Cambridge University Press, 1976.

Smith, Gregory Bruce. "The End of History as a Portal to the Future: Does Anything Lie Beyond Late Modernity?" in *After History? Francis Fukuyama and His Critics,* edited by Timothy Burns. Lanham, Md.: Rowman and Littlefield, 1994.

Smith, Norman Kemp. *A Commentary on Kant's Critique of Pure Reason*. 2d ed. New York: Humanities Press, 1962.

Smith, T. V. *The Philosophical Way of Life in America.* New York: The Kennikat Press, 1943.

Spinoza, Benedict de. *A Political Treatise.* In *The Chief Works of Benedict De Spinoza.* Translated by R. H. M. Elwes. New York: Dover Publications, 1901.

Stern, S. M. *Aristotle on the World State.* Columbia, S.C.: University of South Carolina Press, 1968.

Stone, Julius. *Visions of World Order.* Baltimore: Johns Hopkins University Press, 1984.

Strange, Susan. *The Retreat of the State: The Diffusion of Power in the World Economy.* Cambridge: Cambridge University Press, 1996.

Strauss, Leo. *Natural Right and History.* Chicago: University of Chicago Press, 1953.

———. *The Political Philosophy of Hobbes.* Translated by Elsa M. Sinclair. Oxford: The Clarendon Press, 1936.

Suarez, Francisco. "De Legibus ac Deo Legislatore." In *Selections from Three Works of Francisco Suarez S. J.* Vol.2. Washington, D.C.: Carnegie Endowment, 1944.

Tagore, Rabindranath. *Nationalism.* London: Macmillan, 1917.

Taylor, Charles. *Hegel.* Cambridge: Cambridge University Press, 1975.

———. *Sources of the Self.* Cambridge, Mass.: Harvard University Press, 1980.

———. *The Ethics of Authenticity.* Cambridge, Mass.: Harvard University Press, 1992.

"The Writings of Myres S. McDougal." 84 *Yale Law Journal* 965–68 (1975).

Thomas Aquinas, St. *Treatise on Law.* Chicago: Henry Regnery Company, n.d.

Thompson, Kenneth W., ed. *Masters of International Thought.* Baton Rouge: Louisiana State University Press, 1980.

Toynbee, Arnold. *Civilization on Trial.* New York: Meridian, 1958.

Treitsche, Henrich von. *Politics,* edited by Hans Kohn. New York: Harcourt Brace & World, 1963.

Trilling, Lionel. *Sincerity and Authenticity.* Cambridge, Mass.: Harvard University Press, 1972.

Tussman, Joseph. *Obligation and the Body Politic.* New York: Oxford University Press, 1960.

Unger, Roberto Mangabeira. *Knowledge and Politics.* New York: The Free Press, 1975.

Vattel, Emeric. *The Law of Nations: Or Principles of the Law of Nature Applied to the Conduct and Affairs of Nations and Sovereigns.* 6th ed. Chitty, 1844.

Vitoria, Francisco de. *The Principles of Political and International Law in the Works of Francisco De Vitoria.* Edited by Antonio Truyol Serra. Madrid: Ediciones Cultural Hispanica, 1946.

Voegelin, Eric. *From Enlightenment to Revolution,* edited by John Hallowell. Durham, N.C.: Duke University Press, 1975.

————. *In Search of Order*. Baton Rouge: Louisiana State University Press, 1987.

————. *The New Science of Politics*. Chicago: University of Chicago Press, 1952.

————. *Order and History*. Vol. 2, *The World of the Polis*. Baton Rouge: Louisiana State University Press, 1957.

Von Laue, Theodore H. "From Fukuyama to Reality: A Critical Essay." In *After History? Francis Fukuyama and His Critics,* edited by Timothy Burns. Lanham, Md.: Rowman & Littlefield, 1994.

Walsh, W. *Hegelian Ethics*. New York: Garland, 1984.

Watkin, E. I. *The Bow in the Clouds*. New York: Macmillan, 1932.

Webb, Eugene. *Eric Voegelin*. Seattle: University of Washington Press, 1981.

Weil, P. "Toward Relative Normativity in International Law?" 77 *American Journal of International Law* 413 (1983).

Westlake, John. *Principles of International Law*. Cambridge: Cambridge University Press, 1894.

Wheaton, Henry. *Elements of International Law with a Sketch of the History of the Science*. 2 vols. London: B. Fellows, 1836.

Wheeler, Harvey. *Democracy in a Revolutionary Era*. New York: Frederick A. Praeger, 1968.

Whitehead, Alfred North. *The Function of Reason*. Boston: Beacon Press, 1962.

Whitney v. California, 274 U.S. 357, 373 (1927). See Justice Brandeis's concurrence.

Wicksteed, Philip H. *Dante and Aquinas*. New York: Haskell House, 1971.

Wight, Martin. *Power Politics*. Edited by Hedley Bull and Carsten Holbraad. New York: Holmes & Meier, 1978.

Williams, Bernard. *Ethics and the Limits of Philosophy*. Cambridge, Mass.: Harvard University Press, 1986.

Wilson, Edmund O. *Consilience*. New York: Knopf, 1998.

Wilson, James. *Works of James Wilson*. Vol. 1. Edited by R. J. McCloskey. Cambridge, Mass.: Belknap Press of Harvard University Press, 1967.

Wolff, Christian. *Jus Gentium Methodo Scientifica Pertractatum* (The Law of Nations Treated According to a Scientific Method)(1764). Vol. 2. Carnegie trans., 1934.

INDEX

Theories of World Governance: A Study in the History of Ideas was composed in Bembo by Graphic Composition, Inc., Athens, Georgia; printed on 60-pound Glatfelter and bound by Cushing-Malloy, Inc., Ann Arbor, Michigan; and designed and produced by Kachergis Book Design, Pittsboro, North Carolina.